C++

FOR

GAMERS

2004

BY SALVATORE A. BUONO

ISBN-13: 978-1724452702
ISBN-10: 1724452703

About the Book

This is an old C++ 2004 edition. It's been sitting on a CD-ROM in a small box for 14+ years. I wanted to put it out there so that it wouldn't be lost.

Preface

This is an introductory textbook that covers the C++/CLI (Common Language Infrastructure) subset. Written in accordance with the ECMA (European Computer Manufacturers Association) certified standard. ECMA C++/CLI is a product of the binding of the ISO (International Standards Organizations) C++ language extensions and the Common Language Infrastructure. C++, is known world wide as a cross-platform, vendor-neutral programming language, while CLI is a ISO-standardized language-neutral runtime environment. The purpose of this book is to define the C++ language as it applies to this new standard. Those with pervious knowledge of C++ should note the reduction in the vocabulary available to C++/CLI, while those with a familiarity of C# will note the addition of several communal terms.

How to Use this Book

When I designed this book, I knew it had to serve two purposes: The first being to teach the C++ language in an entertaining, yet practical, context, and the second to introduce the novice programmer to the more advanced concepts of object-oriented programming and .Net design. I accomplished both of these tasks by first designing a traditional programming text and then adding several Window's applications (including a few arcade style games), thus defining the integrated nature of the newly bond language. The book is meant to be enjoyable, motivational, with a collective relationship in regards to skill level and object-oriented principles. The examples orchestrated to emphasize an easy flow and a simple approach to programming. Nevertheless, don't mistake that to mean that it won't be a handful. The course material should take several months to complete with its concepts serving as an invaluable references for many years to come.

What You'll Need

The graphics and sound portions of this text are based on the Windows XP (Home or Professional) and 2000/ME operating systems. C++ .Net as a whole will potentially be available on any number of operating systems, including UNIX, Linux, IBM's O/S2, BeX OS, Apple-Macintosh X, and Alpha's OpenVMS[1]. The basic requirements for leaning this version of the C++ language include a computer and a .Net level compiler. However, do to current restrictions, you'll also need to be running your compiler under either Windows XP, 2000 or NT. The hardware requirements listed to run Microsoft's .Net 2004 include a Pentium II Class PC with a minimum of 450MHz, 160 megabytes of RAM, 3.5 gigabytes of free hard drive space, 4x Speed CD-ROM/DVD-ROM, and a SVGA monitor. Those who wish to take advantage of Microsoft's .Net's 64-bit features, must be running that compiler with a compatible processor. Additional components required and/or referred to in this book include a mouse, sound card (with speakers), and (optional) modem - see your compiler's manual for additional restrictions.

---

[1] Please check with those vendors for the appropriate compiler(s)...

What I Used

The programs written for this text were developed with the understanding that not everyone can afford the very best in technologies. The compilers referenced include a list of student, beta, and trail editions, with the more advanced coding progressing into the standard and professional versions. Again, the compilers where installed under several Windows environments including Window's XP through NT. I also used a host of hardware configurations ranging from AMD & Intel's latest to a few much older AMD and Cyrix type machines.

~~About the CD-ROM~~
NOTE: THE CD-ROM IS NO LONGER AVAILABLE
(CODE SHOWN IN BOOK)

The companion CD-ROM included with this book covers the source code (programming text) and several previously compiled programs, all labeled and listed in the order they're discussed in the text. Each set of programs is placed in a folder titled after that chapter (as in chapter1, chapter2, etc...). In addition, I have included an assortment of games, all meant to aid in your learning and productivity. To load the source codes off the CD-ROM just follow the instructions listed on the next page.

To load and use the source code that accompanies this book:
1. Create a new directory and/or subdirectory. This will be used to store the programs from the CD-ROM and to store programs you create on your own. Name your folder and note where you've place it (in the C drive, D drive, etc,) including which subdirectory and/or subdirectories you chose to place it under. If you use the default, you'll more than likely find your lost files under C:\Documents and settings*YourUserName*\My Documents\Visual Studio Projects*ProjectsNameHere*.
2. Make sure your compiler is installed and working properly.
3. Load and make active the C++ compiler. Close any and all nonessential windows (this includes the C++ tour box). Closing unnecessary background programs will also help to speed up your system.
4. Insert the CD-ROM into the appropriate drive.
5. Select "Open" from your C++ compiler's file menu (see Screen Shot 1).

Screen Shot 1

6. From the "Open" Window's menu, select the folder titled "Source" and then the appropriate subfolder(s). The subfolder titled "MSNET" contains all of the source code for the Microsoft .Net compiler(s)[2] (see Screen Shots 2 and 3).

Screen Shot 2

Screen Shot 3

7. Select "Save as" from that files menu and save it to the directory you created in step 1 (see Screen Shot 4).

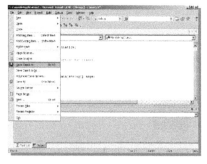

Screen Shot 4

---

[2] The programs depicted in this text were intended for use with Microsoft's .Net compiler.

Your program is now linked to that directory. You can remove the CD-ROM from its drive (remember to repeat these steps for each program as needed). To edit the source code and/or to proceed with compiling, see the instructions listed in chapter one.

How to Read this Book

This book is written for everyone wanting to learn the C++ language in a entertaining yet practical context. The contents have been broken up to accommodate three skill levels.

Part 1: Programming Basics covers the most fundamental portions, including programming history, how to setup your compiler, and algorithms. It also introduces critical material on the .Net framework, data types, input and output commands, legacy coding, mathematics, the Base Class Library, comparisons and loops, switch statements, type casting, predefined/ user-defined functions, and method manipulations (arguments, polymorphism, and recursion).

Part 2: Programming Essentials also covers some very basic concepts–namely single and multidimensional arrays, pointers, string functions, and streams–but eventually leads the reader out of the novice stage with topics including reflection, threads, synchronization, CLS (Common Language Specifications) complaints, Interoperability, and a further study of the Base Class Library.

Part 3: Object-Oriented Programming begins with structures, but quickly migrates into classes and the principles behind object-oriented design. Fields, methods, and operator overloading are discussed early on, with inheritance, virtual functions, delegates, and exception handling expanding our capabilities. Here, we'll also expand upon the principles of the .Net environment using Window's applications for graphics and sounds, GDI+ custom controls and game programming techniques.

This book was also written for anyone taking C++ through a standard college course. Thus, the text covers topics such as bubble sorting, search algorithms, and most teachers' favorite, default settings (although I personally prefer using parenthetical expressions).

In addition to following the book from chapter to chapter, you could also reroute your studies to include alternate paths or approaches. One such example would be to proceed from Chapter 2 straight to Chapter 4, since the gaming portions might not interest you. Alternatively, you could skip some of the more difficult gaming concepts listed in Chapters 3 through 5 and then return to that material after finishing the traditional studies. It is, however, recommended that you do eventually work though those games in order to apply some of the more advanced concepts on object-oriented programming and .Net design.

Getting Help from the Author

Since this book was meant to teach one of the vast and often expanding C languages, I felt that it was necessary to include a continuously updated e-mail forum & internet newsletter, that is, a forum that will include any new or improved features, including programming errors and ways to fix problems. I'd also like to encourage all the beginner programmers by generating a list of web sites, source coding (including arcade style clones), and any other new developments. To register for your FREE Internet newsletter or to write in with a problem or request, please address your e-mails to Plague@iwon.com.

The Students Perspective

This book was written from the perspective of the student. Every attempt was made to move the reader along in a logical and progressive manner. Nearly every keyword and command is followed up with a working (live code) example, and when necessary, the reader is presented with a list of background information and trouble shooting sections that are usually covered by an instructor or gained in some previous programming language.

There are several sections that cover the secondary steps of programming such as C++ to Windows setups, compiler setups, and topics on game coding. The game coding, while considered trivial by many instructors, is one of the most effective ways of demonstrating C++'s object-oriented potential. Each new game is constructed with the intent of maximizing the use of the coding studied in that chapter. The games, while entertaining, also force the reader to press beyond simple logic and answer questions that are not staged or limited to simple text based outputs.

The chapters follow an almost evolutionary pattern that begins with the basics of C++ and progresses through the techniques of structured, modular, and Object-Oriented Programming (OOP), with the last section obviously concluding with the latest advances in Microsoft's new .Net architecture. Both our text concepts and the games developed are part of that evolution, which primarily defines which games can and will be developed with the keywords and commands available.

Remember: for the best results, I'd suggest using the same compiler and operating system(s) I used, Microsoft's Visual C++ .Net 2004, under Window's XP Home or Professional.

Dear Abby, last night I went to the movies with my girlfriend Lora C. She was very excited and when we got home, well, we played all night. We have no problems, but my family really dislikes her. They tell me that I should find a non-fictional girlfriend.

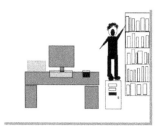

So how long do you think he'll keep trying to suffer the web?

PART ONE
PROGRAMMING
BASICS

Chapter One

"Imagination is more important than knowledge" **Albert Einstein**

C++ from the Beginning

This chapter covers the truly basic aspects of the C++ language including its history, compilers, and algorithms. Each section is designed to facilitate a quick and easy introduction and to insure a strong foundation in programming and problem solving. Special attention was placed on what the new programmer needs to know and/or might be confused about; the sections can, however, be covered quickly. There are a few sections set aside to cover history and theory, but the core of this chapter is about programming. Two sections promote good programming habits and there is a section on runtime, programming, and compiler errors (recommended reading even if you don't get into trouble). If you've skimmed the lessons, you know that this first chapter doesn't include any games, but don't let that fool you. All the concepts covered here are just as important for games as they are for business and/or math related topics.

An Overview of C++ Language

C++ is a high to mid-level programming language (and just in case you didn't know, a programming language is the collection of words, phrases, and syntax rules used to communicate with the computer). Although there are many high-level programming languages (BASIC, JAVA, FORTRAN, Pascal, Lisp, ADA, Modula-2, and Logo), few have reached the popularity of the original C and C++ languages. C and C++ have been used to create everything from operating systems and word processing packages to compilers for other high-level languages. C and C++ have been the programming languages of choice for more than 50 percent of all programming applications, and with their advances in object-oriented programming and Internet applications, both Managed C++ and C# are sure to push the popularity of C languages well into this new millennium.

A Little History on the Cs

C was developed in the 1970s by a man named Dennis Ritchie while working for AT&T Bell Laboratories. Before C, there was a language called B developed by Ken Thompson. While there was an A language, B was actually developed from Basic Combined Programming Language (BCPL), which was developed from a combination of another two languages, namely CPL and Algol60. C++'s object-oriented portions are attributed to still another language known as Simula67. CPL begot BCPL; BCPL begot B; B begot C; C begot C++; C++ begot Managed C++ and Managed C++ begot C++/CLI. In 1979, Bjarne Stroustrup (also at AT&T Bell Laboratories) developed the first version of C++ to be an enhanced version of the C language (initially referred to as C with classes). C++ was significantly enhanced with the addition of the Standard Template Library (STL) developed by Alexander Stepanov and Meng Lee at Hewlett-Packard. STL was based heavily on previous work done by both Stepanov and Musser, from Rensselaer Polytechnic Institute.

   Both C and C++ spread quickly in power and use, but eventually all the added features and expansions lead to incompatibilities and frustrations. In the 80's and 90's two standards were created, first with the American National Standards Institute (ANSI) C standard of 1983, and then the American National Standards for Systems Information and International Standards Organization (ISO) C/C++ standards of 1998 (Note: C was also updated in this second standard). The 1998 ANSI/ISO standard is generally referred to as Native C++, while Microsoft's .Net Extensions was known as Managed C++. C++ became C++/CLI with the 2004

ECMA standard. C++/CLI is intended to supplement the development of applications required for both stream users and Intranet/Internet programmers. C++/CLI is definitely one of the most sophisticated languages ever developed, destine to dominate the world of computer programming for at least the next decade.

As you can see, C++ has evolved into a hunter and gatherer language.
Hey, can I go to the bathroom?

What is the .Net Framework?

The .Net framework is a multitasking, class-based programming library and interface that allows for both the interoperable exchange and execution of data. As a library, the .Net base classes are as powerful as the traditional Windows API function set, but with the added advantage of being completely object-oriented. Object-oriented programming (as explained throughout this book) is a practical method used to develop programs that promotes both the reusability and reliability of coding. The .Net runtime (also known as the Common Language Runtime or CLR) serves as a shell or intermediate environment that assists the operating system with program execution(s).

The .Net framework also allows for program interoperability, requiring a Common Type System (CTS) governed through the *Intermediate Language* also commonly known as Microsoft's Intermediate Language (MSIL) and/or the *Common Intermediate Language* (CIL). Intermediate Language should not be confused with Java's interpreted byte-type coding, which does not have the ability to be compiled. Microsoft has also developed a secondary type of compilation known as JIT (just-in time) compilations. Under JIT, programs are not only installed into our systems, but that coding is optimized for individual processor. In addition, JIT compilation shortcuts the basic startup time by limiting compilation to only the required portions, which also improves overall performance.

The .Net architecture also offers some interesting advantages, including memory management (also known as garbage collection) and zero impact installation. Garbage collection (stemming from Java) is a systematic approach to eliminating previously allocated memory that is no longer being referenced. While garbage collection diminishes the programmer's power to control memory deallocation, it does help to prevent dangerous memory leaks, and saves the programmer additional time that would normally be spent implementing destructors. Likewise, zero-impact installation has been developed to save the programmer and consumer many hours of frustration by eliminating the errors caused by faulty reversioning. Under normal Window's operations, a typical *.dll* type file would be included as part of a centralized reference, which in turn would make it subject to deletion whenever a new version is installed. If that new version is not entirely backward compatible, then that replacement file can cause the program to fail. With zero-impact installation, alternate versions of otherwise identical files can exist side by side, thereby eliminating this problem.

In addition, .Net offers an increase in code security, application domain restrictions, strong typing, and namespaces. The increase in security then allows the consumer to control the level of access granted to any single program, with MSIL also determining the level of access requested by a program before its execution (This may help to prevent some unscrupulous programmers form damaging our files.). *Application domain restrictions* prevent memory conflicts between interrelated applications through the use of *virtual memory barriers*, which are barriers that restrict access, but which do not impose processor delays. (This process is controlled through the MSIL). *Strong typing,* also governed by the MSIL, requires that we specifically state our data types, thus preventing several ambiguous runtime errors.

Managed Code and Assemblies

Managed code is the term used to define the coding implemented under the .Net framework, while the terms native and unmanaged code are used to indicate coding that bypasses this new architecture and is implemented directly through the Window's API. *Assemblies* are units in which our managed coding is stored. Assemblies also contain information packets referred to as *metadata*: *metadata* packets are used to keep track of our assembly's contents including their objects, methods, and types. Shared Assemblies are stored in a central area referred to as the assembly's cache. Metadata packets are stored in an area inside these assemblies known as the *manifest*.

Algorithms

Before we can jump into writing programs, we'll have to learn a little bit about designing them. The first step in designing a program is writing its algorithm. Writing an algorithm is not the same as writing a program; it doesn't require the use of a computer language, or even a computer. An algorithm can be applied to any task or set of tasks. Writing down directions is probably one of the most common examples of an algorithm; recipes, diets, and math solutions are others. Some beginner programmers don't understand the need for algorithms, believing instead that they can plan their programs as they go, or after completing the introductory part of their coding. However, such programming styles often lead to hazards such as additional time spent problem solving and/or more time spent rewriting code to incorporate each new idea or feature. Thus, it is always best to start with an algorithm. Therefore, I've included an outline of the algorithm used to write a native C++ version of the first arcade style game taught in a later chapter –Paddle Tennis (see Example 3.5).

Example 1.1. Abbreviated Algorithm for Paddle Tennis.

1. Create a viable Windows handle accessible through the Windows console settings.
2. Write a function to draw the player's characters
3. Include a function that paints/clears the screen:
4. Define most of our variables as a member of a single class, with the most notable exception being the color settings.
5. Set the variables/members: Setting the ball to a random direction:
6. Create a while-loop that ends when the game ends:

Inside the while loop
7. Write a function that removes our residual images using a combination of calls to blank characters and/or a full-blown clear screen function.
8. Set the colors: Since these colors never change, this can be done from either the do-while or internal while loop.
9. Display the players, ball, and the scores (0 to 0 as we start):
10. Write a function that reads the players input from the keyboard.
11. Write a function to propel the ball.
12. Write a function to limit the area in which the players can traverse.
13. Include sounds when the ball bounces
14. Check to see if the ball and player have collided (see Collision Detection II:

The Ball in Motion). The ball should bounce off the player.

15. If the ball gets to the end of the screen and the player is not there, give the other player a point. Now, reset the ball.
16. Repeat the loop until either player scores some number.
17. Ask player(s) if they want to play again. Remember a good game loop should always allow the player(s) the option of playing again.
18. End or repeat game.

If this seems a bit long, keep in mind that the actual Paddle Tennis subroutines are part of a program that's more than 100 pages long, and even the simplest professionally designed program will tend to run over a 1000 pages. Algorithms do not have to include complete sentences, have correct grammar, or even need to be entirely in English. Yet, having something that you can actually read and that lists the steps to the solution would be important. Further, when writing an algorithm shared by others, never assume that they can read something written in C++; after all, they might be planning to write the program in another language such as VISUAL BASIC, C# or just plan old fashion C.

The .Net Compiler

A traditional compiler translates higher-level languages into the machines own language, appropriately named *Machine Language*. Programmers developed higher-level languages such as C and C++ to bridge the gap between our human languages and the computers binary code of ones and zeroes. As difficult as C++ and other high-level languages seem, their difficulty doesn't compare to the complexity of trying to understand the endless rolls of ones and zeros, such as 01010011 00010100 00011101 found in Machine Language. In addition to machine language, there is also a low-level language known as *Assembly Language*, which also serves as an intermediary between C and that binary code. However, the advent of Managed C++ and the .Net framework replaced this concept.

The new way of thinking about compilation is to break it into two steps: The first step is, a conversion to MSIL, which allows for both the construction and testing of our products from within our compiler's simulated environment. The second step, JIT compilation, isn't implemented until the moment of execution, hence the pun just-in time. With this new form of compiling, Microsoft has been able to implement several new features, including role-type and code-type based security, memory type safety, and interoperability. *Role-type and code-type based security* relate to a program's base of identity and the level of access granted to that code. If an unauthorized program attempts to access/alter any other applications without MSIL's express permission, the execution of that program is not allowed. The same is true for *type-safety*, if the MSIL environment detected that any newly executed program will cause a memory address conflict, that program is also denied system access. In addition, this new method opens up our coding to an entirely new level of code interoperability; with it, we can intermix between objects written in different languages, step between references, and even use those objects as inheriting classes. There is also the potential for reflective comparisons with respect to both interoperable and internal files (See later chapters for details).

Note:
Common Language Specifications: While the .Net framework is designed to promote language interoperability, the use of the Managed C++ language does not guarantee that level of interaction. We can, however, make Managed C++ CLS compliant with what are generally only minor adjustments to our overall method of programming. For example, we must adjust our programs to avoid the use of noncompliant references, data types, and conflicts do to poor naming practices. In addition, we'll have

to restrict our naming practices to avoid conflicts with Visual Basic's inability to distinguish between upper and lower case settings (e.g., Class1 and class1).

Compiling and Executing

While the theories behind proper compilation and execution were outlined in the previous sections, we still haven't established a practical method for the implantation of our applications. Before our programs can be executed either with or without an external .Net environment, they must fist go through a process known as *compilation*. Hence, to start, you'll need a computer program known as a *compiler*. I recommend Microsoft's C++ .Net 2004 in any of its packaged standards (trail, standard, professional, or enterprise). I've also included simple step-by-step instructions on how to setup those compilers.

Quick Setup for Microsoft Visual C++ .NET 2004:
1. Make sure your compiler is installed and working properly.
2. Load and activate the C++ compiler. Close any nonessential windows.
3. From the "File" menu, Select "New" and then "Project" (see Screen Shot 1.1).

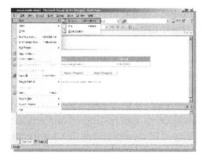

Screen Shot 1.1

4. At this point, a second window should open. Select the icon labeled "Managed C++ Application" (see Screen Shot 2).

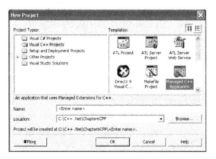

Screen Shot 1.2

You will need to enter a name in the box titled "Name." I called this first example "Chapter1," but you can use any name you'd like. Once you have entered a name, the "OK" button is enabled; click it to continue.

Your compiler is now set up and ready for input. For further details on how to setup the C++ compiler, see the Troubleshooting section at the end of this chapter, check your compiler's help files, or check out Microsoft's online guide at http://msdn.microsoft.com/visualc/.

Now, without regard for any particular compiler or series, we'll want to test to make sure that everything is setup and running correctly. We'll do this by inputting what is known as a "do- nothing" program, that is, a program that creates no significant output, yet by compiling, conveys the message that our compilers are ready. The actual commands used in this program are unimportant at this time.

5. Typing in your C++ source coding is as simple as entering text into a word processor. Just make sure that the larger window to the right is active. Note that an active window is usually marked by a blinking cursor.

Example 1.2. Our first program.

```cpp
#include "stdafx.h"
// programs entry point
void main(void) {


}
```

6. Now, from the main "Build" menu select the submenu option also labeled as "Build" (see Screen Shot 1.3).

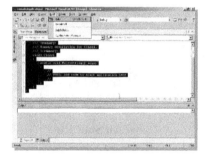

Screen Shot 1.3

You should notice a stream of information appearing in the lower compiler window, normally located at the bottom of the screen. Make sure your getting a message saying zero errors and zero warnings (see Screen Shot 1.4).

Screen Shot 1.4

If you got an error at this step, it means the project was not set up correctly. Repeat all the steps again or see Troubleshooting at the end of the chapter.

7. Finally, to execute the program, simply click on the "Build" menu and select "Execute." Your do-nothing program will now produce a large window asking you to "Press any key to continue." Doing so will end the program (see Screen Shots 1.5 and 1.6).

Screen Shot 1.5

Screen Shot 1.6

Example 1.2 Explained

C++ uses several data types, including integers, real numbers, characters, and void. Void, for all practical purposes, means without a type. Moreover, since the main function doesn't usually require a data type, void is the simplest to use. Data types such as int, float, double, char, and void are explained in detail later in this chapter.

The command void main (void) is used to declare are programs entry point. Void, the logical choice, given that our programs will not return values to the operating system. Main technically is not a keyword, but it is the first word our C++ compilers seek, main includes several modified versions defined by there suffixes (examples include _tmain, wmain, and WinMain), each represents a different aspect to the language, thus, in order to teach C++ in a complete sense, we will be switching between these formats. (Note: _tmain requires the use of *mscorlib.dll* and *tchar.h*, while managed projects required the *stdafx.h* reference).

The main methods sever as the controller to the rest of the program. In these beginning stages, we'll write all commands inside of this main method, but later, as our programs advance, we'll migrate out to other subprograms that will do specific tasks. The main method will then serve as a controller to these subprograms. Writing programs in this manner is still akin to an older method of programming known as *structured programming*, which was a very important part of both C and Native C++ that the object-oriented approach will eventually surpass.

The *opening* and *closing braces* (also know as a block) simply mark the beginning and ending to the program's environment. The computer recognizes these symbols as markers telling it were to start and were to end. Without such markers, programs would not know which coding belonged to which method. Each block, then, indicates a subenvironment, whereas the namespace's exterior block represents the global environment (Note: Comments are explained in the next section).

Comments

Comments are nothing more than system notes, usually written by a programmer, to mark or explain a certain passage that may not seem as obvious to us at a later date. For example, we might mention that the main method ends with a particular brace or that we need to alter or repair a line or two to increase system performance. Examples 1.3 and 1.4 demonstrate the general use of single and multiple line comments.

Example 1.3. Single line comments.

```
// single line comments
#include "stdafx.h"
#using <mscorlib.dll>
#include <tchar.h>
// program entry point
void _tmain(void) {
  // executable statements
} // terminate main function
```

Example 1.4. Multiple line comments.

```
/* Multiple line comments */
/* longer comments (comments spanning two lines or more) are
 * Often set aside with these special markers.
 * Comments are ignored by the compiler and thus
 * do not affect the programs speed. */
#include "stdafx.h"

void wmain(void) { // program entry point
  // executable statements
} // terminate main function
```

Managed Output

Now that we have the basics of writing a few do-nothing programs, let's see if we can add something other then comments to it. Traditionally, a first program will display the message "Hello, world!" However, it is my custom to begin my books with the words "Game Over!" (see Example 1.5).

Example 1.5. Screen output 1.

```
/* Screen Output 1 */
#include "stdafx.h"
#using <mscorlib.dll>
#include <tchar.h>

using namespace System;

void _tmain(void) { // space saving
  Console::Write("Game Over! \n");
}
```

Now there are two commands added to our do-nothing program that, in fact, .make it do something. The command that make the words "Game Over" appear can be simplified to:

```
Console::Write ("Game Over! \n");
```

While the command that moves the cursor to the next line is:

```
"\n"
```

Note: .Net's Console::Write replacing Native C++'s *cout, printf, and puts* commands. Write is formally defined as System::Console::Write("''"), where System is reference as `using namespace System.`

Replacing *Console::Write ("Game Over!");* with *Console::Write ("''");* would result in a program that would seem to do nothing, since there was nothing written between the inner and outer quotes (changing that command to Console::WriteLine would include an automatic newline character (see Example 1.6).

Example 1.6: Screen output 2.

```
/* Screen Output 2 */
#include "stdafx.h"
#using <mscorlib.dll>
#include <tchar.h>

using namespace System;

// Purpose: Displays the words "Hello, world!"
void _tmain(void) {
  Console::WriteLine("Game Over!");
}
```

You can replace the words "Game Over" with virtual any sentence, you could also add additional sentences to the program by repeating the Write/WriteLine commands. Example 1.7 displays a program with several lines of output. Feel free to input a few lines of your own.

Example 1.7. Screen output 3.

```
/* Screen Output 3 */
#include "stdafx.h"
#using <mscorlib.dll>
```

```
#include <tchar.h>

using namespace System;

void _tmain(void) {
  Console::Write("Hello, Programmer.\n");
  Console::WriteLine("How are you today?");
}
```

Unmanaged Output

As mentioned in pervious sections, C++ has included several ways of producing screen output. Two common C language commands were puts and printf. Even with the addition of the C++'s command cout, printf remained very popular. Thus, even though the .Net's Console::Write and Console::WriteLine commands combined the advantages of these three expressions. The ability to recognize unmanaged references becomes especially important. The file <iostream> is also a necessary compiler reference and is the namespace std (see Example 1.8).

Example 1.8. Screen output 4.

```
/* Screen Output 4 */
#include "stdafx.h"
#include <iostream>
using namespace std;

void main(void) {
  printf("Hello, Programmer.\n");
  cout << ("How are you today?\n");
  puts("Fine, and you?");
}
```

Symbols	Purpose
\a	Alert (bell)
\b	Backspace
\f	Formfeed
\n	Newline
\r	Carriage return
\t	Horizontal tab
\v	Vertical tab
\?	Literal quotation mark
\'	Single quotation mark
\"	Double quotation mark
\\	Backslash

Table 1.1. Escape Sequences

The Newline Character

The symbols backslash and n (\n) were used in the previous section inside a pair of quotes, but they were not displayed to the screen with the words "Game Over." This combination, known as the *newline* character, serves as a marker telling the program when to move to the next line. This newline character is one of many specialized characters referred to as the *escape sequences* (see Example 1.9). For a complete list of escape sequences, see Table 1.1.

Example 1.9: The newline character.

```
/* this program demonstrate the newline character */
#include "stdafx.h"
#using <mscorlib.dll>
#include <tchar.h>

using namespace System;

void _tmain() {
  Console::Write ("Hello, programmer. ");
  Console::Write ("How are you today? \n");
}
```

> Note:
> In this program, the newline character was not placed after the phrase "Hello, programmer." As a result, the program did not move to a new line, and thus "How are you today" did not transfer to the second line, producing, instead, the single line "Hello, programmer. How are you today?" A similar result is shown in Example 1.10.

Example 1.10. More practice with the newline character.

```
/* More practice with the newline character */
#include "stdafx.h"
#using <mscorlib.dll>
#include <tchar.h>
#include <iostream>

using namespace System;
using namespace std;

void _tmain() { // Begin main
  printf("This is line 1\n");
  printf("This is line 2\n");
  cout << ("This is line 3");
  puts (" This is still line 3");
  Console::Write ("This is line 4\n");
}
```

Note: We can also disable the automatic formatting of the newline character (or any other escape sequence), thus reproducing the codes as actual text. This is done using an additional \ symbol as shown in Example 1.11.

Example 1.11. Disabling the escape sequences using the \ symbol.

```
/* disabling the escape sequences using the \ symbol */
#include "stdafx.h"
#using <mscorlib.dll>
#include <tchar.h>
#include <iostream>

using namespace System;
using namespace std;

void _tmain() {
  Console::Write ("\\n This is line 1");
  Console::Write ("\n This is line 2");
               ("\n This is line 3");
  cout << ("\\n This is still line 3");
  printf ("\n This is line 4\n");
  puts ("\\n This is line 5\\n");
}
```

The WriteLine Command

An alternate to returning one's cursor position with the newline character is to replace it with that of the WriteLine command.

```
Console::WriteLine ("");
```

The WriteLine command is written in a manner similar to the Console::Write command, but it does not require the newline character (this is also true of the puts command). It can also be used as an output stream or statement, and (as shown above) it can be referenced without any other comments or information. To demonstrate, we'll revise our last example, replacing its Write command with a WriteLine statement (see Example 1.12).

Example 1.12. WriteLine Command.

```
/* WriteLine Command */
#include "stdafx.h"
#using <mscorlib.dll>
#include <tchar.h>
using namespace System;

void _tmain() {
  Console::WriteLine ("This is line 1");
  Console::WriteLine ("This is line 2");
  Console::Write ("This is line 3");
  Console::WriteLine (" This is still line 3");
```

```
  Console::WriteLine ("This is line 4");
}
```

We can also replace WriteLine with the older puts command (see example 1.13).

Example 1.13. Puts command.

```
/* WriteLine, write and puts */
#include "stdafx.h"
#using <mscorlib.dll>
#include <tchar.h>
#include <iostream>
using namespace System;
using namespace std;

void _tmain() {
  puts ("This is line 1");
  Console::WriteLine ("This is line 2");
  Console::Write ("This is line 3");
  Console::WriteLine (" This is still line 3");
  puts ("This is line 4");
}
```

From the users perspective there will be no difference, yet to the programmer there is quite a change in coding.

The EndLine Command

Another option, used in combination with the cout command, with similar properties to the newline character is the endline command –written:

$$cout << endl;$$

The endline command also has some benefits; for example, it does not need to be encapsulated, it can be placed before or after an output-stream, and it can be reference without any other comments (see Example 1.14).

Example 1.14. Using the Endline command.

```
/* Endline command */
#include "stdafx.h"
#using <mscorlib.dll>
#include <tchar.h>
#include <iostream>
using namespace System;
using namespace std;

void _tmain() {
  cout << "This is line 1" << endl;;
  cout << "This is line 2" << endl;
  cout << "This is line 3";
```

```
    cout << " This is still line 3" << endl;
    cout << "This is line 4" << endl;
}
```

The Semicolon

When the compiler detects a semicolon (;), it knows that the command line has ended and that it should move to the next set of instructions. This is especially important when dealing with commands that are often written in varying sizes or those that extend over more than one line. Having such a requirement also limits or restricts the potential for overlapping errors found during compilation. The semicolon is always placed at the end of a complete statement and is always used to signal the end of that statement. Commands that do not require a semicolon often do not terminate until the end of a particular section or set of commands. Some programming commands do not terminate until the program itself ends, and hence, do not require a semicolon.

Whitespaces

Whitespaces are simply blank spaces used to separate coding terms, this is also known as Free Formatting, which all modern compilers support. Variable names as well as keywords require these separations, but in many other cases, these whitespaces are just ignored. It is however, important to remember that these spaces do not indicate the end of a line, terminations of any coding, or any other such control. You should be careful not to abuse this ability to separate command lines (abuse would be any instances were such spacing cause's visual confusion on the part of the programmer).

#Include

The include statement written *#include,* is a C++ preprocessor directive that allows us to add specialized subroutines to our programs. The word "include" literally means to include that file with the project. The sharp/pound symbol (#) is always placed in front of the include statement with the file name marked with quotes or greater and lesser symbols (the style of notation depends on the type of file being accessed).
  Included files (also known as header files) are subroutines usually built into our compilers. They are essentially borrowed programs that usually add something useful like printed words to the screen or even words that are sent to the printer. To beginners the distinction between commands and keywords can become blurred, but it should be noted that included files and the command option that they create are distinctly different. The Iostream header for example gave us the cout, printf, and puts commands; if we removed the link, the commands could not be used. Keywords on the other hand are always available regardless, including as we bridge to different brands of compilers.

Indenting

Indenting is a simple way to keep your programs looking neat and organized. Indenting has been shown in all of the examples, and simply means to set commands several spaces inward from the first line of a segment, which is done to indicate that they are part of that segment. When a line is not indented, it can mean that it is not part of the segment. Indenting, while easier on the eyes, had only a cosmetic effect on source coding and will not affect the computer's/compiler's view of the material.

Trouble Shooting

Before going through the steps involved with the processes of troubleshooting, let's make sure that we understand the four basic types of errors. The first type, known as the *syntax error,* is what might be described as a grammatical error. The compiler, acting as a spell-checker, looks through our programs trying to find any and all misspelled commands and/or forgotten punctuation marks. If it finds any errors, the compiler immediately sends notification and directs us to the problem. Programs with this type of error cannot be "built," and thus no linkable objects are produced.

The Second type of error, described as a *linking error*, occurs when data is missing, faulty or just unavailable at the time of compilation. If your program compilers without errors, but there are errors when you build/rebuild them, then you've more then likely made a mistake setting up your program. If your compiler is not mentioned in this chapter, you must consult your user manual to find the problem. If you're using Microsoft Visual Studio .Net 2004 or any of the earlier versions, repeating the aforementioned procures should solve your problem.

The third type of error is known as a *runtime error*. Runtime errors usually involve asking the computer to doing something it can't, such as dividing by zero or storing a character as a number. This type of error will not be detected by the compiler and will almost always produces a program that will be prone to problems and crashes, or one which will just not run.

The fourth type of error is known as the *logic error*, which could also be called the poor planning error. Examples of this type include telling the computer to subtract when you meant for it to add, or telling it to skip a line when you wanted it to print. Not thinking out the problem and/or not writing out an algorithm usually causes this type of error. Logic errors, like runtime errors, won't usually show up when you're compiling, but they're sure to show up at some point. The best way to detect a problem of this nature is to rerun the program for several situations and, if possible, to recheck the results against a secondary source.

Common Errors, Problems, and Pits:

1. Like C and Native C++, C++ .Net is a case-sensitive languages; thus, any discrepancy in case settings will result in an error. For example, incorrectly writing *void* as either *VOID* or *Void* would result in a syntax error. (Hint: Most compilers identify keywords with a change in color).
2. The main method should have the word main, _tmain, or wmain followed by both the opening and closing parentheses.
3. The program should begin with an opening brace, e.g., {and end with a closing brace}.
4. Comments require two forward slashes, as in //, not backslashes \\. In addition, comments spanning two or more lines require both an opening forward slash and an asterisk, and a closing asterisk and forward slash, as in /* comments here */.
5. If you can't find the error, try removing all the comments and any other unnecessary coding, saving the file under a different name so that you can revert back to the original after you've isolated the error.
6. Braces placed after a comment (as in // this is a note}) are included as part of the comment and will not be read by the compiler.
7. The newline character must be written as forward slash n (/n); using the back slash will result in a syntax error.
8. Both the Write and WriteLine commands require encapsulating parentheses.
9. If you're using an older C++ compiler, you'll need to use the #include <iostream> and using namespace std or <iostream.h> header without using the namespace commands.

If your program compiles without errors, but there are errors when you build/rebuild them, then you've more then likely made a mistake setting up your program. If your compiler is not mentioned in this chapter, you must consult your users manual to find the problem. If you are using Microsoft's Visual Studio .Net 2004 or any of the earlier versions, you more than likely selected something other than the Managed C++ Application's format. In any event, you should repeat the steps given for setup.

Things to Remember

1. When creating a new compiler project always set it to "Managed C++ Application."
2. Most compilers change keywords to blue, green, or red (Microsoft uses blue) if a keyword didn't change color it's probably misspelled.
3. Comments should be used to explain source coding and to mark important points.
4. Indenting makes things easier to read but does not affect the way the computer reads the material.

Questions

1. Define the terms .Net and C++.
2. Who is the author of this book?
3. What are ANSI and ISO certification?
4. What is ECMA certification?
5. What is CLI?
6. When was C++ last standardized?
7. Define the term Managed code.
8. Define JIT?
9. Define MSIL and IL?
10. Write an algorithm that explains how to get to your nearest coffee shop.
11. Write an algorithm that explains how to play the card game fifty-two pickup.
12. Write and compile a "do-nothing" program.
13. Define the types of comments used in C++.
14. Write a "do-nothing" program that includes an initial comment describing the programs purpose and then two other comments marking the beginning and the ending of the main method.
15. Write a program that displays the words "Hey, look at me! I've written a program!"
16. Continuing from Question 15, use the newline character to separate "Hey, look at me!" from "I've written a program!"
17. Continuing from Question 16, using the WriteLine command, replace the newline character without altering the program's output.
18. Continuing from Question 17, rewrite the program to use the cout and endline commands.
19. Continuing from Question 17, rewrite the program to use the puts command.
20. Write a line of coding that requires a semicolon and one that does not.
21. Define the term Whitespace.
22. Using the program created in Question 18, insert three lines of whitespaces that do not disrupt the program's ability to compile.
23. Using the program created in question 19; insert one line of whitespaces that will cause that program to error on compilation.
24. List three included files, (optional) look them up and view there coding.
25. Explain the purpose of indenting.

Chapter Two

"A multitude of rulers is not a good thing. Let there be one ruler, one king." **Homer, The Iliad**

Variables

This chapter covers the concepts related to variables, their data types, naming, declarations, integers, floating point, characters, strings, and the use of arithmetic. We'll also be working with data input, memory management, and data conversions. To begin we'll start with the basics of variable naming.

Naming Variables

  Regardless of the language, the simplest method of storing and/or manipulating generalized data has always been through the use of variables. A *variable* is used by programs to store and retrieve both character and numeric data. While we'll save the technical/coding portions for the next few sections, we'll want to at least understand the naming procedures before moving forward. There are three basic rules when naming variables:

1. Variables can consist of only letters, numbers, and the underscore symbol.
2. Variables must always start with a letter or the underscore symbol. (Note: Underscores and coded prefixes are usually reserved by large projects, companies).
3. Variables cannot have the same name as a reserved word or keyword (see Table 2.1 for a complete list of keywords). It is possible to use the keyword __identifier to override this limitation as in __identifier(C++_keyword), but this is generally only done to allow managed classes access to external classes.

Table 2.1. Keywords.

__abstract	__alignof	__asm	__assume
__based	__box	__cdecl	__declspec
__delegate	__event	__except	__fastcall
__finally	__forceinline	__gc	__hook
__identifier	__if_exists	__if_not_exists	__inline
__int8	__int16	__int32	__int64
__interface	__leave	__m64	__m128
__m128d	__m128i	__multiple_inheritance	__nogc
__noop	__pin	__property	__raise
__sealed	__single_inheritance	__stdcall	__super
__try_cast	__try/__except, __try/__finally	__unhook	__uuidof
__value	__virtual_inheritance	__w64	bool
break	case	catch	char
class	const	const_cast	continue
default	delete	deprecated	dllexport
dllimport	do	double	dynamic_cast
else	enum	explicit	extern
false	float	for	friend
goto	if	inline	int
long	mutable	naked	namespace

new	noinline	noreturn	nothrow
novtable	operator	private	property
protected	public	register	reinterpret_cast
return	selectany	short	signed
sizeof	static	static_cast	struct
switch	template	this	thread
throw	true	try	typedef
typeid	typename	union	unsigned
using declaration, using directive	uuid	virtual	void
volatile	__wchar_t, wchar_t	while	

In addition to these variable rules, there are also some good naming practices that should be followed.

Naming suggestions

1. Give the variable a descriptive name such as Account1, tax, or joystick2; descriptive names reduce the likelihood of confusion.
2. Use a consistent style when writing variables, such as alien_1 and alien_2 or Alien_1 and Alien_2. Do not randomly mix upper and lower case letters as in AliEN_1, AliEn_1. C++, like C and C#, is a case sensitive language–it reads uppercase and lowercase letters as different symbols, and thus, these randomly named variables will not be read as the same value.
3. To remain consistent, you can adopt one of two naming styles. *Humpback*, which capitalizes the first letter of each word (PlayerOne); Camel (also known as Pascal), which capitalize the first letter of interior words, but not the initial letter (playerOne). These notations are the standard for most companies, including Microsoft.
4. Windows programmers follow a special naming procedure known as *Hungarian Notation*, which was also developed by Microsoft. This notation involves giving data types beginning letters that identify their declared types (see the Hungarian Section later in this Chapter).

Example 2.1 demonstrates how to use a variable named OurVariable, and uses several commands not yet completely explained in this section. Therefore, we'll only need to focus on the highlighted lines. You should edit and recompile this program several times, testing different variable names. Remember, you can use any name you want as long as it follows the rules stated above.

Example 2.1. Naming Variables

```
/* Naming Variables */
#include "stdafx.h"
#using <mscorlib.dll>
#include <tchar.h>
using namespace System;

void _tmain() {
  int OurVariable; // an integer data type.
  OurVariable = 1; // we can assign the value 1 to the variable
  Console::Write("The number is ");
  Console::WriteLine(OurVariable);
```

}

Remember that if you change the name in the declaring line, you'll also have to change it in the assigning and referencing lines.

Other possible variable names include:

Other possible variable names include:

-     Number   integer whole_number   computer_data
-     Lives   game_lives   deaths   bombs_on_ship

Declaring Variables and the Integer Data Types

There are five basic data types integer (int), float, double, character (char), and void. Each of these has a specific purpose, but to apply these variables properly we must first learn how to declare them. An integer is any positive or negative whole number (see Example 2.2). To declare an integer, use the keyword *int* followed by the variable name and a semicolon (Remember the semicolon ends the command line). We can declare our data types using either the common method or by expressly stating their CTS type. We can also declare multiple variables in any one program by either repeating the int keyword or adding additional variables to the line as is implied by the use of the comma operator (see Examples 2.3 and 2.4).

Example 2.2. A simple number line of integers.

$$-10, -9, -8, -7, -6, -5, -4, -3, -2, -1, 0, 1, 2, 3, 4, 5, 6, 7, 8, 9, 10\ldots$$

Example 2.3. Declaring variables using common method.

```
/* declaring variables using common method */
#include "stdafx.h"
#using <mscorlib.dll>
#include <tchar.h>
using namespace System;

void _tmain() {
  int Number1, Number2;
  // these variable were declared using the data type integer
  Number1 = 1; // Their assignment values both equal one.
  Number2 = 1;

  Console::Write("The first number is ");
  Console::Write(Number1);
  Console::Write("\nThe second number is ");
  Console::WriteLine(Number2);
}
```

Example 2.4. Declaring variables using the CTS type.

```
/* declaring Variables using the CTS type */
#include "stdafx.h"
```

```
#using <mscorlib.dll>
#include <tchar.h>
using namespace System;

void _tmain(void) {
  System::Int32 Number1, Number2;

  Number1 = 1;
  Number2 = 1;

  Console::Write ("The first number is ");
  Console::Write (Number1);
  Console::Write ("\nThe second number is ");
  Console::WriteLine(Number2);
}
```

The integer data type uses less memory than the other basic numerical data types; thus, it is the format of choice for programming tasks that do not require a floating point (real number) variable. You can also increase or reduce an integer's storage size by replacing that keyword with any of the other predefined integer data types: unsigned short, short, unsigned int, unsigned long, long and the Microsoft specific __int8, __int16, __int32, __int64, The characters reference char technically is also part of this list with a range of -128 to 127, as is the Boolean type were true equals 1 and false equals 0 (char and bool will be explained later in this Chapter). _int8 requires the least amount of systems RAM with 8 bits, with __int16 being equivalent to a *short* variable. Note: While most compilers allow the long variable to have up to twice the range as its integer (int) counterpart, Microsoft's compilers do not, restricting their long values to the same range as the integer data type.

Note: The keyword __box is a managed extension; it is used to create a managed object. Managed objects are derived from the System::ValueType. When working with Console::Write and Console::WriteLine placeholders as in {0}, {1}… are used to mark the insertion of variables. The keyword __box then includes the variable(s) to be displayed. Warning, while it is possible to compile a program where the accompanying variable is not preceded by a __box reference, the output will then will not be formatted correctly and the literal "{0}, {1}…" will be displayed. Managed objects are allocated to the heap, they are bitwise, and their addresses are returnable (see Example 2.5).

Example 2.5: Using data types unsigned short and long.

```
/* using data types unsigned short and long */
#include "stdafx.h"
#using <mscorlib.dll>
#include <tchar.h>
using namespace System;

void _tmain() {
  unsigned short Number1; // unsigned short
  long Number2;   // long integer

  Number1 = 1;
  Number2 = 1;
  Console::WriteLine ("The first number is {0}",
```

```
    __box(Number1));
  Console::WriteLine ("The second number is {0}",
    __box(Number2));
}
```

The keyword **unsigned** is used to reference a variable that does not require negative numbers (all other variables by default are signed), these include weights, distances, and other physical measurements. By adding the unsigned modifier we can double a variables range without increasing the required memory. An unsigned short, for example, gives us twice the upper limit by shifting the total range from -32,768-32,767 to 0-65,535 (for a complete list of ranges, see Table 2.2).

The Data Types **Float** and **Double**

The data types **float** and **double** are both floating point data types, and thus can be explained together. Floating point arithmetic allows for higher precision in calculations. Some floating point values are shown in Example 2.6.

Example 2.6. Floating point values.

1.0	2.5	5.15
7.146	18.001	178.01

C++ uses the keywords **float** and **double** in the same way, but doubles have twice the precision. Doubles are twice as accurate as floats and do not suffer the same risk of data loss when they're assigned to constants. The precision range of a float is seven digits (±1.5 x $10\text{-}45$ to ±3.4 x 1038), while the range for doubles is 15-16 digits (±5.0 x $10\text{-}324$ to ±1.7 x 10308). Examples 2.7 and 2.8 demonstrate these keywords.

Example 2.7: Using the date type float.

```
/* using data type float */
#include "stdafx.h"
#using <mscorlib.dll>
#include <tchar.h>
using namespace System;

void _tmain() {
  float Number1, Number2;    // float comes from the word floating point
  Number1 = 1.0f; // using the f converter
  Number2 = 1.1f; // to convert to float

  Console::Write ("The first number is ");
  Console::Write (Number1);
  Console::Write ("\nThe second number is ");
  Console::WriteLine(Number2);
}
```

Example 2.8. Using the data type double.

```
/* using data type double */
#include "stdafx.h"
#using <mscorlib.dll>
#include <tchar.h>
using namespace System;

void _tmain() {
  double Number1, Number2;
  Number1 = 1.0;
  Number2 = 1.1;

  Console::WriteLine ("The first number is ",
    __box(Number1));
  Console::WriteLine ("\nThe second number is ",
    __box(Number2));
}
```

Example 2.9. Using doubles and floats.

```
/* Using doubles and floats */
#include "stdafx.h"
#include <iostream>
using namespace std;

void main() {
  double Number1, Number2;
  Number1 = 1.0;
  Number2 = 1.1;

  cout << "The first number is " << Number1 << endl;
  cout << "The second number is " << Number2 << endl;
}
```

The Data Type Decimal

In addition to the basic data type, there are also several expanded data types (including the predefined integer types listed earlier and several advanced types that we'll hold off on until later). This section introduces the .Net extended type Decimal (written with a capital D). The Decimal is used to calculate monetary equations that bring the highest level of accuracy to the dollar amount (see Example 2.10).

Example 2.10. Using the .Net extension Decimal.

```
/* Using the .Net extension Decimal */
#include "stdafx.h"
#using <mscorlib.dll>
#include <tchar.h>
using namespace System;
```

```
void _tmain() {
  Decimal Number1, Number2;
  Number1 = 1.0;
  Number2 = 1.1;

  Console::WriteLine ("The first number is {0}
    \nThe second number is {1}",
    __box(Number1), __box(Number2));
}
```

The Data Type *character*

The data type character (char) is declared and accessed in the same manner as the numeric variables, the main difference being that they allow for the storage of characters rather than numeric information. Technically, numbers are also included in this list of characters, but their values are not equivalent to their numeric counterparts. Character variables are declared using the keyword char, and can be assigned through user input and/or as a part of a declaration/assignment. They are only capable of holding a single character value, and are assigned using single quotation marks (see Example 2.11).

Example 2.11. The character data type.

```
/* the character data type */
#include "stdafx.h"
#using <mscorlib.dll>
#include <tchar.h>
using namespace System;

void _tmain() {
  char Symbol;
  Symbol = 'A';

  Console::WriteLine
    ("And the first letter in the alphabet is {0}.",
    __box( __box(Symbol)->ToChar(0)));
}
```

Note: Here we could have also switched to the .Net extension Char, bypassing the need for the secondary boxing and character data conversion (data conversions will be explained later in this chapter). See Example 2.12.

Example 2.12. The Char .Net Extension.

```
/* the Char .Net Extension */
#include "stdafx.h"
#using <mscorlib.dll>
#include <tchar.h>
using namespace System;

void _tmain() {
```

```
   Char Symbol = 'A';

   Console::WriteLine
   ("And the first letter in the alphabet is {0}.",
     __box(Symbol));
}
```

Table 2.2 (Approximate storage capacities)

Types	Description	Range
char unsigned	Character type (ASCII)	-128 to 127, 0 to 255
short, unsigned short	Integral type	-32768 to 32767, 0 to 65,535
int, long unsigned	Integral type	-2,147,483,648 to 2,147,483,647 0 to 4,294,967,295
__int8 __int16 __int32	Microsoft specific integral type	Char short int/long
__int64		-9223372036854775808 to 9223372036854775807, 0 to 18,446,744,073,709,551,615
Float	32-bit single precision floating-point	$\pm1.5 \times 10^{-45}$ to $\pm3.4 \times 10^{38}$
Double	64-bit double precision floating-point	$\pm5.0 \times 10^{-324}$ to $\pm1.7 \times 10^{308}$
System::Decimal	.Net Extension	$\pm1.0 \times 10^{-28}$ to $\pm7.9 \times 10^{28}$
_m64	N/A	MMX and 3DNow!
_m128	N/A	SIMD Extension
_m128d/_m128i	N/A	SIMD Extension

Storage Capacities: *Sizeof* and *__alignof*

Most computers/compilers use the same standard ranges when declaring their data types (see Table 2.2). Microsoft differs by making the integer and long equivalent (replacing the traditional long with the __int64 type). C++ can use the keywords *sizeof* and *__alignof* to gather the exact range of each data type as part of a test program run by the compiler (see Examples 2.13 and 2.14).

Example 2.13. sizeof.

```
/* sizeof */
#include "stdafx.h"
#using <mscorlib.dll>
#include <tchar.h>
using namespace System;

void _tmain() {
  Console::Write ("unsigned short = ");
```

```
  Console::WriteLine (sizeof (unsigned short));
  Console::Write ("short = ");
  Console::WriteLine (sizeof (short));
  Console::Write ("unsigned int = ");
  Console::WriteLine (sizeof (unsigned int));
  Console::Write ("integer = ");
  Console::WriteLine (sizeof (int));
  Console::Write ("unsigned long = ");
  Console::WriteLine (sizeof (unsigned long));
  Console::Write ("long = ");
  Console::WriteLine (sizeof (long));
  Console::Write ("float = ");
  Console::WriteLine (sizeof (float));
  Console::Write ("double = ");
  Console::WriteLine (sizeof (double));
  Console::Write ("long double = ");
  Console::WriteLine (sizeof (long double)) ;
}
```

Example 2.14. __alignof.

```
/* __alignof */
#include "stdafx.h"
#using <mscorlib.dll>
#include <tchar.h>
using namespace System;

void _tmain() {
  Console::Write ("unsigned short = ");
  Console::WriteLine (__alignof (unsigned short));
  Console::Write ("short = ");
  Console::WriteLine (__alignof (short));
  Console::Write ("unsigned int = ");
  Console::WriteLine (__alignof (unsigned int));
  Console::Write ("integer = ");
  Console::WriteLine (__alignof (int));
  Console::Write ("unsigned long = ");
  Console::WriteLine (__alignof (unsigned long));
  Console::Write ("long = ");
  Console::WriteLine (__alignof (long));
  Console::Write ("float = ");
  Console::WriteLine (__alignof (float));
  Console::Write ("double = ");
  Console::WriteLine (__alignof (double));
  Console::Write ("long double = ");
  Console::WriteLine (__alignof (long double)) ;
}
```

The Data Type *void*

As previously mentioned, *void* is a data type that holds no data. It thus severs the purpose of telling the compiler that a variable or returning function requires no data, which is logical since the ending of the main function is also the ending of the program, and there would be no program to receive information. *Void* is also most commonly associated with user-defined functions that use reference and generalized pointers variables (explained in later chapters). Unlike the other data types, void does not take a position in memory. Therefore, we won't need to measure its size in bytes.

Assignment Statements

One other aspect to the above examples remains to be explained, namely, the equal sign (also known as the assignment operator). Quite obviously, using an equal sign means to make the variable equal to whatever number we assign, and is therefore known as an assignment statement. This works equally well for assigning a variable to a literal constant or a referenced variable (as demonstrated in Example 2.15).

Example 2.15. Using the assignment operator.

```
number_shown = x + 1;
// Arithmetic will be explained later in this chapter
```

Unlike mathematical expressions, assignment statements are always formulated with the receiving variable positioned to the left. Example 2.15, although similar to an algebraic expression does not involve any inference of data. In fact, an unreferenced or undefined variable used to assign such a value would result in the minimum of a compiler warning (see Example 2.16).

Example 2.16. Compiler warning resulting from an undefined variable.

```
/* Compiler warning resulting from an undefined variable. */
 - int n, x = 2, y;
// Any variable assigned to another
// variable must by requirement be
 - n = x + 1;
// assigned a value itself, before
// that secondary assignment can occur.
 -  n = y + 1;
// variable referenced without being declared.
```

Type Compatibility: Implicit Conversions

Before we begin to combine numbers in the form of equations, we have to make sure that their data types are compatible. Numeric data types, as you remember, were short, int, long, float, double, and Decimal. The best way to calculate and assign these data types is to use their matching data types (for examples; short to short, float to float, and double to double), but when this is not possible, converting between data types is an option. The safest data conversions always involve converting from smaller to larger data types e.g. short to int, int to long, long to float, and float to double or any of the smaller to larger types. Any other type of conversion may result in the loss in data and/or in a calculation error. Since float, double, and Decimal are all floating point values, you many not notice a problem when preparing your algorithm (that's not to say there wouldn't be a problem, just that you might not notice it). The worst type of intermixing would be from floating point to integer, which would be allowed, but should sight a warning. That said, many programmers still write programs that involve the intermixing of these larger to smaller data types relying on compiler defaults to calculate them in their favor.

Dear IRS, in regards to my last SEVEN tax returns; there was a slight error in my program's ability to convert data types and although it was quite an amusing error…

Formatting Strings

In addition to being able to display our simple text layouts using the Write and WriteLine commands, we can also format that text to give our programs a more controlled output. This works especially well when dealing with variables. A single numeric value then indicates a reference to the appropriate variable: {0} {1}, and {2} reference the first, second, and third variables, respectively. Moreover, we can also apply right and left justifications by inserting a secondary control sequence, inserting a positive number as {0, 6}, denotes a 6 space shift of the right, whereas the insertion of a negative control sequence results in a left-shift {0, -3} e.g. three spaces to the left. We can also exert a third level of control, which involves string formatting, for example {0, -3:C2}, where C stands of our local currency and the 2 represents the number of decimal places to be displayed (See Table 2.3 for a complete list of formatting strings). Finally, we can use the numeric symbol (#) as a placeholder, as in Console::WriteLine ("{0.#.00}", variables); (for further examples, see the Arithmetic section).

Table 2.3. String Formats.

String Format	Description
C	Currency (local)
D	Decimal (decimal point)
E	Exponential (Scientific Notation)
F	Fixed-point
G	General (E or F, to reduce space)
N	Number (inserts commas as in 1,313.02)
P	Percent
X	Hexadecimal

Arithmetic

Using arithmetic operators in C++ is much like using a handheld calculator or doing arithmetic on paper. There aren't any formulas or fancy codes to remember, it's just adding, subtracting, multiplying, dividing, and finding remainders (yes, remainders, like the ones you use to find before learning long division). Since we've already seen an example of adding that's where we'll start. To add two or more numbers together we'll have to use the plus sign (+). Nevertheless, you can't just write "1 + 1 =" and expect the computer to do the rest –you'll have to write it out into a program as was done for us in example 2.17.

Example 2.17. Integer addition.

```
/* Integer Addition */
#include "stdafx.h"
#using <mscorlib.dll>
#include <tchar.h>
using namespace System;

void _tmain() {
   int number1 = 5, number2 = 2, total;
   total = number1 + number2;
   Console::WriteLine("{0} + {1} = {2}",
      __box(number1), __box(number2), __box(total) );
}
```

Program Walkthrough:
This program starts with the normal introductory comments–the using and namespace references (remember these references are required when working with our base class library). Next, there's the *void* data type linked to main. Then as we start the main method, we declare three variables, all of type integer. We assign the first two values 5 and 2 using the assignment operator (=). Then, something new: We tell the computer to make the third variable equal to the sum of the other two. Finally, we displayed the equation "5 + 2 = 7."

Try compiling and running this program and you'll see that the WriteLine command displays our equation. You can also change the variables to any positive or negative whole number. Recompile and watch the display change. Not surprisingly, subtraction, multiplication, and division are used in exactly the same manner (see Examples 2.18 – 2.20). You can retype each example or just reedit the first one to match the changes; you might also want to experiment with alternate data types, comments, and the variables names.

Example 2.18. Integer subtraction.

```
/* Subtraction 5 - 2 with integers    */
#include "stdafx.h"
#using <mscorlib.dll>
#include <tchar.h>
using namespace System;

void _tmain() {
   int number1 = 52, number2 = 22, total;
   total = number1 - number2;

   Console::WriteLine("{0} - {1} = {2}",
      __box(number1), __box(number2), __box(total));
}
```

To multiply and divide we use the asterisks (*) and the forward slash (/), respectively.

Example 2.19. Multiplication with data type *float*.

```
/* 5 Multiplied by 2 - with data type float */
#include "stdafx.h"
#using <mscorlib.dll>
#include <tchar.h>
using namespace System;

void _tmain(){
  float number1, number2, total;
  number1 = 5.0F;     // When using float include an F
  number2 = 2.0f;
  total = number1 * number2;
  Console::WriteLine (" {0, 3:C2}\nx {1, 3:C2}\n  ----\n {2, 3:C2}",
    __box(number1), __box(number2), __box(total));
}
```

Example 2.20. Division with data type *double*.

```
/* 5 divided by 2 - with data type double   */
#include "stdafx.h"
#using <mscorlib.dll>
#include <tchar.h>
using namespace System;

void _tmain() {
  double number1 = 5.0, number2 = 2.0, total;

  total = number1 / number2;
  Console::WriteLine (" {0, 3:E}\n/ {1, 3:E}\n ---\n {2, 3:E}",
    __box(number1), __box(number2), __box(total));
  Console::WriteLine ("\n {0, 3:F}\n/ {1, 3:F}\n ---\n {2, 3:F}",
    __box(number1), __box(number2), __box(total));
  Console::WriteLine ("\n {0, 3:G}\n/ {1, 3:G}\n ---\n {2, 3:G}",
    __box(number1), __box(number2), __box(total));
}
```

We can also use combinations of symbols, as shown in Example 2.21. This example maintains the values for number1 and number2 as previously introduced; it multiplies them together (5 x 2 equaling 10) and then adds the value of number1 to that product (10 + 5 = 15).

Example 2.21. Order of operations 1.

```
Total = number1 * number2 + number1;
        12 = 5 * 2 + 5
```

To change the order of the calculation, use parentheses as shown in Example 2.22. This equation now adds the last two numbers first and then multiples their sum by the first value working in the default from left to right, multiplication and division take precedence over addition and subtraction, making the total 35, showing the importance of defining the order of operations.

Example 2.22. Order of operations 2.

```
Total = number1 * (number2 + number1);
        35 = 5 * (2 + 5)
```

In some cases, the order of our calculations can still be left to the default settings, but most of the time we'll want to guarantee the order of execution through the enlistment of parenthetical expressions. Example 2.23 shows how confusing an undistinguished expression can be, while Example 2.24 clears up much of the confusion with a minor bit of effort.

Example 2.23. Order of operations 3.

```
Total = number1 * number2 / number1 + number2 - number1;
        By order of operations: 5 * 2 / 5 + 2 - 5 = -1
```

Example 2.24. Order of operation 4.

```
Total = ((number1 * number2)/number1) + number2 - number1;
        By order of parentheses: ((5 * 2) /5) + 2 - 5 = -1
```

There is one last arithmetic symbol, but its meaning isn't as obvious. It is the remainder, as in, to find the remainder of a number divided by a second number. Example 2.25 gives a sample of how this in a program.

Example 2.25. The remainder symbol.

```
Total = number1 % number2;
// the remainder of 5 divided by 2 is 1.
```

Since we have been using the data type integer, 5 divided by 2 is not 2.5, but 2, because, the result is the truncated integers (by definition are whole numbers) and therefore a whole number; thus, we use the remainder symbol (%) to find the remainder (see Example 2.26).

Example 2.26. The remainder symbol with data type integer.

```
/* The remainder symbol with data type integer */
#include "stdafx.h"
#using <mscorlib.dll>
#include <tchar.h>
using namespace System;

void _tmain() {
  int number1 = 5, number2 = 2, total, remainder;

  total = number1 / number2;
  remainder = number1 % number2;
  Console::WriteLine ("\n  {0, 7:N}\n/ {1, 7:N}\n ---\n  {2, 7:N}",
    __box(number1), __box(number2), __box(total));
  Console::WriteLine ("And the remainder is {0, 7:N}",
    __box(remainder));
  Console::WriteLine ("\nAnd the remainder is {0:#.00}",
    __box(remainder));

  double percent, num1 = 5.0, num2 = 2.0;
  percent = num2/num1;
  Console::WriteLine ("\n{0} is {1, 0:P} of {2}",
    __box(num2), __box(percent), __box(num1));
}
```

If you find any of the equations confusing, try rewriting them out on paper, choose some new numbers, and see if you can predict their outcome; then when you're ready move on to the next section, which, by the way, finally explains how to input data from the keyboard.

Table 2.4. Arithmetic Operators.

Function	Symbol	Written as
1. Addition	+	`total = number1 + number2;`
2. Subtraction	-	`total = number1 - number2;`
3. Multiplication	*	`total = number1 * number2;`
4. Division	/	`total = number1 / number2;`
5. Remainder	%	`total = number1 % number2;`

Keyboard Input

The cin, Read, and ReadLine commands, as their names imply, allow us to input information from the keyboard. Read and ReadLine statements are written using the console reference, similar to the Write commands, while the cin >> command is associated with the cout << reference, the difference being that these are used to extract information rather than to project it. The basic Read and cin commands are only capable of storing single character inputs, while the ReadLine command is capable of storing whole strings (see Examples 2.27 and 2.28).

Example 2.27. The Read and cin commands.

```
/* The Read and cin commands */
#include "stdafx.h"
#using <mscorlib.dll>
#include <tchar.h>
#include <iostream>

using namespace System;
using namespace std;

void _tmain(){
  int integer;

  Console::Write ("Enter a number here: ");
  cin >> integer;

  Console::WriteLine ("And the number you entered is {0}",
    __box(integer));

  Console::Write ("Enter a number here: ");
  integer = Console::Read();

  Console::WriteLine ("And the number you entered is {0}",
    __box(__box(integer)->ToChar(0)));
}
```

Program Walkthrough:
The .Net system is referenced (including the iostream header) the *void* data type declares the main function. The first statement prints the text line "Enter a number here." Now the cin function waits for the user to input a number. When a whole number is entered, the program will store this information into the variable integer. The program will then reprint its value after the words "The number you entered is:" This process can be repeated for any real number data types, as well as the data character type – see Example 2.28.

Example 2.28. The ReadLine command with various data types.

```
/* The ReadLine command with various data types */
#include "stdafx.h"
#using <mscorlib.dll>
#include <tchar.h>
#include <iostream>

using namespace System;
using namespace std;

void _tmain() {
```

```
    String *Name, *convert;
    float RealNumber;

    Console::WriteLine ("Enter a number here: ");
    convert = Console::ReadLine ();

    Console::WriteLine ("Enter your name here: ");
    Name = Console::ReadLine ();

    RealNumber = (float) convert->ToDouble(0);
    Console::WriteLine ("Your name is {0}", Name);
    Console::WriteLine ("And the number you entered is {0}",
        __box(RealNumber));
}
```

Uninitialized Variables

Another key component of the bond C++ language/ .Net 2004 compiler, is the inaccessibility of undeclared variables. This new standard produces an error rather than a warning upon any attempt to access an unassigned memory location. The decision to change was based primarily on the need to offset the abundance of minor errors found when those unassigned values were represented by random data access. Understandably, if we could not filter out those random values, our results become unpredictable and subsequently useless in any matter of importance. Keep in mind that we have been properly declaring and initializing variables throughout this text. Moreover, in our last few examples, we even expanded upon the methods used to assign those variables. However, the most practical of all the methods is to include an assignment statement at the moment of declaration, thereby removing any chance of error (see Example 2.29).

Example 2.29. Declaring and initializing variables.

```
/* Declaring and initializing Variables */
#include "stdafx.h"
#using <mscorlib.dll>
#include <tchar.h>
using namespace System;

void _tmain() {
  int OurVariable = 1;
  Console::WriteLine("Our variable was assigned as {0}",
      __box(OurVariable));
}
```

The Access Modifiers constant and volatile

We can also simultaneously declare and initialize variables using the variable type constant. A constant variable cannot change its value after it has been specified. Declaring a constant variable is similar to our last example, but with the added keyword const which, of course, stands for constant. Adding the keyword *const* notifies the compiler of its unchanging nature and allows it to optimize storage space for that value (see Example 2.30).

Example 2.30. Declaring constant variables.

```
/* Declaring Constant Variables */
#include "stdafx.h"
#using <mscorlib.dll>
#include <tchar.h>
using namespace System;

void _tmain() {
  const int OurVariable = 1;
  Console::WriteLine("Our Variable was assigned as {0}",
    __box(OurVariable));
}
```

Adding the keyword const to a variable of type float, double, or char would make them constants. Keep in mind that their values would also have to be assigned as they are declared (see Example 2.31).

Example 2.31. Constant variables of various data types.

```
/* Constant variables of various data types */
#include "stdafx.h"
#using <mscorlib.dll>
#include <tchar.h>
using namespace System;

void _tmain() {
  const int number1 = 1;
  const float number2 = 2.5F;
  const double number3 = 3.14159;   // PI
  const char symbol1 = 'A';

  Console::WriteLine ("This is a constant of type integer {0}",
    __box(number1));
  Console::WriteLine ("This is a constant of type float {0}",
    __box(number2));
  Console::WriteLine ("This is a constant of type double {0}",
    __box(number3));
  Console::WriteLine ("This is a constant of type char {0}",
    __box(__box(symbol1)->ToChar(0)));
}
```

In contrast, the keyword volatile (written as const volatile char varaible1) expresses that the variable it proceeds will change dramatically. For example, a value may be altered by the system's clock, or used to pass data to a component in hardware. In either case, foregoing the volatile command will result in the compiler automatically limiting that variable (this is done to optimize the program's performance). Thus, in order to keep our variable's access open to many possibilities, we'll need to insert the volatile command before such variables.

#define

You can also rewrite numeric constant using a native C/C++ preprocessor directive #define (preprocessor directives are covered in greater detail later in this text). #define, works much like a combination of multiple data types and constant identifiers. The #define directive must be placed before the main function and does not require an equal sign or semicolon (see Example 2.32).

Example 2.32. The preprocessor directive #define.

```
/* The preprocessor directive #define */
#include "stdafx.h"
#using <mscorlib.dll>
#include <tchar.h>
#include <iostream>
using namespace System;
using namespace std;

#define number1    1
#define number2    2.5
#define number3    3.14159

void _tmain() {
  Console::WriteLine("This value reflects an integer {0}",
    __box(number1));
  Console::WriteLine("A floating point variable {0}",
    __box(number2));
  Console::WriteLine("A double {0}",
    __box(number3));
}
```

Incrementing & Decrementing Operators

The incrementing (++) and decrementing (--) operators increase and decrease their variables by one numeric value, respectively. This holds true for all numeric data types, including the extended integer, floating point, or Decimal references (character data is handled differently). The operators can be used in either postfix mode (x++) or prefix mode (++x). Prefix mode refers to a calculation that must occur before a variable is accessed by a secondary equation, whereas postfix mode allows for that variable to be read, equated, and then altered after the completion of the equation. There are, of course, advantages to each type, and the latter explains the pun C++. Use examples 2.33 and 2.34 to test these operators. You should revise these examples using several of the other numeric data types, as well as both postfix and prefix modes.

Example 2.33. Incrementing operators.

```
/* Incrementing operators */
#include "stdafx.h"
#using <mscorlib.dll>
#include <tchar.h>
using namespace System;

void _tmain() {
  int number = 1;
  number++; // 2
  Console::WriteLine ("The number is {0}",
     __box(number++)); // 2
  Console::WriteLine ("The number is {0}",
     __box(number)); // 3
}
```

Example 2.34. Decrementing operators.

```
/* Decrementing operators */
#include "stdafx.h"
#using <mscorlib.dll>
#include <tchar.h>
using namespace System;

void _tmain() {
  int number = 1;
  number++; // 2

  Console::WriteLine ("The number is {0}",
     __box(++number)); // 3
  Console::WriteLine ("The number is {0}",
     __box(number)); // 3
}
```

Metonym Data Types

A metonymic expression is a word or phrase used to redefine an object for either casual or systemized reference. This secondary name may or may not add clarity to the definition, but sometimes this is not the purpose of the naming scheme. For example, in terms of language, this could mean anything from naming your pet to referring to a friend by their screen name. In C and C++ we can use the keyword typedef (which literally means defining what you've entered) to add additional names for data types. Applying a new declaratory reference won't actually alter our variables data type, but it will give us additional benefits later (see Example 2.35).

Example 2.35. Metonym data types.

```
/* Metonym data types */
#include "stdafx.h"
#using <mscorlib.dll>
#include <tchar.h>
using namespace System;

void _tmain() {
  // cat becomes a metonym for int
  typedef int cat;
  cat number = 1;

  Console::WriteLine("Data type cat = {0}",
    __box(number));
}
```

Keyword Defaults

The C++ language includes a few older keywords, namely **auto**, and **signed**, used to declare actions that are equivalent to the system's default settings. These keywords are not required or commonly used in current C++ programs, but they are still necessary in the understanding of the complete C++ language. The first of these, **auto**, a storage class specifier, is used when declaring localized variables. Localized meaning; created as part of a function that is opened and destroyed as the block is closed. This action is part of the definition used to describe local variables and hence auto is not needed when declaring our variables. Auto's origins lead back to the days of the B language, and only existing now for backward compatibly with some older C programs.

   Signed, allows variables to hold both positive and negative values; again, something we assume when declaring variables. Using the reverse, **unsigned**, is very common when attempting to save memory while increasing an integer's positive range, but alas, it too has no practical value, i.e., you won't see it much, but when you do, you'll need to understand the concept behind it.

Using Namespace

One very noticeable change from Native C++ to C++ 2004 is the altered use of the **iostream** classes, and hence the keywords **using** and **namespace**. These redefined commands are a result of a larger object-oriented change found in the Base Class Libraries. The most notable alterations include the reference to the namespace System (as in **using System**), and the external user-defined **namespaces** (as in Chapter1, etc.). System is one of the larger namespaces developed for the Base Class Library. We can also nest and/or expand[3] those namespaces to include a hierarchical structure. While we've already worked with many of the abbreviated examples, it is also important to become familiar with the extended form (as in Example 2.36).

---

[3] That is to include within a secondary or multiple set of files.

Example 2.36. Not using "using."

```
/* not using "using" */
#include "stdafx.h"
#using <mscorlib.dll>
#include <tchar.h>

void _tmain() {
  System::Console::WriteLine ("Hello, World!");
}
```

Hungarian Notation

Hungarian notation, named for the ethnicity of its developer Charles Simonyi, is Microsoft's formal way of identifying variables based on their data types. This notation is used by many programmers, especially those that work for Microsoft and it is not limited to the C++ language. The notation uses prefixes attached to variables that are always written in lowercase. For example, the prefix that identifies a character is simply the letter c, thus a declaration of a character can be as simple as (char cVariable;). The integer data type is identified with the letter i, the letter n identifies a short integer, and l indicates a long integer (e.g., int ipassword; short nID; long lAccount). (Note: While there is less of a need for such notation, it is still very popular with many C++ programmers -see Table 2.5).

Table 2.5. Data Types.

Data Types:	Prefixes
Boolean	B
BYTE (unsigned char)	By
Character (for types char, WCHAR, and TCHAR)	C
Integer used as x, y lengths (c stands for count).	Cx, cy
Double WORD (unsigned long integer)	Dw
Function	Fn
Handle	H
Integers	i
Integer used as x, y coordinates	X, y
f stands for "flags"	F
Long Integers	l
String	S
String terminated by 0 character	Sz
Pointer	P
Short Integers	N
WORD (unsigned short integer)	W

Note: Hungarian Notation does not include prefixes for the data types *float*, *double*, or *Decimal*. This actually makes sense, since they're all floating-point variables and the lack of notation is in essence a form of notation.

We might also consider the reasoning that floating point variables should always reflect their data requirements, and should only be converted or declared using higher precision data types in order to avoid data loss.

Trouble Shooting

It's time for another deep breath and a bit of problem solving. Remember that if you don't find the answers here they might have been explained in the last chapter under troubleshooting (see Chapter 1). First let's look at the problem for a logical standpoint; let's assume that you've worked, successfully, with all of the programs listed in the last chapter. If so, then any problems would have to relate to syntax. Question, does the program error at compilation? Try resetting the warning level to a lower setting, did those errors become warnings, –Perhaps you had a syntax error, look for errors caused by using the wrong symbols in your comparisons. If there are no compiling errors, but the program's data is still producing incorrect output try look for reversed symbols, typographical errors, incomplete coding errors.

Common Errors, Problems, and Pits:

1. Did you follow the rules given in this chapter on naming variables? Breaking these rules usually causes syntax errors.
2. One error can cause your compiler to spit out several compiling errors; thus you should always attempt to recompile your program if no other errors seem likely.
3. Did you misspell the variables name? Undefined statement errors are usually caused by such misspellings.
4. Did you forget the comma when adding several variables to a single line?
5. Did you forget a semicolon or did you put one were it wasn't suppose to be?
6. Did you forget the single quote or use double quotes when assigning a character variable?
7. You must use an integer value when calculating the remainder.
8. Symbol combinations such as ==, !=, and >= cannot be written with spaces between them (= =, ! =).
9. Reversing != with =! and >= with => is defiantly and error and should always be avoided even if the program seems to work.
10. Do not confuse = with ==. Remember = is used to assign a value and == is used to compare two values.
11. Listing any keywords or variables with a space between the letters is always an error.

Things to Remember

1. Using integers or bytes reduces the amount of RAM (Random Access Memory) that your program will need. Games that use less RAM can be played on more computers (also the extra RAM can be used to improve graphic, sounds or just plan speed things up).
2. When using floating point variables, you can save memory by choosing **float** over **double**.
3. The character data type can only hold one letter or symbol and uses the single quote (don't worry, there are ways to store whole words, and sentences, but they're several chapters away).
4. Variables should not be read without first being initialized.
5. User cannot change variables declared as constants, using the keyword **volatile** prevents unwanted optimization.
6. Although your compiler doesn't care about good grammar, you should make sure to use proper spacing, including adding one space after each comma and spaces between arithmetic operators.
7. You should take the time to study your operating system and compiler; feel free to experiment with keywords and commands–try to get a feel for what they do and where on the screen they do it.
8. Avoid variable names that start with single or double underscores these may cause conflicts with advanced assignment statements.

9. Use parentheses rather than relying on the order of operations when using arithmetic operators. Using excess parentheses won't harm your program, but leaving necessary ones out will. The key is to make things clear through the use of spacing and a comfortable amount of parentheses.
10. Finally, don't worry about rushing to the end or trying to jump right into the advanced code. Everything you'll need is in this book; you'll just have to be patient.

Questions

1. Write a program that declares four separate variables using the data-types int, float, double, and char.
2. Continuing from Question 1, add four additional lines of coding that assign appropriate values to each of the listed variables.
3. Continuing from Question 2, using only the declared statements, assign appropriate values to each variable.
4. How many keywords are listed for the CLI bond C++ languages?
5. Using only integers, write a program that adds and then subtracts two numbers.
6. Revise Question 5, so that it uses the Microsoft specific data type __int64.
7. Using either single or double precision values, write a program that first multiplies and than divides two numbers.
8. Revise Question 7, so that it uses the .Net data type Decimal.
9. Write a program that finds the digits after the decimal point for any irrational number.
10. Write a program that reads in a character and echoes it back using both Write and WriteLine.
11. Write a program that demonstrates at lest three forms of arithmetic (addition, subtraction, multiplication, division, or remainders), also use at least one string format (Currency, Decimal, Exponential, Fixed point, General, Number, Percent, or Hexadecimal).
12. Write a program that uses preprocessor directives rather than standard data types, have it calculate the sum of two numbers and display their total.
13. Write a program that uses the keyword typedef to create three metonymic integers, demonstrate both addition and subtraction with those values.
14. Write a program that using both incrementing and decrementing operators.
15. Write a simple "Hello World" program, that does not use the using namespace reference.
16. Using different data types, list three variable names following the rules of Humpback, Pascal, Camel, and Hungarian notation (label each).

Chapter Three

"Do not go where the path may lead, go instead where there is no path and leave a trail."
Ralph Waldo Emerson

Branches & Loops

This chapter begins with the basic control sequences: if, else, switch, and the && (and), || (or), and ! (not) operators. It also covers the iteration processes as in the while, do-while, and for loops. Mathematical abbreviations are also discussed in this chapter, as well as Boolean expressions, short circuit evaluations, and type casting.

The If Statement

Before we can begin to write even the simplest of interactive programs, we'll have to first learn to create programming branches. Branches are alternate paths developed inside a single program to respond to the unique actions of the user. The paths then are sets of coding that include instructions relating to the choices made by the user. When combining these blocks with specifically designed responses we can create program interaction. C++ offers an abundance of ways to accomplish this task; the simplest of these is the if statement, thus, this is where we'll begin.

To this point, all of our programs have followed a single path. That is, they do one-step and then the next without regard for our input. Example 3.1 demonstrates this nonresponsive, linear form of programming. To test this program, try inputting something other then the requested data.

Example 3.1. A nonresponsive program.

```
/* A nonresponsive program */
#include "stdafx.h"
#using <mscorlib.dll>
#include <tchar.h>
using namespace System;

void _tmain(void) {        // Begin main
  int iResponse; // Step 1 - try typing N for NO
  Console::WriteLine ("Input <Y> for YES: ");
  iResponse = Console::Read (); // Step 2
  Console::WriteLine ("\n You typed Y\n");
}
```

Now, in order to make this program respond correctly (i.e, responding where the proper key is depressed), we'll have to give our program the ability to compare data. This is done with the keyword if and the comparison operator (e.g., = =, see Table 3.1). The first step, then, will be to rewrite the last program using the if statement (see Example 3.2).

> Note:
> Remember the C++ language is case sensitive, thus the letters Y and y are not
> considered equivalent inputs. For the correct response, the uppercase Y is required.

Example 3.2. Using the if statement.

```
/* using the keyword if */
#include "stdafx.h"
#using <mscorlib.dll>
#include <tchar.h>
using namespace System;

void _tmain(void) {
  int iResponse;
  Console::Write ("Input <Y> for YES:  "); // Step 1
  iResponse = Console::Read (); // Step 2
  if ((char) iResponse == 'Y') // Step 3 - if response equals 'Y'
    Console::WriteLine ("\n You typed Y\n");
}
```

This program still displays the message "You typed Y," but now only if the letter Y is actually entered. If any other character is entered, the program simply ends and nothing is written to the screen. This is true for any letter or character data as long as it equals the variable. Try reediting this program so that it responds to both upper and lowercase letters ('Y' || 'y'). If you alter the required input, remember to alter the accompanying inquiry. For our next task, we'll modify the program so that it uses numerical data (see Example 3.3).

Table 2.1. Comparison Operators.

1. Two equal signs "= =" meaning "equal to" as in
  -   if (variable1 = = variable2)
  -   // 5 is equal to 5

2. Less than symbol "<" meaning "less than" as in
  -   if (variable1 < variable2)
  -   // 5 is less than 10

3. Less than or equal to "<=" meaning "less than or equal to" as in
  -   if (variable1 <= variable2)
  -   // 5 is less than or equal to 10

4. Greater than ">" meaning "greater than" as in
  -   if (variable1 > variable2)
  -   // 20 is greater than 10

5. Greater than or equal to ">=" meaning "greater than or equal to" as in
  -   if (variable1 >= variable2)
  -   // 20 is greater than or equal to 10

6. Not equal "!=" meaning "Not equal" as in
  -   if (variable1 != variable2)
  -   // 20 does not equal 10

Example 3.3. Using the if statement with numerical data.

```
/* Using the keyword if II */
#include "stdafx.h"
#using <mscorlib.dll>
#include <tchar.h>
using namespace System;
```

```
void _tmain(void) {
  String* sAnswer;
  Console::Write ("1 + 1 =  ");      // Step 1
  sAnswer = Console::ReadLine ();      // Step 2
  // Step 3 - numbers do not require quotes
  if (sAnswer->ToUInt32(0) == 2)
  Console::WriteLine ("\n That is correct!\n");
  // Step 4
  if(sAnswer->ToUInt32(0) != 2)
  Console::WriteLine("\n Wrong!!!\n");
}
```

Floats and doubles will work equally well in these comparisons. You might also want to try a varied list of operators such as __int8, *unsigned short*, and *unsigned long*. The next section actually continues with the if statement, combining if with the keyword **else**. Everything that we've studied here still applies, but **else** gives if some added control.

> Note:
>   Your programming abilities should now enable you to alter the programs data type, add comments, rename variables, and edit the output message without further mention. However, I will still mention any opportunities to use the unsigned data types, should they arise.

The **else** Statement

Else is the first logical extension to the questioning if statement. It adds an additional line of reasoning and an additional path for our programs to follow. **Else** cannot be used by itself; it links easily to the tail end of the if structure. Example 3.4 uses the If-**else** statement to redefine the previous program. The addition of **else** negates the need for the second if statement, and its simplicity adds a more elegant feel to our coding.

Example 3.4. The if-else statement.

```
/* Using the keywords if and else */
#include "stdafx.h"
#using <mscorlib.dll>
#include <tchar.h>
using namespace System;

int _tmain(void) {
  String* input;
  double Answer;

  Console::Write ("1 + 1.5 =  ");
  input = Console::ReadLine ();
  Answer = input->ToDouble(0);

  if (Answer == 2.5)
    Console::WriteLine ("\n That is correct!\n");
```

```
  else
     Console::WriteLine("\n Wrong!!!\n");
}
```

The if-**else** statement works in basically the same manner as did the if statement. The term **else** implies "in all other cases" or an "everything else here" type situation. This ability to alter the direction of our programs is what defines it as a programming technique. If-else, however, is still limited to two directions, of which the second is nonspecific. To specify the second or multiple paths, we would have to use the third type of if statement known as the **else-if** statement.

The *else-if* Statement

Else-if, like **else** is a dependent or secondary extension to the original if statement. Yet **else**-if definitely adds something new to the table. Since **else**-if must be added after an if, we'll alter the previous program once again, this time giving the user a little more to go by than just the word wrong–see Example 3.5.

Example 3.5. The else-if statement.

```
/* Use if with else-if */
#include "stdafx.h"
#using <mscorlib.dll>
#include <tchar.h>

using namespace System;

int _tmain(void) {
  String* input;
  double Answer;

  Console::Write ("1 + 1.5 =  ");
  input = Console::ReadLine ();
  Answer = input->ToDouble(0);

  if (Answer == 2.5)
     Console::WriteLine ("\n That is correct!");
  else if (Answer > 2.5)
     Console::WriteLine ("\n Wrong, too high!!!");
  else if (Answer < 2.5)
     Console::WriteLine ("\n Wrong, too low!!!");
}
```

Else-if includes a second conditional response with respect to if. Because **else**-if statements are dependent, they are only read by the computer if the first if statement is false (see Example 3.6).

Example 3.6. The else-if statement as a dependent statement.

```
/* Use if with else-if and else */
#include "stdafx.h"
#using <mscorlib.dll>
#include <tchar.h>
```

```
using namespace System;

void _tmain(void) {
  String* input;
  double Answer;

  Console::Write ("1 + 1.5 =   ");
  input = Console::ReadLine ();
  Answer = input->ToDouble(0);

  if (Answer == 2.5)
    Console::WriteLine ("\n That is correct!");
  else if (Answer > 2.5)
    Console::WriteLine ("\n Wrong, too high!!!");
  else
    Console::WriteLine ("\n Wrong, too low!!!");

  Console::WriteLine ("I hate the if statement!");
}
```

Program Walkthrough:
  The last two programs are essentially identical; with the minor exception of the altered **else** statement, which concludes Example 3.6. This emphasizes the key points on how the **if**, **else-if** and **else** statements are linked. Following the logic of the if statement, we find that if our number is not 2.5, the program proceeds to the next **else-if**. If we then find that the number is not greater than the 2.5, we again move to the next **else**. In order to reach the **else** statement, our number would have to be smaller then 2.5. Therefore, we do not need to test to see if that value is actually smaller.

Compounding **If** Statements

A compound statement is a group of statements combined into a bundle enclosed by a pair of braces. A compound if statement is an if statement that executes this bundle as if it were a single action. The proper way to write such a compound statement is demonstrated in example 3.7. (Note: Either **else** or **else-if** could still be used simply by placing those keywords at the end of the compound statement.)

Example 3.7. A compound if statement.

```
/* repeating the if statement   */
#include "stdafx.h"
#using <mscorlib.dll>
#include <tchar.h>
using namespace System;

void _tmain(void) {
  String* input;
  float MyNumber;
```

```
Console::WriteLine ("How old are you? ");
input = Console::ReadLine ();
MyNumber = (float)input->ToDouble(0);

if (MyNumber >= 18)  {  // compound statement
   Console::WriteLine ("\n You're an adult\n You can vote\n");
}
else
   Console::WriteLine ("\n Your turn will come");
}
```

The rules guiding the execution of compound if statements are simple. When the if statement is true, all the statements inside the compounded statement our executed, and when the if statement is false, all the statements are ignored. This may not seem like much when discussing a compound statement made up of only two lines, but imagine dealing with compound statements of over two hundred lines. Many C++ commands can be placed inside of these compound statements including other if statements, but we'll leave such matters to the sections ahead. The **else** and **else-if** statements can also use compound statements, as demonstrated in Example 3.8. Notice how important it becomes to comment when programs become longer and more complicated.

Example 3.8. Compound if and else-if statements.

```
/* repeating the if statement   */
#include "stdafx.h"
#using <mscorlib.dll>
#include <tchar.h>
using namespace System;

void _tmain(void) {
   String* input;
   float MyNumber;

   Console::Write ("How old are you? ");
   input = Console::ReadLine ();
   MyNumber = (float)input->ToDouble(0);

   if (MyNumber >= 18)
      Console::WriteLine ("Your an adult\n You can vote\n");
   else if (MyNumber == 17)
      Console::WriteLine ("Your turn will come \n");
   else if (MyNumber == 16) { // compound statement
      Console::Write
        ("\n Don't rush it boy you'll only be young once\n
         How old are you again? ");
      input = Console::ReadLine ();
      MyNumber = (float)input->ToDouble(0);
   } // end else-if
else
   Console::WriteLine ("\n You're just too young!!!\n");
}
```

This is the last example for this section, but if statements are explained further in the next two sections. As for compound statements, they'll be used repeatedly in several types of loops including the while and for loops coming up shortly. These new commands also follow the same rules (i.e., run when true; ignore when false); after a while this type of behavior should seem natural. The next section discusses three new decision operators: and, or, and not. These, like the comparison operators, can be combined with if statements and programming loops to define programs paths.

And, Or, and Not

There are three decision operators; and (written as &&), or (written as ||), and not (written as !). Of these, and (&&) and or (||) are used to combine if and else-if statements while the third operator not (!), is used to reverse our comparison's outcomes, the operators && and || are placed inside the parenthetical structure of if statements (see Table 3.2). By adding an && or a || we can reduce wasteful and repetitive if statements. Example 3.9 shows how the || operator can turn two *ifs* and six commands into one if and three commands.

Table 3.2: The And, Or and Not Operators

1. And "&&" meaning "both must be true for the statement to be true"
    -    if (variable1 > variable2 && vaiable2 == variable3)
    -    // 20 > 10 and 10 = 10

2. Or "||" meaning "only one needs to be true for the statement to be true"
    -    if (variable1 == variable2 || variable2 < variable3)
    -    // 20 = 20 or 20 < 10

3. Not "!" meaning "makes true statements false and false statements true"
    - if !(1 == 1)   // 1 = 1 then   not (true) or false
    - if !(1 == 2)   // 1 = 2 then   not (false) or true

Example 3.9. Reducing if statements by using the or operator.

```
/* if this, if that or just if this and that */
#include "stdafx.h"
#using <mscorlib.dll>
#include <tchar.h>
using namespace System;

int _tmain(void) {
  String* input;
  double Age, Weight;
  int iQuickAnswer;
  Console::Write ("How old are you? ");
  input = Console::ReadLine ();
  Age = input->ToDouble(0);

  Console::Write ("How much do you weigh?");
  input = Console::ReadLine ();
  Weight = input->ToDouble(0);

  if (Age < 3 || Weight < 35) {
```

```
      Console::Write
        ("\nThe law requires you to sit in a car seat\n
        \n Do you have a car seat? ");
      iQuickAnswer = Console::Read ();
  }
}
```

The not operator is placed directly in front of an expression (as show in Table 3.2). Although the not operator can be useful, it can also be confusing. I suggest reediting example 3.9 so that it uses the not operator. [Hint: the if statement would be written as (age > 3 || weight > 35)].

Nested If Statements

Just as it is possible to write a program using more than one if statement, it is also possible to place one or more if statements inside a compound if statement. These internal or *nested* if statements have nothing to do with the controlling if statement, but since we're using the same keyword, it can become confusing. Nested if statements work just as independently as any other if statement placed anywhere in the program, including inside a compound else or else-if statement. Example 3.10 demonstrates a complex blend of nested if and else-if statements.

Example 3.10. Nested if and if-else statements.

```
/* Complex/ nested if and if-else statements */
#include "stdafx.h"
#using <mscorlib.dll>
#include <tchar.h>
using namespace System;

int _tmain(void) {
  String* Input;
  float Age, Weight;
  char iQuickAnswer;
  // note: you'll want to hit return before entering the second answer
  Console::Write ("How old are you?");
  Input = Console::ReadLine ();
  Age = (float)Input->ToDouble(0);
  Console::Write ("And how much do you weigh? ");
  Input = Console::ReadLine ();
  Weight = (float)Input->ToDouble(0);

  if (Age < 3 || Weight < 35) { // start compound if statement
   Console::Write
     ("\nThe law requires you to sit in a car seat\n
     \n Do you have a car seat? ");
   iQuickAnswer = Console::Read ();

  if (iQuickAnswer == 'y')  // nested if statement
   Console::Write ("\n Good, but using it would be better.\n");
  else {  // nested else compounded
   Console::Write ("\n No, do you care about your baby?\n");
```

```
if (iQuickAnswer == 'y') // nested if in nested else
  Console::Write ("\n Well then get a car seat!\n");
else if (iQuickAnswer == 'n') // nested else-if in nested else
  Console::Write ("\n You sicken me!\n \n Your bay is worth it!\n");
else          // nested else in nested else
  Console::Write ("\n Your bay is worth it!\n");
      }
}       // end compound if statement
else if (Age > 85 || Weight > 500)
  Console::WriteLine ("\n Sorry I asked!\n");
}
```

Mathematical Abbreviations

Sometimes, as programs become larger and more complex, they also become wordy and drawn out. To alleviate this problem, programmers often used abbreviations. Our coverage here mimics what we've already studied under the section on arithmetic. Table 3.3 defines these shortcuts, and Example 3.11 demonstrates how they're written. I've included arithmetic statement in both longhand and shorthand forms to make them easier to compare. I've also thrown in several if statements, which were already covered in this chapter. You'll need to rerun this program a minimum of five times, entering the proper characters once for each shortcut. You might also want to try removing the longhand statements or rewriting the program using the *while* loop (explained in the next section).

Table 3.3 - Numeric Abbreviations:

Arithmetic	(int iNumber = 5;)	Abbreviates to	Returns
Addition:	iNumber = iNumber + 1;	iNumber += 1;	6
Subtraction:	iNumber = iNumber – 1;	iNumber -= 1;	4
Multiplication:	iNumber = iNumber * 2;	iNumber *= 2;	10
Division:	iNumber = iNumber / 2;	iNumber /= 2;	2
Remainders:	iNumber = iNumber % 2;	iNumber %= 2;	1

```
// Assume variable1 = 5 and variable2 = 2 and that their of a
numeric data type.
1. Variable1 = Varaible1 + Variable2
   Variable1 += Variable2
 // variable1 now equals 7 since -    7 = 5 + 2
2. Variable1 = Variable1 - Variable2
   Variable1 -= Variable2
 // variable1 now equals 3 since -    3 = 5 - 2
3. Variable1 = Variable1 * Variable2
   Variable1 *= Variable2
 // variable1 now equals 10 since -   10 = 5 * 2
4. Variable1 = Variable1 / Variable2
   Variable1 /= Variable2
        // variable1 now equals 2.5 since -   2.5 = 5 / 2
(When variable1 is either float or double)
        // variable1 now equals 2 since -   2 = 5 / 2 (When
variable1 is of type integer)
5. Variable1 = Variable1 % Variable2
```

```
     Variable1 %= Variable2
// variable1 now equals 1 since -   1 = 5 % 2 (variable1 should
only be used with integers)
// Remember % stands for the remainder of 1 as in 5 / 2
```

Example 3.11. Shorthand notation.

```
/* Shorthand notation */
#include "stdafx.h"
#using <mscorlib.dll>
#include <tchar.h>
using namespace System;

void _tmain(void) {
  String* Input;
  int iVariable1, iVariable2, iVariable3;
  char cCharacter;
  /* Note: later we'll learn techniques that will allow us to read
partial bits of info, but until then we'll still want to enter each
number with a return statement */
  Console::Write ("\n Enter a number: ");
  Input = Console::ReadLine ();
  iVariable1 = Input->ToInt32(0);
  Console::Write("\n Now, a second number: ");
  Input = Console::ReadLine ();
  iVariable2 = Input->ToInt32(0);
  iVariable3 = iVariable1;

  Console::WriteLine ("\n Enter one symbol: \n addition (+) \n
   subtraction (-) \n multiplication (*) \n division (/), or \n
   remainder (%): ");
  cCharacter = Console::Read ();

  if (cCharacter == '+') {
    iVariable1 = iVariable1 + iVariable2;
    Console::WriteLine ("\n Your longhand sum is {0}",
      __box(iVariable1));
    iVariable3 += iVariable2;
    Console::WriteLine ("\n Your shorthand sum is also {0}",
      __box(iVariable3));
  }

  if (cCharacter == '-') {
    iVariable1 = iVariable1 - iVariable2;
    Console::WriteLine ("\n Your longhand sum is  {0}",
      __box(iVariable1);
    iVariable3 -= iVariable2;
    Console::WriteLine ("\n Your shorthand sum is  {0}",
      __box(iVariable1));
  }
```

```
if (cCharacter == '*') {
  iVariable1 = iVariable1 * iVariable2;
  Console::WriteLine ("\n Your longhand sum is {0}",
    __box(iVariable1));
  iVariable3 *= iVariable2;
  Console::WriteLine ("\n Your shorthand sum is  {0}",
    __box(iVariable1));
}

if (cCharacter == '/') {
  iVariable1 = iVariable1 / iVariable2;
  Console::Write ("\n Your longhand sum is  {0}",
    __box(iVariable1));
  iVariable3 /= iVariable2;
  Console::WriteLine ("\n Your shorthand sum is  {0}",
    __box(iVariable1));
}

if (cCharacter == '%') {
  iVariable1 = iVariable1 % iVariable2;
  Console::WriteLine ("\n Your longhand sum is  {0}",
    __box(iVariable1));
  iVariable3 %= iVariable2;
  Console::WriteLine ("\n Your shorthand sum is  {0}",
    __box(iVariable1));
}
}
```

The *While* Loop

In the last section, we were forced to restart our program five times in order to test the results of five characters. Although this might be acceptable in a book which teaches programming, it would not be acceptable for a real program. This section therefore shows us how to repeat a program, or portions of a program, in a repeating cycle or loop. The first type of loop we'll examine uses the keyword while; thus, it is called the while loop. The while loop can be set up to repeat and/or terminate in several different ways: the most common include using a predetermined count (as in to repeat an iteration five times then end); using the user's input (end by request); and a termination command (a command that short-steps or breaks the loop–we'll learn about these shortly).

A while loop compares most directly to a compound if statement. while, like if, is written first, followed by a comparison operator and then a set of compound statements. When while is true, all the statements between its brackets will be executed, and when it is false, all of its statements will be skipped. while, unlike if, will not terminate when its last statement is executed. Rather, assuming it remains true, it will repeat, re-executing the compound statement. This process repeats indefinitely, ending only when something is altered to cause the comparison to become false or other special steps are taken to reroute the computer's line of execution. The techniques for terminating a while loop are thus just as important conceptually as the keyword while. Example 3.12 demonstrates a limited or predetermined type of while loop; this example terminates when our variable tests at a value greater then four.

Example 3.12. A while loop limited to five passes.

```
/* This loop is limited to 5 passes */
#using <mscorlib.dll>
#include <tchar.h>
using namespace System;

void _tmain(void) {
  int iCounter_1 = 0;

  while (iCounter_1 < 5) {   // while loop
    Console::WriteLine (iCounter_1++);
  }
  Console::WriteLine ("Program complete!\n");
}
```

Program Walkthrough:
  When the while loop is first executed, the value of the counter is compared to 5. Since, zero is less than five, the loop is executed and our variable "iCounter_1" is incremented by one. The loop retests itself, finding the variable at one, which is still less than five. The loop continues to run until the counter variable is incremented to 5, at which point, the loop ends. The program moves to the next line–Console::WriteLine ("Program complete!"); and the program ends. This would hold true if we had made the value 15 or even 50 million, although that would take a bit longer to execute.

We could have used an arithmetic statement or shortcut to alter our indexing variable's value e.g., counter = counter + 1 and counter += 1. We could have even rewritten five as negative 5 instead of 5 and counted backwards using the decrementing operator or shortcut -= 1. Any such combination would work just as long as we made sure the variable would eventually reach a value that terminates the loop. Otherwise we have written a program with a *nonterminating* or *infinite* loop; which usually locks up programs, making them unusable. The second type of termination is by users input; this can be done either with the user's knowledge, as in asking the user "Would you like to continue?" or without the user's knowledge, as in when his ship is destroyed, the loop automatically ends. Example 3.13 demonstrates a simple user-terminated loop.

Example 3.13. This while loop ends when I say it ends, got it?

```
/* While loop with user termination */
#include "stdafx.h"
#using <mscorlib.dll>
#include <tchar.h>
using namespace System;

void _tmain(void) {
  String* Quit = "no";

  while (!Quit->Equals("yes")) {
    Console::Write ("\n Would you like to end this loop? ");
    Quit = Console::ReadLine ();
  }
```

```
  Console::WriteLine ("Program complete!\n");
}
```

Program Walkthrough:
   The first we'll need to declare and initialize the variable Quit. We'll use "no" as its initial value (note: "no" has no real meaning to the program). Next, we'll set up a while loop that compares the value of Quit to "yes" and makes the loop comparison true only when Quit's value does not equal "yes." We then ask the user from inside the compound statement whether he or she wishes to end the loop. The user's input is then stored to Quit; the loop will continue to repeat until the user enters "yes." Then, the last statement "Program complete!" will be executed and the program will terminate.

As with counting loops, user input loops can be made nearly infinite if you forget to tell the user how to end them (which, of course, should be avoided). For the third type of termination, we'll have to add the keyword **break**. **break**, as its name implies, terminates any enclosed loop or conditional statement. Example 3.14 demonstrates this final while termination technique.

Example 3.14. Hey, you broke my while loop!

```
/* hey, you broke my loop! */
#include "stdafx.h"
#using <mscorlib.dll>
#include <tchar.h>
using namespace System;

void _tmain(void) {
  String* Quit = "no";

  while (!Quit->Equals("yes")) {
    break;                    // breaks loop
    Console::Write ("\n Would you like to end this loop? ");
    Quit = Console::ReadLine ();
  }

  Console::WriteLine ("Program complete!\n");
}
```

When **break** is executed, it simply breaks the loop and moves down to the next statement, skipping the remaining loop statements, and the while loop is considered complete. The program executes the last command "Program complete! \n" and then terminates. **break** works as an instant end to an otherwise structured loop.
   Another interesting keyword is **continue**, which, like **break**, shortcuts its iterations; but rather than ending the loop, it merrily brings the loop back up to the top. The loop continues from the top with a new iteration and everything else continues accordingly (see Example 3.15).

Example 3.15. The keyword continue.

```
/* Continue */
#include "stdafx.h"
#using <mscorlib.dll>
#include <tchar.h>
using namespace System;

void _tmain(void) {
  int iVariable1 = 10, iVariable2 = 0;

  while (iVariable1 == 10) {
    iVariable2 = iVariable2 + 1;    // while loop
    if (iVariable2/iVariable1 < 1)
      continue;
    iVariable1 = iVariable1 - 1;
  }

  Console::WriteLine (iVariable2);
}
```

Battle Bit

Finally, after many painful hours of lost sleep, burning eyes, screams of madness, and dogged determination, you've reached the pentacle of gaming knowledge and can now create dynamically animated, graphically breathtaking, and hardware accelerated three-dimensional video adventures capable of running on all platforms using all technologies. Hey, wake up! This is chapter 3. Real game programming isn't even introduced until the latter part of this text, and there's nothing in those chapter about hardware acceleration or three-dimensional programming. As for your abilities up until this point, well maybe, just maybe, you might be ready to try out a little text style program that, at least partially, will ease you into the whole gaming concept. The game is called Battle Bit and the player's objective is to destroy the aliens before they land. To play, you simply guess the aliens' location, which is represented by numbers typed into your computer's keyboard. To win you must guess the correct answer before you use up your shots. Oh, and if you fail, I've setup a bug that will automatically erase your hard drive–but don't fret, it shouldn't take too long to reinstall everything!

Example 3.16. Battle Bit: The Text Adventure.

```
/* Battle Bit the Text Adventure
 * Your a lieutenant in earth's toughest military fleet
 * Your current mission watchdog earth's intergalactic conference hall
 */
#include "stdafx.h"
#using <mscorlib.dll>
#include <tchar.h>
using namespace System;

void _tmain(void) {
  String* input;
  int iAmmo = 12, // player has 12 guesses
```

```
   iAlienShip = 49, // the alien ship starts here
   iTarget = 50;    // This variable stores your input

/* Game introduction -explains to the player what he needs to do, why he
is doing it… * The introduction should also, be used to set the games
mood and excite the player. */

   Console::WriteLine ("\n Captain, aliens are attempting"
    "to land peacefully!\n"
    "What? How dare they and on the day were suppose "
    "to start peace talks.\n"
    "It just goes to show you, you just can't trust "
    "those alien scum.\n"
    "Lieutenant, lock target,"
    "I don't want to see one "
    "alien left alive.\n"
    "But captain, isn't that the ambassadors ship…\n"
    "And wasn't he suppose to be coming today?\n"
    "Lieutenant, are you going to target the alien "
    "ship or not?\n"
    "But sir. \n Type in the ships location and fire soldier…\n"
    "But sir…\n"
    "Lieutenant, you'll take out that alien scum or I'll "
    "take you out…\n"
    "(The captain's gun points oddly at your head.) "
    "Got it? Yes sir!\n");
// location of ship - this just makes it harder to find the ship
   iAlienShip = ((iAlienShip * iAmmo) / (iTarget + 1)) + 3;

   while (iAmmo > 0)  {
    // when ammo runs out the loop ends
     Console::WriteLine ("\n\n Enter targeting information?");
     input = Console::ReadLine ();
     iTarget = input->ToInt32(0);

     if (iTarget == iAlienShip) {
      // if your input equals the ships location
       Console::WriteLine ("Alien ship hit, the ships"
        "been destroyed sir.");
       break;
     }    // break ends loop
     else if (iTarget > iAlienShip) {   // when input is too high
       Console::WriteLine ("You missed, try aiming a little lower");
       iAmmo--;
     }     // ammo-reduces the total ammo by 1
     else  {         // when input is to low
       Console::WriteLine ("You missed, try aiming higher");
       iAmmo--;
     }   // also reduces ammo by 1
     // The location of the ship moves with each shot
     iAlienShip = (iAlienShip * iAmmo) / iTarget;
   }
```

```
if (iAmmo > 0)
  // if you have ammo you must have hit the alien
    Console::WriteLine
    ("\n Good work soldier, remind me to promote you.");
  else  // if your out of ammo you can't protect the hall
    Console::WriteLine ("\n BOOM!!! Your dead.\n");

  Console::WriteLine ("\n Game Over\n");
}
```

The do-while Loop

The second type of while loop, which is known as the do-while loop, is essentially the while loop turned upside down. Here we insert the while loop comparison at the end of the loop, which also allows for one complete execution before the 1st comparison takes place.

Example 3.17. A do-while loop I.

```
/* Basic do-while loop */
#include "stdafx.h"
#using <mscorlib.dll>
#include <tchar.h>
using namespace System;

int _tmain(void) {
  String* Quit = "no";

  do {    // this is an endless loop
  } while (!Quit->Equals("yes"));
    // notice the semicolon
}
```

The keyword *do* is placed at the top of the loop and the keyword while is placed at the end. The compound statement is written directly after the keyword do, just as it was with while and if. One obvious difference between the while loop and the do-while loop is that the comparisons are not made until the loop is already running. Again, this guarantees us at least one execution before the coding is tested. Example 3.18 demonstrates the do-while loop in action.

Example 3.18. The do-while loop II.

```
/* do-while loop II */
#include "stdafx.h"
#using <mscorlib.dll>
#include <tchar.h>
using namespace System;

void _tmain(void) {
  String* Quit;
```

```
  do {  // do-while loop
    Console::WriteLine ("\n Would you like to end this loop? ");
    Quit = Console::ReadLine (); // users input
  } while (Quit->Equals("yes"));

  Console::WriteLine ("Program complete!\n");
}
```

Needles to say, the while and do-while loops also take advantage of the and (&&), or (||), and not (!) operators. They can be rewritten without compound statements as in single line while and do-while statements (although, that would be considered poor programming style). Moreover, you can nest while/do-while loops inside of each other. Example 3.19 gives us an example of both the nesting technique and the && operator. You may also want to test this program using either the || or ! operators, but I'll leave the exact phasing of those two operators up to you.

Example 3.19. Nested while and do-while loops.

```
/* nested while loop */
#include "stdafx.h"
#using <mscorlib.dll>
#include <tchar.h>
using namespace System;

void _tmain(void) {
  int iNumber = 0;              // Begin main
  String* Quit;

  do {             // begin do-while loop
    Console::Write ("\n Would you like to end this loop? ");
    Quit = Console::ReadLine ();          // users input

    while (Quit->Equals("yes") && iNumber < 10) { // nested while loop
      Console::WriteLine ("Were sorry the exit you have chosen"
       "is not available at this time\n please try again");
      Quit = Console::ReadLine ();
      iNumber++;
    }
  } while (!Quit->Equals("yes"));          // end do-while

  Console::WriteLine ("Program complete!\n");
}
```

Program Walkthrough:
   If you're trapped, the secret to escaping is in understanding the comparisons. First, if you enter anything other then "yes," you can't exit the do-while loop. If you enter "yes," the program goes into the nested while loop. After entering the while loop, if you enter anything other that "yes," you're forced to repeat the do-while loop and the process starts all over. However, if you enter "yes" the nested while-loop keeps repeating itself.
   The solution, you'll have to enter "yes" eleven times. Once to get into the while loop and ten times to get out. The incrementing variable iNumber will cause the nested while loop, to become false, and since the character's string "Quit" is still equal to "yes," the do-while loop will also become false and

64

the loop will end.

Note: You don't have to use the same variable in both loops; in fact, the use of the same variable is what made this example so confusing. In addition, for preset numbers such as zero to ten you might be better off using the for loop, which just happens to be the subject of the next section.

The For Loop

The for loop, also known as the for statement, is a repetitive process that is set up under certain conditions to run a particular number of times. This terminating factor will also help us to separate it from the other two looping processes, because it's not dependent on an unknown variable. The for-loop thus predefines its variable as part of its initial statement. The comparison operators are still used to determine whether to continue or terminate, but this will always happen at a predetermined point in the loop, as when our variable equals 10, 100, or x number of cycles. The for statement is constructed much like the while loop, but with its initializing variable and its incrementing operator both becoming one with its declaration (see Example 3.20).

Example 3.20. The for loop.

```
/* the for-loop */
#include "stdafx.h"
#using <mscorlib.dll>
#include <tchar.h>
using namespace System;

void _tmain(void) {
  int iCounter_1;

  for (iCounter_1 = 0; iCounter_1 < 5; iCounter_1++) {
    Console::WriteLine (iCounter_1);
  }
}
```

Program Walkthrough:
The for statement begins by assigning our variable the value zero. This value is then compared to 5 and found true since zero is less than five. The incrementing operator then adds one to the value of our variable making its value one. The loop is then executed and our variable iCounter_1 is displayed. The loop then finds the variable is still less than five, and the variable is then incremented a second time. The third time the loop runs, our value is increase to three, which is still less than five, so the loop runs again. The fourth iteration increases our value to four and the loop is run again. Finally, our variable equals five and the loop terminates. The program moves to the next line "Program complete!" and the program ends.

Nesting is just as legal and useful in for loops as it is in while and do-while loops, but it is also just as dangerous (or as trying) when you are caught in an infinite loop. Thus, you should avoid using the for loop's tracking variable for anything other than keeping track of that for loop. If you think you're up to it, you can go back and rewrite the while and do-while programs using only for loops.

The for loop can become an infinite loop or mindless hole with even the most subtle of errors. For example:

```
for (iCounter_1 = 0; iCounter_1 < 5; iCounter_1++)
  {iCounter_1 = 1;
    Console::WriteLine (iCounter_1); }
```

Will never reach its termination mark of iCounter_1 equaling 5, because iCounter_1 will always be reset to 1 inside the loop, thus editing a for loop's count from inside the body of the for loop should be a well thought-out choice.

That's it for the looping processes, but there is still one additional comparison process namely the *switch* statement, which we'll be looking at in the next section. Switch is similar to the *if-else-if*–else combinations, but it can handle much longer lists of comparisons without becoming cluttered.

The switch Statement

The switch statement, like the if and else-if statements, is used to execute a statement or set of statements, depending on a value. However, unlike the if and else-if statements, the switch statement doesn't use comparison operators; instead, it simply reads the value of the variable and attempts to direct the program to the proper channel. A second keyword, case, is also used in this process. The keyword case is written and used multiple times from within the switch statement; each switch statement holds a numeric or character value for comparison. If the value held by a case statement matches the value read by the switch statement then everything following that case statement would be executed.

Another useful keyword used with the switch statement is the term default, meaning when no other case matches. Default is usually placed at the end of the switch statement, thus allowing us to execute selected statements based on the fact that they do not match any of the pervious values (see Example 3.21).

Example 3.21. The switch statement.

```
/* Switch Statement */
#include "stdafx.h"
#using <mscorlib.dll>
#include <tchar.h>
using namespace System;

int _tmain(void) { // Begin main
  int Grades;
  Console::Write ("How would you grade yourself so far "
    "A, B, or C? ");
  Grades = Console::Read ();

  switch (Grades) {     // switch statement
    case 'A':
    case 'a':
      Console::WriteLine ("You'll make a great programmer");
      break;

    case 'B':
    case 'b':
      Console::WriteLine ("You're sure of yourself");
      break;
```

```
   case 'C':
   case 'c':
    Console::WriteLine ("You don't let hard work keep you down");
   break;

   default:
    Console::WriteLine ("A, B, and C inputs only!");
   break;
  }
}
```

Note that the termination sequence is actually only the keyword **break**, which does nothing more then to move us out of a block and onto the next segment. **break**, like **case**, is repeated for each comparison.

Unlike C#, C++ allows us to drop between cases, that is, all coding listed after a specific **case** can still be executed, as long as there are no **break** statement to end the comparison (see Example 3.22).

Example 3.22. The Switch statement continued.

```
/* Switch Statement Continued */
#include "stdafx.h"
#using <mscorlib.dll>
#include <tchar.h>
using namespace System;

void _tmain(void) {
  String* input;
  int byNumber;

  Console::Write ("Enter a number greater than one: ");
  input = Console::ReadLine ();
  byNumber = input->ToInt32(0);

  switch (byNumber) {
    case 0:
     Console::WriteLine ("\n Zero is not greater than one!\n");

    case 1:
     Console::WriteLine ("\n I said a number greater than one!");

    default:
     Console::WriteLine ("\n Good job now take a lap!");
    break;
  }

Console::WriteLine ("\n Program complete\n");
}
```

It is possible to have **switch** statements using either **character** or **integer** data types, but the set case types must be literal or variable constants. You cannot set two cases to the same value even if it's written as a variable, and you cannot have more than one default in any single **switch** statement. **switch** statements can have if statements in their cases, and if statements can have switch statements in there compound statements. In addition, you can place switch statements in while and do-while loops or write those loops into case statements, but switch statements inside of other switch statements should be used sparingly to avoid confusion.

> Note:
> Defining a Block:
>   A block (opening and closing brackets { }) although technically identical to a compound statement, can in fact mean any set of brackets placed anywhere in a program. For example, the main program is enclosed by opening and closing brackets but it is not considered a compound statement. Blocks allow programmers to separate special sections of code, opening up new ways to use local variables, or enclose certain code including confining subroutines (discussed in chapter 4). When a block is nested within another block, the outside block is considered global to the inner block, just as coding written outside of the main program is considered global to the program. Global and local concepts are very important when working with C++ and will be discussed in greater detail throughout this text.

Optimizing Tip: The keyword __assume is used to represent a expression that is known to be true and will remain true until the expression is altered. Select use of __assume can improve optimization/ overall program speed. __assume is most commonly used as part of the switch statement as in __assume(0) (see Example 3.23).

Example 3.23. __assume.

```
/* __assume */
#include "stdafx.h"
#using <mscorlib.dll>
#include <tchar.h>
using namespace System;

void _tmain(void) {
  String* input;
  int byNumber;

  Console::Write ("Enter a number greater than one: ");
  input = Console::ReadLine ();
  byNumber = input->ToInt32(0);

  switch (byNumber) {
    case 0:
     Console::WriteLine ("\n Zero is not greater than one!\n");

    case 1:
     Console::WriteLine ("\n I said a number greater than one!");

    default:
      __assume(0);
     Console::WriteLine ("\n Good job now take a lap!");
    break;
  }
```

```
Console::WriteLine ("\n Program complete\n");
}
```

Converting from Native to Managed C++

While most of us remember the older C and C++ I/O notations, it is safe to assume that not everyone reading this text can do so without some type of reference. This section defines the C/C++ commands that were replaced by our Write and WriteLine extensions. When these older commands are encountered, the trick is to replace them with the appropriate combination of extensions and formatting strings.

The printf and cout functions are alternatives to the Write and WriteLine commands and the scanf and cin function are alternatives to the Read and ReadLine commands. Like our Reads and Writes, these functions are not keywords, but instead they are added commands linked by the older included file structure (see Chapter 1). The included file that controlled these commands were <cstdio> (written as #include <cstdio> and #include <stdio.h>) and iostream (written as #include <iostream> and #include <iostream.h>); <stdio.h> actually reaches back to the original C language. printf, and for that matter scanf, have the most in common with our C++'s new notation, which becomes obvious when comparing them directly. For an extended list of printf / scanf notations, see Table 3.4.

Two interesting command functions that continue to evolve through the C languages are the old style and member functions puts and gets. The original puts was accessed in essentially the same manner as was printf, but with the restriction that it could only display character data (as in puts ("this is a test 1, 2, 3."); gets, like scanf, was also used to read data, but everything read is interrupted as a character string. This can also be thought of as an array (which we'll explain in a later chapter). The extended member function versions of these two types are unfortunately limited to only single character references as in cout.puts ('A'); and cin.get (character), so their practicality is limited. Two ANSI/ISO alternative replacements for these older style functions were cin.getline (characters, sizeofline) and cout.write (characters, sizeofline) These will also be explained in a later chapter (see Example 3.24). Note that while the puts function automatically moves data to the next line, cout.write does not.

Table 3.4 – Using Conversion Specifiers with printf () and scanf ()

	Specifier	Definition	Example
1.	%d	Holds positive or negative whole numbers -int variable1 (signed int variable1)	scanf("%d", &variable1); printf("Your number is %d", variable1);
2.	% u	Holds only positive whole numbers -unsigned int variable1	scanf("%u", &variable1); printf("Your number is %u", variabe1);
3.	%f	Holds floating point (real) numbers -float variable1	scanf("%f", &variable1); printf("Your number is %f", variable1);
4.	%c	Holds a single character data type -char variable1	scanf("%c", &variable1); printf("Your symbol is %c", variable1);
5.	%s	Holds a string or array of characters -char variable1[7] (or any positive number)	scanf("%s", &variable1); printf("Your word is %s", variable1);

Example 3.24. C, native C++ vs. managed C++ and C#.

```
/* C/C++ vs. managed C++/C# */
#include "stdafx.h"
#using <mscorlib.dll>
#include <tchar.h>
```

```cpp
#include <iostream>

using namespace System;
using namespace std;

void _tmain(void) {
    int Number;
    char name [10];
    String* Answer;

    Console::Write("\n Hello, please enter a number: ");
    //Console.Write ("\n Hello, please enter a number: ");
    printf ("\n Hello, please enter a number: ");
    cout << "\n Hello, please enter a number: ";
    std::cout.write("\n Please enter a name: ", 24);
    puts("\n Please enter your name:");

    Answer = Console::ReadLine();
    Number = Answer->ToInt32(0);
    // Number = int.Parse(Answer = Console.ReadLine ());
    scanf("%d", &Number);
    cin >> Number;
    std::cin.getline(name, sizeof(name));
    gets(name);

    Console::Write ("You entered ");
    Console::Write (Number);
    Console::Write (" is that correct? ");
    // Console.WriteLine ("You entered {0} is that correct?", Number);
    printf ("\n You entered %d is that correct?", Number);
    cout << "\n You entered " << Number << " is that correct?";

    Answer = Console::ReadLine ();
    // Answer = Console.ReadLine ();
    scanf ("%s", &Answer);
    cin >> name;
}
```

We could also convert multiple references, including formatting strings to represent the change in notation (see Example 3.25).

Example 3.25. Converting multiple references.
Console::WriteLine ("\n You entered the number {0, D} and also the letter {1}",
  __box(iNumber), __box(cAnswer));
printf ("\n You entered the number %d and also the letter %c\n",
  iNumber, cAnswer);

Boolean Expressions

Boolean expressions are mathematical representations for the concepts of both true and false. That is, while their actual evaluations are based on mathematical data, their outcomes are in fact determined by a conceptual understanding. This type of determination is represented in the C++ as the data type *bool*, with its variables assigned to the Boolean constants *true* or *false*. In managed C++, as with C and native C++, this process can include a numeric substitute, namely the numeric constants one and zero with the zero equaling false and the value one or any nonzero positive or negative number equaling true. However, this numeric substitution should be avoided. Example 3.26 demonstrates this sequence for a while loop, but you should attempt to rewrite the program as a do-while loop before proceeding to the next section.

Example 3.26. Boolean Expressions –true or false.

```
/* true or false */
#include "stdafx.h"
#using <mscorlib.dll>
#include <tchar.h>
using namespace System;

void _tmain(void) {
  bool Variable1 = true;
  String* Test;

  while (Variable1) {
    Console::Write ("\n Would you like to end this loop? ");
    Test = Console::ReadLine ();  // yes will break the loop
    if (Test->Equals("yes") || Test->Equals("YES"))
    Variable1 = false;
  } // end while loop

  Console::WriteLine ("Program complete!");
}
```

Short Circuit Evaluation

Short circuit or *partial comparisons* are comparisons that can be deduced without testing the entire statement. This deduction can be made for either logical types && or ||, but with opposite results, as shown in Table 3.5.

Table 3.5 – True and false determinations:

	Non-specific Equations	Evaluation Process	Reasoning
1.	(True && True)	Complete evaluation	True + True = True
2.	(True && False)	Complete evaluation	True + False = False
3.	(False && True)	Short circuit evaluation	False + Test Skipped = False
4.	(False && False)	Short circuit evaluation	False + Test Skipped = False
5.	(True || True)	Short circuit evaluation	True + Test Skipped = True
6.	(True || False)	Short circuit evaluation	True + Test Skipped = True
7.	(False || True)	Complete evaluation	False + True = True

| 8. | (False \|\| False) | Complete evaluation | False + False = False |

As you can see, Tests 1 and 2 required complete evaluation because neither outcome could be determined without the second evaluation. This is not the case when using short circuit or partial comparison reasoning (as shown in Tests 3-8). In such cases, the decision to label the comparison as true or false is done without the second test, and thus saves us time and trouble of the second comparison. In addition, we can use this partial comparison to safeguard against runtime errors such as dividing by zero–Example 3.27.

Example 3.27. A partial comparison used to safeguard runtime errors.

```
-   Console::WriteLine("Enter any number other than zero: ");
-   variable1 = Console::Read ();
-   // Some smart user enters zero, the system crashes.
-   while (5/variable1 < 1);
-   // Later that day... you're fired!
-   // Alternatively, you could have used short
-   // circuit evaluation. And later that same day,
-   while (variable1 != 0 && 5/variable1);
-   // you could have been surfing the web as RedHotPartyPants.
```

The Conditional Operator

The *conditional operator*, which is also described as a *ternary operator* (because of its three operands), is essentially an abbreviated if-else expression that uses two symbols: a question mark (?) and a colon (:). The statement requires three expressions: an if-else comparison, a true calculation, and a false calculation as shown below.

First, the comparison is made:
```
x = y ? 41 : 71
if(x == y)   // followed by an assignment
     x = 41;
else    // and then an else statement
     x = 72;
```

Where x equals y, the comparison is true and x is reassigned as 41. When x does not equal y, x is reassigned as 72.

```
Comparison ? Equation1 : Equation2:
```

Note: The conditional operator can also be placed inside of other commands and statements (including the *while*, *do-while*, and Write commands).

Cartoon 3.1:

Hey, would you like a second cup of coffee? Yes, I think I would like a second cup of coffee.

OH NO! Funny, Jim never goes digging in the trash after a second cup of my coffee.

Always remember to backup your work.

Trouble Shooting

Common editing and setup errors were covered in the last two chapter (see Troubleshooting), thus in this chapter we'll begin learning about our compiler's help files. Most compilers include a set of error identification codes that are displayed at the time of compilation. Using those codes, we can lookup the definition of errors, thereby, at least theoretically, isolating those errors. If this fails the next best, way to find an error is to rebuild the project, inputting the coding in steps, testing each step until the error reappears. Once the error reappears, we can isolate and repair it. If there are no logical answers, look for text misprints and compiler incompatibles (also consider new compliance errors); (For solutions to new compliance errors email the author Plague@iwon.com). If no obvious errors are found, try skipping to the next example or reverting to the pervious example, do you get the same errors? Other common errors are listed under Commons Errors, Problems, and Pits (see that list for details).

Common Errors, Problems, and Pits:

1. Symbol combinations such as ==, !=, and >= cannot be written with spaces between them. (i.e. = =, ! =).
2. Dot not confuse = with = =. Remember = is used to assign a value and = = is used to compare two values.
3. while loops do not require a semicolon, but do-while loops do (as in do…while (something);).
4. Most compilers don't recognize names beyond the first thirty characters so be careful with long names that are too similar.
5. Leaving off a closing bracket usually causes several errors. In addition, forgetting to delete an excess bracket usually causes an unexpected error.
6. Forgetting to terminate a while loop is a prime example of a logical/ runtime error. The program does everything it's told to do, but that causes it to become stuck. The solution is simply to cancel the program either with a Ctrl-<C> or by closing the executable window with the mouse and then rewrite the loop to include an event that will end it at the right time. This type of error is most commonly called an *infinite loop* error.
7. All values should be initialized before any information is taken from them, not doing so will result in a *corrupted data* error.
8. Of course, you still can't divide by zero, so don't even try it. However, if you fear that occasionally your data might total zero, you'll need to test for that result and work around it. This can be done in many ways, but the easiest is with the if statement (think about short-circuiting).
9. You cannot increment or decrement a complex variable. For example, you wouldn't be able to increment the sum of two numbers e.g., [(x+5)++].
10. One of the most common errors is to mistakenly reverse a less than or greater than symbol from inside a loops termination sequence, causing the comparison to never find its match: this is a typographical error that creates a runtime error (an infinite loop).
11. Did you place a semicolon at the end of the first line of an if statement, for statement, or switch statement? Doing so would indicate to the compiler that these lines were blank or null and your block or single statement would not be viewed as part of that sequence.

Things to Remember

1. If statements are used with limited comparisons, while **switch** statements are used in multiple cases.
2. A compound statement is a set of statements that are contained between to braces.
3. Mathematical shortcuts should only be used if they make things simpler to read. (Note: some compilers will convert these shortcuts into faster running code).
4. System::Console::Write and using namespace System; with Console::Write do exactly the same thing.
5. The **while** loop test first then runs its first cycle, while the **do-while** loop runs first, and tests after running its first cycle.
6. When writing a statement that stretches over a single line try to break it up. Break at a comma or other marking to make the split easier to read.
7. When using **if-else** statements try to place the most common occurrence first; this will speed up your program by moving you to the right segment with fewer comparisons.
8. Converting several if statements into fewer **if-else** statements also speeds up programs, since more comparisons can be skipped and tasks are reduced.
9. Some programmers use brackets to enclose every **if-else** statement, this is not required, but is considered good form.
10. It should be noted that **switch** statements do not require a concluding default statement, although they are considered good form; *defaults* are not restricted to the concluding portion of a **switch** statement, but concluding with the **default** is also considered good form.
11. Loops based on counters such as **for** and **while** will become infinite if their marks are counting the wrong way or start after the mark. These are also considered *infinite* loops, with these errors being much harder to detect.
12. Be careful when comparing real numbers: Remember 4.001 does not equal 4.00005, and neither equal the integer value 4.
13. Avoid using floating point variables e.g., (**float, double** or **Decimal**) as loop counters, they require larger amounts of memory and more processing time without additional benefits.
14. When using Boolean expressions, restrict yourself to actual true and false concepts, do not use 0 and 1 comparisons–it's considered bad form.
15. Managed C++, like C and native C++, always attempts to shortcut a comparison when it is written using an && symbol, this will save time by reducing tasks. Thus to speed up your programs you should try to place the more commonly false tests first.
16. Some programmers feel that keywords such as **break** and **continue** are in violation of the structured programmer's ideals. These keywords, however, speed up programming tasks and are considered valuable by many programmers.

Questions

1. Using three if statements, write a program that tests two variables such that if it finds that the first variable is equal to, less than, or greater than the second, a corresponding message is displayed.
2. Using the keywords **else** and **if**, simplify the previous program (Hint: Use one if statement and two else-ifs).
3. Using the keyword **else**, simplify the first program to use one **if** statement, one **else-if** statement, and one **else** statement.
4. From Question 3, revise each comparison to include the compound if, **else if**, and **else** statements.
5. Write a program that uses a nested if statement that first asks the user if he has two numbers to compare and then repeats question 4.
6. Revise the program from Question 5 using the **or** operator as is ('Y' || 'y').
7. Revise the program from Question 5 using the "and" and the "not" operators.
8. Find the sum of two numbers using the abbreviated form +=.

9. Repeat Question 8 for subtraction, multiplication, division, and remainders.
10. Write a program that allows the use to choose from any one of the five basic math types. Use a while loop to repeat the choices after each calculation.
11. Revise the program from Question 10 using a continue statement that forces the while loop to skip the actual calculation.
12. Revise the program from Question 10 using the do-while loop.
13. Revise the program from Question 10 using the for loop.
14. Alter the program from Question 10, replacing all the if statements with switch statement.
15. Revise the program from Question 14, replacing Console Read and Write with cin and cout.
16. Revise the program from Question 14, replacing Console Read and Write with scanf and printf.
17. Revise the program from Question 14, replacing Console Read and Write with gets and puts.
18. Write a program that tests an if statement using the Boolean data type (bool test).
19. Write a program that uses short circuit evaluation to safeguard against division by zero.
20. Write a program that uses the conditional operator, include the screen outputs "If:" and "Else:"

Chapter Four

"I long to accomplish a great and noble task,
but it is my chief duty to accomplish small tasks as if they were great and noble."
- **Helen Keller**

Functions

This chapter covers the fundamentals of structured/modular programming, concepts such as predefined and user-defined functions, type casting, variable scope, black box theory, mathematical abbreviations, calls by mechanism, calls by reference, basic polymorphism (overloading), recursive and inline functions.

Predefined Functions

There are two types of functions used in C++: Those that are written by us and used like little subprograms, and those that were written for us and used to save us the time of writing them ourselves. The first type, referred to as user-defined function, are a bit more complicated, and aren't completely explained until the end of this chapter. The second type are most commonly referred to as a predefined function, which I actually began using them back in Chapter 1. The section takes a moment to introduce formally the concept of the predefined function.

The good news is that with the advent of the .Net architecture we no longer have to memorize dozens upon dozens of included file references in order to use a few simple commands. The bad news is that most of us have already memorized so many of them that it just might feel a little bit unfair, to which I say not to worry –the basics of the new structure aren't that different from the old ones and everyone including the newbies, should pick it up pretty quickly. Again, all predefined functions referenced under this new architecture involve a object (class); thus, the procedure for referencing those functions are very similar to what you might expect when referencing a standard C/C++ method (or member function). Now, not all of our user-defined functions are accessed in the same way (this should become apparent with time). Moreover, not even the best of us can truly claim to know them all, but they're now much easier to access, especially when you're using a visual compiler. The next few paragraphs then explain some of the most common extensions.

Characters

The first function we'll define is **ToUpper**, which literally means to make a letter that is lowercase into one that is uppercase. This function also has an antonym named **ToLower**, which changes uppercase letters into their lowercase counterparts. The **ToUpper** function is useful when you cannot control the user's input, as we couldn't in Example 3.2. In that example, I had to ask that you limit your responses to uppercase Y. This was necessary at the time, but is no longer the case, since we can easily rewrite this program to use the ToUpper function (see Example 4.1).

Example 4.1. Using ToUpper.

```
/* Using ToUpper - see how far we've come */
#include "stdafx.h"
#using <mscorlib.dll>
#include <tchar.h>
using namespace System;
```

```
void _tmain(void) {
  String* Response;
  Console::Write ("Input <Y> for YES:   ");
  Response = Console::ReadLine ();
  Response = Response->ToUpper();

  if (Response->Equals("Y"))  {
    Console::WriteLine ("\n You typed {0}",
      __box(Response));
  }
}
```

Math

The next few functions we'll cover are from the predefined method Math. These functions can be extremely useful when calculations are required. Our first function is Math::Sqrt ( ), which stands for the square root of a number. This function returns the square root of any value placed within its parentheses.

A second function linked to Math is the Math::Pow ( ), which stands for an exponential power of a number (remember we can always substitute variables for literal constants). This could be used to reverse the square root, or with other powers as in cubes.

Our third and fourth functions are Math::Ceiling ( ) and Math::Floor ( ), which are used to round real numbers to their highest or lowest whole value, respectfully. The most important points to remember when working with these functions are that Ceiling always rounds up and that Floor always rounds down, regardless of the size of the decimal value they're reading. That is, Math::Ceiling ( ) would round 3.2 to 4 and Math::Floor ( ) would round 3.9 to 3.0. Therefore, you'll have to decide which way you want to go before using either one (see Example 4.2).

Trigonometric Functions [where x is a double/floating point value read in radians]:

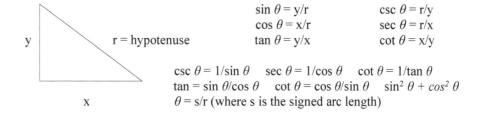

$$\sin \theta = y/r \qquad \csc \theta = r/y$$
$$\cos \theta = x/r \qquad \sec \theta = r/x$$
$$\tan \theta = y/x \qquad \cot \theta = x/y$$

$$\csc \theta = 1/\sin \theta \quad \sec \theta = 1/\cos \theta \quad \cot \theta = 1/\tan \theta$$
$$\tan = \sin \theta/\cos \theta \quad \cot \theta = \cos \theta/\sin \theta \quad \sin^2 \theta + \cos^2 \theta$$
$$\theta = s/r \text{ (where s is the signed arc length)}$$

Example 4.2. A few common math functions.

```
/* Just a few of the most common math functions */
#include "stdafx.h"
#using <mscorlib.dll>
#include <tchar.h>
using namespace System;

void _tmain(void) {
  String* input;
  double number1, number2, number3 = 2.0;
```

```
Console::Write
  ("Enter a number and I'll give you its square root: ");
input = Console::ReadLine ();
number1 = input->ToDouble(0);
number2 = Math::Sqrt (number1);
Console::WriteLine ("\nThe square root of {0} is {1}",
  __box(number1), __box(number2));
number2 = Math::Pow (number2, number3);
Console::WriteLine ("Do these numbers match {0} and {1}",
  __box(number1), __box(number2));
number1 = Math::Ceiling (3.2);
number2 = Math::Floor (3.9);
Console::WriteLine ("Math::Ceiling (3.2) = {0}",
  __box(number1));
Console::WriteLine ("Math::Floor (3.9) = {0}",
  __box(number2));
}
```

Additional extensions include some useful functions that determine absolute values and references that convert from character to numeric data types. One particularly interesting extension is the random number generator (a pseudo-randomly generated number cruncher, based on the internal clock), which we can use to create the text adventure Battle Bit II: this is war! (see Example 4.3).

Example 4.3. Battle Bit II: This is War!

```
/* Battle Bit II - THIS IS WAR! Some mad dog soldier
shot down the alien Ambassador's convoy and it sparked
an intergalactic war. Earth's defenses was weak form
warring with several hundred other worlds. So now, it's
all up to you. */
#include "stdafx.h"
#using <mscorlib.dll>
#include <tchar.h>
using namespace System;

int _tmain(void) {
  String* input;
  Random* rnd = new Random ();

  do {    // do-while loop
    double AlienShip1 = Math::Round (rnd->NextDouble () * 100)+1,
    AlienShip2 = Math::Round (rnd->NextDouble () * 100)+1,
    Target = 0,
    AliensMissiles = 0;
    const double YourLocation = 50;

    Console::WriteLine ("Captain, are you in there? Captain?"
      "\n(Crying is herd form his quarters)"
      "\nThis is ground control to lieutenant Bob."
      "\nYour bother major Tom has been shot down,"
```

```
               "\nRepeat he has been shot down."
               "\nThe aliens have destroyed our space outpost and "
               "\nare now on route to Earth."
               "\nI know it's a long shot lieutenant,"
               "\nbut I promised my wife and kids you'd  stop them."
               "\nI'll do my best...");

while ((AlienShip1 > 0) || (AlienShip2 > 0)) {
   Console::Write ("\n\n Enter targeting information: ");
   input = Console::ReadLine ();
   Target = input->ToByte(0);

   Console::WriteLine (AlienShip1);
   Console::WriteLine (AlienShip2);

   if (Math::Ceiling (Target) == Math::Ceiling (AlienShip1) ||
    Math::Ceiling (Target) == Math::Floor (AlienShip1) ||
    Math::Floor (Target) == Math::Ceiling (AlienShip1) ||
    Math::Floor (Target) == Math::Floor (AlienShip1)) {
     Console::WriteLine ("Alien ship hit, you got him!");
     AlienShip1 = -1;
    }

    if (Math::Ceiling (Target) == Math::Ceiling (AlienShip2) ||
     Math::Ceiling (Target) == Math::Floor (AlienShip2) ||
     Math::Floor (Target) == Math::Ceiling (AlienShip2) ||
     Math::Floor (Target) == Math::Floor (AlienShip2)) {
      Console::WriteLine("\n Alien ship hit, "
                         "you took him down!!\n");
      AlienShip2 = -1;
    }

    if ((Math::Round (Target) > Math::Round (AlienShip1)) &&
      (Math::Round (Target) > Math::Round (AlienShip2)))
       Console::WriteLine ("\n You missed, "
         "try aiming a little lower\n");
     else if ((Target < AlienShip1) && (Target < AlienShip2))
      Console::WriteLine ("\n You missed, try aiming higher\n");
     else
      Console::WriteLine ("\n I can't get a lock on them\n");

    if (Math::Ceiling (AliensMissiles) == Math::Ceiling
      (YourLocation) || Math::Ceiling (AliensMissiles) ==
      Math::Floor (YourLocation) || Math::Floor
      (AliensMissiles) == Math::Ceiling (YourLocation) ||
      Math::Floor (AliensMissiles) == Math::Ceiling
      (YourLocation))
       break;
     else
      AliensMissiles = rnd->NextDouble ();
}        // end loop
```

```
    if ((AlienShip1 + AlienShip2) < 0)
      Console::WriteLine
        ("\n Good work lieutenant, or should I say captain.\n");
    else
      Console::WriteLine ("\n BOOM!!! Your dead.\n");

    Console::WriteLine
      ("\n Game Over\n \n Would you like to play again? (Y/N)");
    input = Console::ReadLine ();
    input = input->ToUpper ();
  } while (input->Equals("Y"));
}
```

Type Casting: Explicit Conversions

Before we jump into user-defined functions, let's cover one additional topic that actually allows the conversion of numeric data into other various sized data types without those annoying warnings about truncation and undue data loss. Remember that in chapter 2 we covered implicit conversions, which generally fell under the category of smaller to larger transfers of data. *Type casting* is an explicit conversion and is used for conversion from smaller to larger to protect against calculating errors, or lager to smaller to redefine those parameters when a value's precision overshadows its requirement (see Text Examples 1 and 2). In either case, the action of declaring an explicit conversion notifies the compiler of our intention and automatically reassigns those variables.

Text Example 1:

When a value is larger than is required for practical purposes, that value can be truncated to save space or to refine the final displayed statement, e.g., $10.012 becoming $10.01, the amount owed.

Text Example 2:

When an irrational number is the result in an integer equation, the value is always truncated to an integer value. This will happen regardless of the assigned variables data type and without regard for the truncating variables true value. For example, in the equation 9 divided by 2, the real quotient should be 4.5, but after truncating, using rules of integer division, we are left with the value of 4. Although incorrect, this is the value passed to the variable, even if that variable is of a floating-point data type. The simplest way to correct this is to make at least one of our values a real number, for example 9.0/2 equals 4.5. However, the problem here is that this type of change only works for literal constants and not for variables that hold integer data (as in x = 9, y = 2, x/y yielding 4). A more creative solution then would be to use type casting. Type casting, as explained above, allows us to convert both literal constants and variables by using data type conversions, e.g., (*double*)9 or *double*(9) (see Example 4.4).

Example 4.4. Type casting.

```
/* Type Casting */
#include "stdafx.h"
#using <mscorlib.dll>
#include <tchar.h>
using namespace System;
```

```
int _tmain(void) {
  double number1 = 9/2;
  // Warning - returning 4
  Console::WriteLine (number1);

  double number2 = (double) 9/ (double) 2;
  // returning 4.5
  Console::WriteLine (number2);

  int integer1 = (int) (4.7);      // 4
  Console::WriteLine (integer1);

  if ( 9/2 >= (double)9 / 2 )  // always false
   Console::WriteLine ("4 >= 4.5");
   //Unreachable code detected

  int integer2 = 9;
  double number3 = (double) integer2/2; // 4.5
  Console::WriteLine (number3);

  int integer3 = (int) ((double) 9/ (double) 2 + .5);   // 5.0
  Console::WriteLine (integer3);
}
```

Note: Unsigned values by definition have twice the range of signed values, thus the potential of data loss is increased when attempting to convert to a restricted data type.

Introduction to User-Defined Functions

What are *user-defined* functions? Simply put, they are subprograms (subroutines or secondary methods) linked to a main or secondary method and subsequently used to carry out a list of tasks when that method requests it. They can receive information from other functions (including the main method) and they can send information back to their referencing function. They are both commands (like the predefined functions) and lines of code used to implement those commands, which we create as programmers. Technically, everything placed inside a user-defined function could have just as well have been left inside its main method, but in professional programs, this would lead to confusion and a very large and cluttered main method. In addition, there are many techniques that can be applied to user-defined functions (including *calls-by-references*, *overloading*, and *recursion*), all of which can be applied repeatedly rather than asking the programmer to repeat that coding over and over again in a single linear method. To start, we'll begin with the simpler functions and then expand on these topics one section at a time.

Writing Our First User-Defined Function

Writing a user-defined function isn't that different from writing a main function. In fact, if you compared the two, you'd find that the underlying rules are basically the same. One key advantage then when declaring user-defined functions is their flexibility in descriptive naming, which gives the programmer an instant, if not complete, description of what the function will do. Microsoft's Hungarian notation and Camel notation, along with the simple rules of variable naming (all discussed in Chapter 2) are what we'll use when declaring our user-defined functions. Our first example demonstrates how a simple function is written. You should use this example to compare the two types of functions e.g., Main ( ) versus OurFunction ( ) (see Example 4.5).

Example 4.5. Our first user-defined function.

```
/* Our first function call */
#include "stdafx.h"
#using <mscorlib.dll>
#include <tchar.h>
using namespace System;

static void OurFunction ( ) {
 /* This is a do nothing function */
}

int _tmain(void) {
   OurFunction ( );
}
```

Note: Referencing a user-defined function is not unlike referencing a predefined function.

Although this program is similar to the do-nothing programs of Chapter 1, it still represents a true user-defined function. From here, we could have inserted a slue of information including declared variables, predefined functions, loops, and switch statements. Still, it's best if we hold off on some of these at least until we've completely defined user-defined functions. The next few sections include descriptions of prototypes, global and local variables, data structures, and *return* statements all of which are crucial to that definition, so try to be patient.

Prototypes

A Prototype is similar to this text's table of contents; it gives the compiler a list of user-defined functions that will be found after the main method. If a prototype is missing, the compiler assumes that there is no function to assign too and an error is sighted. Functions listed before *main* do not require a prototype as the compiler as already noted their positions. Prototypes also, usually include descriptive comments (see Example 4.6).

To create a prototype we must follow two rules:

1. The function and prototype must have identical naming schemes including declarative content.
2. Prototypes, unlike their functions counterparts, require a terminating semicolon.

Example 4.6. Prototypes.
```
/* Our second function call */
#include "stdafx.h"
#using <mscorlib.dll>
#include <tchar.h>
using namespace System;

static void OurFunction ( ); // prototype
```

```
int _tmain(void) {
  OurFunction ( );
}
```

Variable Scope

Local variables are variables declared inside the main or subsequent methods. Their values are not known beyond the limitations of their block. Programmers who wish to transfer data from one block to another must do so using a referencing function. There are generally two types of passing variables: *calls-by-mechanism*, where information is merely passed to new variables, and *calls-by-reference*, which allow the programmer to alter the original memory locations. Local variables, as well as their secondary counterparts, can be passed and repassed endlessly, so limitations are minimized. In addiction, user-defined functions have the ability to return data to the main or other calling functions.

  Global variables are variables declared outside of blocks (including the main and user-defined blocks/functions). Global variable exist throughout the program and can be accessed by all functions/subroutines. Global variables are also not subject to automatic garbage collection. The disadvantage to global variables is that they limit program portability, the ability to integrate coding, and reusability (see Example 4.7).

Example 4.7. Local and global variables.

```
/* Are first look at global variables */
#include "stdafx.h"
#using <mscorlib.dll>
#include <tchar.h>
using namespace System;

static void OurFunction (int Total);
static int NumberOne, NumberTwo, GlobalTotal = 0;

// This is the entry point for this application
int _tmain(void) {
  String* input;

  int LocalTotal = 0;
  Console::Write
  ("\n How many apples did Johnny shoplift? ");
  input = Console::ReadLine ();
  NumberOne = input->ToInt32(0);
  Console::Write
  ("\n How many apples did Bobby shoplift? ");
  input = Console::ReadLine ( );
  NumberTwo = input->ToInt32(0);

  LocalTotal = NumberOne + NumberTwo;
  OurFunction (LocalTotal);
}

static void OurFunction (int Total) {
```

```
  GlobalTotal = NumberOne + NumberTwo;
  Console::Write
  ("\n Good news, Johnny and Bobby were arrested"
   "for shoplifting. \n By the way would you like"
   " an apple? I have ");
  Console::Write (Total);
  Console::Write (" of them, ");
  Console::Write (GlobalTotal);
  Console::WriteLine (" apples is a lot.");
}
```

> Note:
>   All global references that conflict with local variables are generally hidden by the
> compiler when those blocks are accessed, thus a local reference will always be chosen
> over a global value. When working with local and global variables that require dual
> references, two important distinctions must be made. First, a new function reference
> must be declared and second, the global variables must be completely defined using the
> class' definition (see Examples 4.8).

Example 4.8. Variables scope.

```
/* Variable Scope II */
#include "stdafx.h"
#using <mscorlib.dll>
#include <tchar.h>
using namespace System;

const double GoldBar = 1000.00; // global variable
        // (also the value of a gold bar on earth).
void _tmain(void) {
  double GoldBar = 0;
  // local variable (also the value of a gold bar in hell).
  // Class1 GlobalCA2 = new Class1 ();
  Console::WriteLine ("The value of gold on earth is {0}",
    __box(::GoldBar));

  Console::WriteLine ("The value of gold in hell is {0}",
    __box(GoldBar));
}
```

Functions that Return Values

Our next step will be to re-equip our user-defined functions with nonvoid data types that require some type
of returning calculation. The keyword return passes back a single value to the calling function. The value in
question must be of the qualified type, and in cases where the returning type is void it can be omitted. return
statements are required with all nonvoid user-defined functions and methods. We'll begin by developing a
simple, but effective function that finds the sum of two values and returns that value to the main method (we
could also revise this example to compute their difference, product, quotient–see Example 4.9).

Example 4.9. Returning values.

```
/* returning values */
#include "stdafx.h"
#using <mscorlib.dll>
#include <tchar.h>
using namespace System;

static int RandomNumber ();

void _tmain(void) {
  String* input;
  int iNumberOne = 0, iNumberTwo = 0; // Local variables

  while (iNumberOne != 99)  {  // 99 ends loop
    Console::Write ("\n Guess the number, hint: ");
    Console::Write ("it's between ten and three.\n");
    Console::Write ("Can you guess it he, he, he? ");
    input = Console::ReadLine ();
    iNumberOne = input->ToInt32(0);

    iNumberTwo = RandomNumber();

    if (iNumberOne == iNumberTwo) {
     Console::Write ("\n Hey you win, with a smile ");
     Console::WriteLine ("with a grin!!!");
    }
    else if (iNumberOne > iNumberTwo) {
     Console::WriteLine ("\n To high smart guy!");
     iNumberTwo = iNumberTwo++;
    }
    else  {
     Console::WriteLine ("\n To low slow Joe");
     iNumberTwo = iNumberTwo--;
    }
  }// end while
} // end main

static int RandomNumber () {
  Random* rnd = new Random ();
  int n2 = (int) Math::Round (rnd->NextDouble () * 10)+1;

  Console::WriteLine (n2);
  return (n2);
}
```

Our next comparison then opens the field a bit by making our random function capable of returning character data. Here we also included a while loop that protects our function from returning anything other than a letter (see Example 4.10).

Example 4.10. Letter generator.

```
/* Letter Generator */
#include "stdafx.h"
#using <mscorlib.dll>
#include <tchar.h>
using namespace System;

static char LetterGenerator (char Letter);

void _tmain(void) {
  char letter = 'a';
  String* input;

  Console::WriteLine ("This program attempts"
   "to guess the first letter of your name.");
   "All you have to do is "
   "reply with a \"y\"\n"
   "or a \"n\" after each guess\n"
   "You can also enter \"q\" to quit "
   "the game at any time.\n"
   "My first guess is...\n");

  do  {
    letter = LetterGenerator (letter);
    Console::WriteLine ("{0} is this correct?\n",
      __box(__box(letter)->ToChar(0)));
    input = Console::ReadLine ();
    input = input->ToUpper();

    if (input->Equals("Y"))
     Console::WriteLine ("Great let's play again");
    else
     Console::WriteLine ("How about...");
    } while (!input->Equals("Q"));
}

static char LetterGenerator (char letter)  {
  Random* rnd = new Random ();
  letter = (char)((int) Math::Round (rnd->NextDouble () * 100));

  while (!(letter >= 65 && letter <= 90)) {
letter = (char)((int) Math::Round (rnd->NextDouble () * 100));}

return (char)(letter);
}
```

The main function/method is also easily adaptable to include both storage data types and the **return** statement (see Examples 4.11 and 4.12). Note that referencing a **return** statement from within the main method also causes the immediate termination of that program.

Example 4.11. Main function with data types.

```
/* Main functions can include data types */
#include "stdafx.h"
#using <mscorlib.dll>
#include <tchar.h>
using namespace System;

int _tmain(void) {
  return 0;
}
```

Example 4.12. Empty return statements.

```
/* empty return statements */
#include "stdafx.h"
#using <mscorlib.dll>
#include <tchar.h>
using namespace System;

void _tmain(void) {
  return;
}
```

Of course, there is also a noreturn command that, as its name implies, tells the compiler that this function will not return a value. This is useful when a attempting to avoid a warning (C4715) or error message (C2202). The command sequence __declspec(noinline) is placed before the function as is shown in Example 4.13.

Example 4.13. noreturn.

```
/* Letter Generator */
#include "stdafx.h"
#using <mscorlib.dll>
#include <tchar.h>
using namespace System;

__declspec(noreturn) static void LetterGenerator (char *Letter);

void _tmain(void) {
  char a = 'a', *letter = &a;
  String* input;

  Console::WriteLine ("This program attempts to guess"
    "the first letter of your name.\n"
    "All you have to do is reply with a \"y\"\n"
    "or a \"n\" after each guess\n"
    "You can also enter \"q\" to quit "
    "the game at any time.\n"
    "My first guess is...\n");
```

```
  do  {
    LetterGenerator (letter);
    Console::WriteLine ("{0} is this correct?\n",
      __box(__box(*letter)->ToChar(0)));
    input = Console::ReadLine ();
    input = input->ToUpper ();

    if (input->Equals("Y"))
     Console::WriteLine ("Great let's play again");
    else
     Console::WriteLine ("How about...");
    } while (!input->Equals("Q"));
}

__declspec(noreturn) static void LetterGenerator (char *letter)  {
  Random* rnd = new Random ();
  *letter = (char)((int) Math::Round (rnd->NextDouble () * 100));

  while (!(*letter >= 65 && *letter <= 90)) {
    *letter = (char)((int) Math::Round (rnd->NextDouble () * 100));
  }
}
```

Passing Variables: Calls-by-Value

The *call-by-value* type *mechanism* is a mechanism used to transfer data between methods that does not allow for continued access to the original fields. The data is then considered to be a value type, which is appropriately stored on the "stack"–the computer's temporary memory–and will be removed, or "popped off," when that method is terminated. Again, the changes in these secondary variables will not affect the original fields, nor will there be deletions. The *call-by-value* formal parameters refer to the variables referenced from inside user-defined functions as demonstrated in Example 4.14 (a simple example that finds the square root of a number).

Example 4.14. Passing our first variable.

```
/* Passing our first variable */
#include "stdafx.h"
#using <mscorlib.dll>
#include <tchar.h>
using namespace System;

static float SquareRoot (float n);

void _tmain(void) {
  String* input;
  float number = 0, root = 0;

  Console::Write ("This program will find the "
    "square root of any number\n"
    "Enter your first value now: ");
```

```
  input = Console::ReadLine ();
  number = (float)input->ToDouble(0);

  root = SquareRoot (number);
  Console::WriteLine (root);
}

// This function generates square roots using Newton's method
static float SquareRoot (float n) {
  float test1, test2;
  test1 = n-(float).01 - ((n-(float).01)*(n-(float).01) - n)/
   (n*(n-(float).01));
  test2 = test1 - ((test1*test1)-n)/ ((n)*test1);

  while (test1 != test2)   {
    test1 = test2;
    test2 = test1 - (test1*test1 - n)/((n)*test1);
  }

  return (test2);
}
```

Note: We could have also replaced that user-defined function with the predefined function Math::Sqrt ( ).

Writing Functions as Black Boxes

The *black box theory* is simply a concept that stresses the idea that most, if not all, functions should be thought of as independent or self-containing subprograms. It also reasons that the coding used to construct such a function does not need to be studied or known by a programmer who only wants to invoke that function. Thus, the only information needed to access a function is the proper passing variables and the knowledge of what would be returned by that function. This is analogous to being able to drive a car, but not knowing how to repair the engine. This is actually quit the norm in C++, since all predefined functions are black boxes to most programmers and the idea of enhancing them would literally force us to open them up and redesign them to some new standard. Of course, if you were to write your own user-defined functions, you'd certainly know how each one of them worked.

  Creating a black box style function requires or restricts us to the use of encapsulated controls. This, of course, means that you must avoid using global variables and that you must include comments with every prototype to alert any other programmer to the variable settings and to their results. In addition, you should keep in mind that in later chapters, we'll be both reading and writing to user-defined functions from separate files, thus creating a real need for detailed comments explaining what these different function calls do.

Note: Applying the black box approach to Example 4.15.
  Let's assume that you didn't really understand the second portion of the last example, but you used the square root function anyway. While it is a bit disheartening to the mathematician in me, this will not affect the way the program executes that data, in fact, it actually makes my point. If however, that coding piqued your interest then enticed your interest then here's a quick overview of the mathematics (see example 4.15).

Example 4.15. The square root function explained.

```
/* The Square Root Function Explained */
static float SquareRoot (float n) {// Newton's Method (Basic Calculus)
  float test1, test2; // X_{n+1} = X_n - f(X_n)/f '(X_n)    n = 1, 2, 3, …
  test1 = n-(float).01 -   // X_0 = Guess-Estimate
  ((n-(float).01)*(n-(float).01) - n)/(n*(n-(float).01));
  test2 = test1 - ((test1*test1)-n)/((n)*test1);

  while (test1 != test2) {// X_1 = X_0 - (X_0^2 - Number)/(Number*X_0)
   test1 = test2;        // X_2 = X_1 - (X_1^2 - Number)/(Number*X_1)
   test2 = test1 -       // X_3 = X_2 - (X_2^2 - Number)/(Number*X_2)
   (test1*test1 - n) /   // X4 = X_3 - (X_3^2 - Number)/ (Number*X_3)
   ((n)*test1);          // X_5 = X_4 - (X_4^2 - Number)/(Number*X_4)
  }

return (test2);    // until X_{n..} = X_{n..+1}
}
```

Again, we can also reconstruct the last program using the predefined function Math::Sqrt ( ) (see Example 4.16).

Example 4.16. User-defined versus predefined functions.

```
/* user-defined vs. predefined functions */
#include "stdafx.h"
#using <mscorlib.dll>
#include <tchar.h>
using namespace System;

void _tmain(void) {
  String* input;
  float number = 0, root = 0;

  Console::Write ("This program will find the "
   "square root of any number\n"
   "Enter your first value now: ");
  input = Console::ReadLine ();
  number = (float) input->ToDouble(0);
  root = (float) Math::Sqrt (number);
  Console::WriteLine (root);
}
```

Note: We'll want to take the black box approach to most, if not all, of the predefined functions listed in this text.

Passing Variables: Calls-by-Reference

The *call-by-reference mechanism* is an assignable mechanism, where the variables that are passed to a function are not just passed as values, but include actual memory references. Thus, by altering those values, we are also altering the values accessed by the main program. These variables, then, are not created and destroyed as part of a temporary stack; rather, they are created and stored by the heap, which is a memory location that exists for the entire life of the program's execution. This has the minor disadvantage of not allowing us to send numeric or literal constants as we could with the call-by-value mechanism, but it does expand our options when dealing with otherwise globally restricted data. To change a call-by-value parameter into a call-by-reference parameter all we need to do is insert the ampersand symbol (&) after the data type (see Example 4.17).

Example 4.17. A day at the races.

```
/* a day at the races */
#include "stdafx.h"
#using <mscorlib.dll>
#include <tchar.h>
using namespace System;

static void TheRace (int* Num);
static void TieBreaker (int Num1, int* Num2);

void _tmain(void) {
  String *input = "Y", *Horse;
  int iNumber1 = 0, iNumber2 = 0, iNumber3 = 0;

  Console::Write ("Let's have a horse race.\n");
  Console::WriteLine ("To play select one of the horses below");

  while (!input->Equals("N")) {
    Console::WriteLine ("(1) for Whitefire");
    Console::WriteLine ("(2) for The Train and, ");
    Console::WriteLine ("(3) for Noisy Glue");
    Horse = Console::ReadLine ();

    TheRace (&iNumber1);
    TheRace (&iNumber2);
    TheRace (&iNumber3);

    TieBreaker (iNumber1, &iNumber2);
    TieBreaker (iNumber2, &iNumber3);
    TieBreaker (iNumber1, &iNumber3);

    Console::Write ("And the winner is ");

    if (iNumber1 > iNumber2 && iNumber1 > iNumber3)
     Console::WriteLine ("The Train"); // 2
    else if (iNumber2 > iNumber1 && iNumber2 > iNumber3)
     Console::WriteLine ("Noisy Glue"); // 3
    else
```

```
      Console::WriteLine ("Whitefire"); // 1

    Console::WriteLine ("Would you like to play again (Y/N)?");
    input = Console::ReadLine ();
    input = input->ToUpper ();
  }
}

static void TheRace (int* Num)   {
  Random* rnd = new Random ();
  *Num = (int) Math::Round (rnd->Next(3));
}

static void TieBreaker (int Num1, int* Num2)    {
  if (Num1 == *Num2) {
    TheRace (Num2);
    TieBreaker (Num1, Num2);
  }
}
```

An Introduction to Polymorphism

Polymorphism (also known as *overloading*) occurs when any reference has a closely matching, but not identical definition. These secondary, or substitute functions, while not technically required, generally tend to stay within the confines of that first function's purpose. If an overloading function were to be altered to a degree that promoted a completely new definition, then overloading would not be necessary. While overloading functions do share the same referencing title, their definitions must defer in arrangement by at least one transferring data type. The use of these differing access points guides our compilers to the correct (overloading) function. Since more than one possible referencing point exists, there is also an increased chance of miscalling that function, thus creating a runtime error. Examples 4.18 and 4.19 give alternate functions that can produce the same results, but only Example 4.18 performs correctly.

Example 4.18. Overloading a function.

```
/* Overloading a function */
#include "stdafx.h"
#using <mscorlib.dll>
#include <tchar.h>
using namespace System;

static int Sum (int iNumber1, int iNumber2, int iNumber3);
static int Sum (int iNumber1, int iNumber2);

void _tmain(void) {
  String* input;
  int iNumber1 = 0, iNumber2 = 0, iNumber3 = 0, iTotal;

  Console::Write ("Please enter two to three ");
  Console::Write ("numbers to be added\n");
  Console::Write ("If you only have two numbers make ");
  Console::Write ("the third number equal to zero:\n");
```

```
  Console::Write ("Your first number is? ");
  input = Console::ReadLine ();
  iNumber1 = input->ToInt32(0);

  Console::Write ("Your Second number is? ");
  input = Console::ReadLine ();
  iNumber2 = input->ToInt32(0);

  Console::Write ("Your Third number is? ");
  input = Console::ReadLine ();
  iNumber3 = input->ToInt32(0);

  if (iNumber3 == 0)
    iTotal = Sum (iNumber1, iNumber2);
  else
    iTotal = Sum (iNumber1, iNumber2, iNumber3);

  Console::Write ("The Sum of these numbers was ");
  Console::WriteLine (iTotal);
}

static int Sum (int iNumber1, int iNumber2)  {
  int iSum;
  iSum = iNumber1 + iNumber2;
  return (iSum);
}

static int Sum (int iNumber1, int iNumber2, int iNumber3) {
  int iSum;
  iSum = iNumber1 + iNumber2 + iNumber3;
  return (iSum);
}
```

Note: If you're not sure if this programs working correctly, try retesting the three variables using two zeros and a negative one.

Example 4.19. This program does not overload the function.

```
/* ERROR: This program does not overload the function */
#include "stdafx.h"
#using <mscorlib.dll>
#include <tchar.h>
using namespace System;

static int Sum (int iNumber1, int iNumber2, int iNumber3);

void _tmain(void) {
  String* input;
  int iNumber1 = 0, iNumber2 = 0,
  iNumber3 = 0, iTotal;
```

```
Console::Write ("Please enter two to three numbers");
Console::Write ("to be added\n");
Console::Write ("If you only have two numbers");
Console::Write ("make the third number equal to zero: \n");

Console::Write ("Enter your first number now: ");
input = Console::ReadLine ();
iNumber1 = input->ToInt32(0);

Console::Write ("Enter your second number please: ");
input = Console::ReadLine ();
iNumber2 = input->ToInt32(0);

Console::Write ("Enter your third number if you have one: ");
input = Console::ReadLine ();
iNumber3 = input->ToInt32(0);

iTotal = Sum (iNumber1, iNumber2, iNumber3);

Console::Write ("The Sum of these numbers was ");
Console::WriteLine (iTotal);
}

static int Sum (int iNumber1, int iNumber2, int iNumber3) {
  int iSum;
  iSum = iNumber1 + iNumber2 + iNumber3;
  return (iSum);
}
```

Introducing Recursion

A *recursive function* is a user-defined function that contains one or more odd iterations caused by the unusual placement of a secondary call to that function. The position or placement of this secondary function call is considered unusual or at least a special topic because it invokes a function from within that function. That is to say, when the programmers created the function, they included it in a call to that causes that function to loop repeatedly, or at least multiple times. (Note: This would also mean that it would have to return to itself multiple times before returning to the main or calling function). The reasons for manipulating a function in this manner are diverse and at times confusing, but ultimately, the coding for such examples is quite simple, as shown in Example 4.20. Note the recursive function used to test our horseracing program earlier in this chapter.

Example 4.20. Recursion.

```
/* Recursion */
#include "stdafx.h"
#using <mscorlib.dll>
#include <tchar.h>
using namespace System;
```

```
static void Password ();

int _tmain(void) {
  Password ();
}

static void Password ()   {
  String* input;
  int password;

  Console::WriteLine ("\n Enter Your Access Code Now: ");
  input = Console::ReadLine ();
  password = input->ToInt32(0);

  if (password == 1024) {
   Console::WriteLine ("\n Access Granted");
   return;
  }
  else
   Password ();
}
```

Inline Functions

Another interesting way to set up and use functions is to make them inline functions. What exactly is an inline function? Well, simply put, it's a function that is inserted into every line that calls it. That is, rather than having the function call actually call the function, the function is compiled into that line of coding. This speeds up the program, but it also increases the coding size.

It should also be noted that *inlining* is only a request, with the compiler giving the final approve. If the compiler finds that inlining will not optimize the coding or if it would cause an error, then your request is denied. This rejected coding will still compile, it just won't include those inline references. Microsoft also offers the keyword __forceinline, if you're sure of that inlining is the best decision. However, if its used incorrectly, it can also slowdown the program (see Example 4.21).

Example 4.21. Inline functions.

```
/* Inline function */
#include "stdafx.h"
#using <mscorlib.dll>
#include <tchar.h>
using namespace System;

inline void StandardFunction(void);
__inline void MicrosoftInlineFunction(void);
__forceinline void MicrosoftForcedInlineFunction(void);

void _tmain(void) {
  StandardFunction();
  MicrosoftInlineFunction();
```

```
  MicrosoftForcedInlineFunction();
}

inline void StandardFunction(void) {
/* Note the word inline doesn't have to be repeated */
}
  __inline void MicrosoftInlineFunction(void) {
/* __inline is a Microsoft specific function */
}
  __forceinline void MicrosoftForcedInlineFunction(void) {
/* Microsoft specific function */
}
```

Of course, there is also a noinline function that, as its name implies, stops a function from being inlined. This is useful when a function is smaller and less likely to produce beneficial results. The command sequence __declspec(noinline) is placed before the function as is shown in Example 4.22.

Example 4.22. Noinline.

```
/* noinline function */
#include "stdafx.h"
#using <mscorlib.dll>
#include <tchar.h>
using namespace System;
  __declspec(noinline) void StandardFunction(void);

void _tmain(void) {
  StandardFunction();
}

  __declspec(noinline) void StandardFunction(void) {
}
```

An alternative to inline is the __fastcall reference. Here __fastcall is used to specify that an argument is best served if included in the register. As with inlining this is merely a request and future compiler versions may use different registers. /Gr compiler options default to fastcall, but main and conflicting functions are not converted. Note: Using the /Gr setting however, disabled the default stack cleanup, though this can be countered using keyword __cdecl, though this also creates larger executables then __stdcall. The /Gd option forces the __cdecl convention.

Trouble Shooting

Troubleshooting review, in chapter 1 we covered the four basic types of errors: *syntax*, *runtime*, *logic* and *linking errors*, in that chapter we also covered set up and the basic "do-nothing" program. In chapter 2, we looked at the *syntax error* as both a *typographical error* and as a change in *compliance error*. With Chapter 3, we began to study the online help reference included with our compilers, looking up codes, examples–I also offered my email address to handle compliance errors (see that Chapter for details).

Now, while this chapter includes several new topics, the errors they invoke have not change. For example, failing to include a header or namespace before calling a predefined function will still result in a linking error, mistyping the signature of a user-defined will still invoke a syntax error, and the online help menu can still help to define nonspecific errors.

Common Errors, Problems, and Pits:

1. Predefined functions require a linked file reference Native C++ used the included file, managed C++ can use both the included file and the namespace reference. Referencing a predefined function without either source will result in a linking either a *syntax* or *linking error*.
2. Failing to include a returning value for a *non-void function* will result in an *compilation error*.
3. Remember, from inside a functions definition, you must declare each data type individually as in int one, int two... attempting to include them without a data type would result in a *compilation error*.
4. *Overloaded functions* must include unique signatures, identical signatures will result in a *compilation error*.
5. Recursive functions must include an exit point, infinite recursion will result in a *runtime error*.

Things to Remember

1. Remember C++ requires function prototypes and included files.
2. Calls-by-reference can completely replace global variables.
3. Overloaded functions must not contain the same arrangement of passing variables.
4. Recursion means nothing more than repeating the same function from within that function.
5. Always use a standard predefined function when possible they speed up programming tasks and increase program portability.
6. The goal of any good programmer is to write code that can be reused in several projects. Don't waste time rewriting the same code.
7. Always remember when asking the user for inputs such as name, social security number... You can echo that information and/or allow for changes.
8. Calls by value let you transfer the content of a value to a new variable, while calls by reference remain linked to the original variables.
9. Try to limit each function to a single task. If one function requires a large list of variables or if it does the job of many functions, then it's probably too big.
10. Remember, the ultimate goal of the programmer is to write for both reusability and portability.

Questions

1. Write a do-nothing program that calls the user-defined function Hello ( ). Hello should display the words "Hello world!" (list the function before the main function).
2. Revise the last the program so that the Hello function is listed after the main function. (Hint: remember to include prototype for Hello ( ).
3. List three of the Character predefined functions.
4. List three of the Math predefined functions.
5. Write a program than sights a warning/error for implicit conversion, as in possible loss of data. Use an explicit type cast to remove the warning/error.
6. Using global variables, write a program that compares two variables inside a user-defined function.
7. Revise the last program using local variables; use Hello (*int* iVal1, *int* iVal2).
8. Revise the last program so that the two variables are declared and assigned inside the user-defined function and only the final value is sent back to the main function.
9. Define the theory of the black box approach.

10. Write a program that uses two user-defined functions, one to add the sum of two numbers, the other to add the sum of three numbers, using an overloaded user-defined function.
11. Write a recursive function.
12. Convert a standard "do-nothing" function into an inline function, and then change it into a Microsoft specific inline function, then a Microsoft forced inline function.
13. Write a user-defined function that uses recursion to count from zero to ten.

PART II

OBJECT-ORIENTED PROGRAMMING

Chapter Five

I found Rome a city of bricks and left it a city of marble.
Augustus Caesar

Arrays, Pointers, & Strings

This chapter addresses a concept that lets us combine variables into a collective or arrogated set, provided they share the same base data and some common purpose. The first portion of this chapter explains this concept—properly referred to as an *array*—from both its singular and multidimensional perspectives. The second portion of this chapter introduces another powerful concept known as the *pointer* and several other keywords and processing commands (including *predefined array/string functions* and *data stream manipulations*). There are also several traditional concepts intermixed in this chapter including *bubble sorting*, *array searches*, and calculations of *mean, median, mode,* and *range*. (Note: Chapter 6 also offers some intermediate array and string examples that involve an extended knowledge of classes).

Arrays

Arrays are referenced values associated with the collective heap. They are instances of the Base Class Library and thus considered objects, which also makes them subject to the automatic garbage collector. In their simplest form, they can be thought of as a collection of variables used under one data type with similar values and identities. These variables often share the same programming tasks with redundant calculation and similar or redundant concluding data. The information generated is stored collectively, but also with an independent reusability that reduces or prevents the need for repetitive coding[4]. The simplest way to demonstrate the conversion from several variables to an array is to express that process visually, as done in Example 5.1.

Example 5.1. Implementing an array.

```
int number1, number2, number3, number4, number5;
                  Is approximately equivalent too
              int [] number = new int [5];
   // number[0], number[1], number[2], number[3], number[4].
```

As you can see, the first line represents the declaration of five variables and the third line represents a value equivalent to five variables. The array's components are broken-down in Example 5.2.

Example 5.2. The components of an array.
Component number [0] is the first variable (or the replacement for number0),
   Console::Write (number0);   can be converted too   Console::Write (number [0]);

Component number [1] is the second variable (or the replacement for number1),

[4] The idea of converting several similarly structured variables to a single or multifunctional array predates the origins of both C++ and C. Arrays could also be thought of as the fathers and grandfathers of structures and classes, respectively.

std::cout << number1;   can be converted too   std::cout << number [1];

Component number [2] is the third variable (or the replacement for number2),
    for (*int* index = 0; index < number2; index++) ... for (*int* index = 0; index < number [2]; index++)

Component number [3] is the fourth variable (or the replacement for number3),
                    if (number3 = = 27)   rewritten as   *if* (number [3] = = 27)

Component number [4] is the fifth variable (or the replacement for number4),
                    while (number4)   ...   *while* (number [4])

Component number [5] is not a usable variable and instead holds the null character that terminates the line. Additional indexed variables (for example, number [6], [7]), will also exceed our array's declared space, which may not be flagged as a compilation error.

> Note:
> In Example 5.2, the first value is zero (not one)[5]. In addition, you might conclude that this array should hold six values since number [5] was not used. This conclusion would be in error since C++ withholds that last space as a termination marker assigning the zero-null character "\0" to that position. Our first chore then will be to convert a simple singular variable program into one that can take advantage of the new array format (the potential of arrays will become obvious very shortly).

Declaring and Referencing Arrays

The declaration of an array doesn't vary greatly from the declaration of either a standard or a constant variable. They are generally written using lowercase lettering, and all of the rules of variable naming still apply. The one significant difference is in the insertion of the square brackets (demonstrated in the last example), which both define an array and allow us to reference their components. The capacity of an array is determined by the size of the value placed inside those initializing brackets. The formal name for this type of value is the *indexed variable*, but it is also known as the *subscripted variable*, or less precisely, as an *element* (i.e., an element of an array). The number of indexed variables (total spaces reserved) is called the *declared size*, or just the size, while the data type used to declare that array is called the *base type* (see Examples 5.3 and 5.4).

Example 5.3. Converting from singular variables to arrays –part 1.

```
/* This program list five student's grades using five variables,
 * while the next program does the same task using only one array. */
#include "stdafx.h"
#using <mscorlib.dll>
#include <tchar.h>
using namespace System;

void _tmain(void) {
```

---

[5] In C++ and assembled languages, the array's numeric notation can be seen as a measure of the distance from one space in the array to another. Since the first space has no space or distance from itself this would be noted as zero. Although it is possible for higher-level languages to alter this value to read one, there are still no formal procedures that allow us to convert those values in C++.

```
String *student0, *student1, *student2, *student3, *student4;

Console::Write ("Enter student 1's grade : ");
student0 = Console::ReadLine ( );

Console::Write ("Enter student 2's grade : ");
student1 = Console::ReadLine ();

Console::Write ("Enter student 3's grade : ");
student2 = Console::ReadLine ();

Console::Write ("Enter student 4's grade : ");
student3 = Console::ReadLine ();

Console::Write ("Enter student 5's grade : ");
student4 = Console::ReadLine ();

Console::WriteLine ("\nYour input was {0} {1} {2} {3} {4}",
 student0, student1, student2, student3, student4);
}
```

Example 5.4. Converting from multiple variables to an array –part 2.

```
/* Arrays: this program is a revision of the last program */
#include "stdafx.h"
#using <mscorlib.dll>
#include <tchar.h>
using namespace System;

void _tmain(void) {
 String* student __gc[] = new String* __gc[5];

 for (int index = 0; index < 5; index++) {
  Console::Write ("Enter student 1's grade : ");
  student[index] = Console::ReadLine ();
 }

Console::WriteLine ("\nYour input was {0}, {1}, {2}, {3}, {4}",
  student[0], student[1], student[2], student[3], student[4]);
 }
```

In addition to displaying its values as fragments, we can also display them as a whole (see example 5.5).

Example 5.5. Converting from variables to an array –part 3.

```
/* Arrays */
#include "stdafx.h"
#using <mscorlib.dll>
#include <tchar.h>
using namespace System;
```

```
void _tmain(void) {
 String* students_grades __gc[] = new String* __gc[5];

 for (int index = 0; index < 5; index++) {
  Console::Write ("Enter student ");
  Console::Write (index+1);
  Console::Write ("'s grade: ");
  students_grades[index] = Console::ReadLine ();
 }

 Console::Write ("Your input was ");
 for (int index = 0; index < students_grades.Length; index++) {
  Console::Write (students_grades [index]);
  Console::Write (" ");
 }

 Console::WriteLine ( ) ;
}
```

Note:
Using Variable Names as Indexed Variables:
You can also use variable names when declaring and referencing arrays of undetermined sizes. The one catch here is that those arrays are then limited by that declaration. This holds true even when the variable used to declare that array's range is not a constant (see the section on dynamic arrays). For a simple example of a variable declaration, see Example 5.6.

Example 5.6. Variable declaration for an array.

```
const int total_students = 35;
// this is equivalent to students_grades [35]
char students_grades[total_students];
```

Assigning Values to Arrays

In addition to declaring arrays, we will need to assign values to them, which can be done either after the array is declared, or as a part of the declaration. There are three standard formats; all include a reference to the data type followed by the array symbol [], and the array's definition. In each case, we will include a host of values contained within an opening and closing set of curly braces, as shown in Example 5.7.

Example 5.7. Assigning values to arrays.

```
int array1[7] = {16, 15, 12, 99, 31, 2, 34};
// Here the zeroth array element equals 16.
double array2[4] = {16.5, 54.95, 3.14159, 34.0};
// The last value (4), equals the line marker
char[] array3[3] = {'a', 'b', 'c'};
int array4[] = {1, 2, 3};
```

Another useful tool is to include a *string value reference*, replacing the older value type character array with a dynamic value. This new format eliminates the need to make arbitrary guestimations about string size, and thus it will be much less likely that we'll have to tamper with the coding in order to deal with any unusual changes (see Example 5.8).

Example 5.8. String value reference.

```
String *String1 = "Damn it boy, its three o'clock in the morning."
String *String2 = "What the hell are you doing up so late? \n";
String *String3 = "I'm just doing my homework dad.\n";
String *String4 = "Oh, I know what your doing, turn those games off and
go to bed! \n";
String *String5 = "That's it; I'm quitting school and joining a software
company! \n";
String *String6 = "Oh no you're not mister! We didn't raise you to
develop software! \n";
```

Passing Arrays to Functions

In addition to using arrays inside of user-defined functions, we can also pass their values either as elements or in their entirety. The techniques for doing so are similar to passing standard arguments, but a few minor changes should be noted. The first type we'll look at are the elements themselves, since they require the least amount of alteration (see Example 5.9).

Example 5.9. Passing the elements of an array.

```
/* Passing the elements of an array */
#include "stdafx.h"
#using <mscorlib.dll>
#include <tchar.h>
using namespace System;

static void Ageism (int tester);

void _tmain(void) {
  String* input;

  int childrens_ages __gc[] = new int __gc[20];

  for (int counter = 0; counter < childrens_ages.Length; counter++) {
    Console::Write ("Enter student ");
```

```
    Console::Write (counter+1);
    Console::Write ("'s age:");

    input = Console::ReadLine ();
    childrens_ages [counter] = input->ToInt32(0);
    Ageism (childrens_ages [counter]);
  }
}

static void Ageism (int tester)   {
if (tester > 6)
Console::WriteLine ("Your child is to old.\n") ;
}
```

Note: We can also pass arrays containing literal constants, such as ages [0], ages [1], and ages [2], etc.

We can also reapply this program using a call-by-reference marker as shown in Example 5.10.

Example 5.10. Calls-by-reference in arrays.

```
/* calls by reference */
#include "stdafx.h"
#using <mscorlib.dll>
#include <tchar.h>
using namespace System;

static void Ageism (int tester);

int _tmain(void) {
 String* input;
 int childrens_ages __gc[] = new int __gc[20];

 for (int counter = 0; counter < childrens_ages.Length; counter++) {
  Console::Write ("Enter student ");
  Console::Write (counter+1);
  Console::Write ("'s age:");

  input = Console::ReadLine ();
  childrens_ages [counter] = input->ToInt32(0);

  Ageism (childrens_ages [counter]);

  if (childrens_ages [counter] > 6)
    Console::WriteLine ("Your child is to old.\n");
 }
}

static void Ageism (int tester)   {
 Console::WriteLine (tester); // we're all too old
 tester += 7;
}
```

The procedure for passing an entire argument differs somewhat from the method used to pass a single element. For example, the initial identifying brackets are not required when sending those values, but they are essential to the receiving statement (see Example 5.11). In native C++, it was also important to include a secondary reference that included the arrays size; however, this is no longer the case since an array's length can always be found using the *length extension* (included as a method that is accessible by all properly declared arrays).

Example 5.11. Passing an entire array.

```
/* Passing an entire array */
#include "stdafx.h"
#using <mscorlib.dll>
#include <tchar.h>
using namespace System;

static void Ageism (int* tester, int index);

void _tmain(void) {
 String* input;
 const int array_size = 20;
 int* childrens_ages = new int[array_size];

 for (int counter = 0; counter < array_size; counter++) {
  Console::Write ("Enter student ");
  Console::Write (counter+1);
  Console::Write ("'s age: ");

  input = Console::ReadLine ();
  childrens_ages [counter] = input->ToInt32(0);
  Ageism (childrens_ages, counter);
 }
}

static void Ageism (int* tester, int index)   {
 if (tester [index] > 6)
  Console::WriteLine ("Your child is to old.\n");
 else
  Console::WriteLine ("Okay.\n") ;
}
```

> Note:
> Although unnecessary, it is quite possible to pass an array's declarative size as a call-by-reference variable. This dangerous maneuver may lead to the accidental alteration of that array's size, thus causing a runtime error and possibly a system crash.
>
> The three most effective ways to prevent such an error are:
> 1) Using the array's length when referring to the array's size;
> 2) Declaring the array using a constant variable;

3) Using call-by-mechanism variables when passing variables representing an array's size.

These steps may seem a bit redundant, but they almost become mandatory when dealing with multidimensional arrays (see the nest section).

Multidimensional Arrays

Multidimensional arrays (also known as *multiple subscript arrays*) are arrays specifically declared to hold more than one set of values. These values are usually linked in a way that makes viewing them simpler than just writing them as independent variables or singular arrays. They are initialized in the same manner as standard arrays, only with the addition of a few more brackets. The practicality of using multidimensional arrays varies from project to project, but in general, they tend to drain the system resources and are usually computed slower than standard arrays; thus, anything beyond four dimensions should be avoided (see Example 5.12).

Example 5.12. Multidimensional arrays.

```
/* Multidimensional arrays */
#include "stdafx.h"
#using <mscorlib.dll>
#include <tchar.h>
using namespace System;

void _tmain(void) {
 String* input;
 char students_grades __gc[,] = new char __gc[5, 5];

 for (int i = 0; i < 5; i++)  {
  Console::WriteLine ("Enter student ");
  Console::Write (i+1);
  Console::Write ("'s grades from first to last:");

  for (int j = 0; j < 5; j++) {
  input = Console::ReadLine ();
  students_grades [i, j] = (char)input->ToChar(0);}
 }
 Console::Write ("Your input was");

 for (int i = 0; i < 5; i++)  {
  for (int j = 0; j < 5; j++)
   Console::Write (students_grades [i, j]) ;
  }
 Console::WriteLine ();
}
```

You should have noticed that our first array didn't have any individual values, i.e., the elements of the first dimension were actually only the first element of each of the secondary arrays. This is usually described as an *array of arrays*, but that tends to confuse people. The best way to think about it is as a set of single arrays listed together in a single column as demonstrated in Example 5.13.

Example 5.13. Array values.

a[0][0]	a[0][1]	A[0][2]	a[0][3]	a[0][4]
a[1][0]	a[1][1]	A[1][2]	a[1][3]	a[1][4]
a[2][0]	a[2][1]	A[2][2]	a[2][3]	a[2][4]
a[3][0]	a[3][1]	A[3][2]	a[3][3]	a[3][4]
a[4][0]	a[4][1]	A[4][2]	a[4][3]	a[4][4]
a[5][0]	a[5][1]	A[5][2]	a[5][3]	a[5][4]
a[6][0]	a[6][1]	A[6][2]	a[6][3]	a[6][4]
a[7][0]	a[7][1]	A[7][2]	a[7][3]	a[7][4]
a[8][0]	a[8][1]	A[8][2]	a[8][3]	a[8][4]
a[9][0]	a[9][1]	A[9][2]	a[9][3]	a[9][4]

Where, a [10] [0] through a [10] [4] are Null (\0).

Just as standard arrays can be initialized, passed, and included as entire arrays inside functions, so can multidimensional arrays. Although slightly different in appearance, they follow the same rules and have the same basic limitations. The next few examples show how this type of coding is implemented (see Example 5.14).

Note:
The program in Example 5.14 accepts a list of six names of five letters each.
The values are stored in a multidimensional array (6x5).

Example 5.14. Two-dimensional arrays.

```
/* 2-Dimensional Array */
#include "stdafx.h"
#using <mscorlib.dll>
#include <tchar.h>
using namespace System;

static void file (String* tester[,]);

void _tmain(void) {
 String* names[,] = new String* [6, 5];

 for (int i = 0; i < 6; i++) {
  Console::Write ("Enter student's name ");
  Console::Write ("(all names must include 5 letters): ");

  for (int j = 0; j < 5; j++) {
   names [i, j] = Console::ReadLine ();
  }
 }

 file (names);
}

static void file (String* tester[,]) {
 for (int i = 0; i < 6; i++) {
```

```
  for (int j = 0; j < 5; j++)
    Console::WriteLine (tester [i, j]) ;
  }
}
```

Three-Dimensional Array

Algebra uses Cartesian coordinates to graph dimensions, e.g., x, y, and z. Physics uses
the letters i, j, and k, which mean exactly the same thing (see Examples 5.15 and 5.16).

Example 5.15. Graphing coordinates x, y, z.   **Example 5.16. Graphing coordinates i, j, and k.**

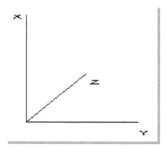 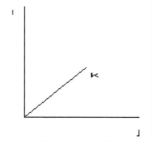

Most programmers use i, j, and k to reference an array's memory locations, as well as to represent nested
loops, three-dimensional space, etc. The values for a three-dimensional array are basically the same in
coding terms, but the data's reference points are quite different, as shown in Example 5.17.

Example 5.17. Three-dimensional array values.

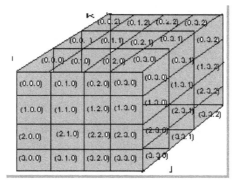

This cube shows us how the values are laid out from 0, 0, 0 to 3, 3, 2. We can assign reference points such
that i equals the list of arrays, j is the first value of each array, and k is the last value stored for each list.

Example 5.18. Declaring, initializing, and passing a three-dimensional array.

```
/* declaring, initializing, and
passing a 3-dimensional array */
#include "stdafx.h"
```

109

```cpp
#using <mscorlib.dll>
#include <tchar.h>
#include <iostream>
using namespace System;

static void Display (String* print[,,]);

void _tmain(void) {
 String* names [, ,] = new String* [8, 5, 6];
 names[0,0,0]="T"; names[0,0,1]="h";
 names[0,0,2]="i"; names[0,0,3]="s";
 names[0,0,4]=" "; names[0,0,5]="i";
 names[0,1,0]="s"; names[0,1,1]=" ";
 names[0,1,2]="a"; names[0,1,3]=" ";
 names[0,1,4]="t"; names[0,1,5]="e";
 names[0,2,0]="s"; names[0,2,1]="t";
 names[0,2,2]=" "; names[0,2,3]="t";
 names[0,2,4]="h"; names[0,2,5]="i";
 names[0,3,0]="s"; names[0,3,1]=" ";
 names[0,3,2]="i"; names[0,3,3]="s";
 names[0,3,4]=" "; names[0,3,5]="o";
 names[0,4,0]="n"; names[0,4,1]="l";
 names[0,4,2]="y"; names[0,4,3]=" ";
 names[0,4,4]="a"; names[0,4,5]=" ";
 names[1,0,0]="t"; names[1,0,1]="e";
 names[1,0,2]="s"; names[1,0,3]="t";
 names[1,0,4]="."; names[1,0,5]="\n";
 names[1,1,0]="F"; names[1,1,1]="o";
 names[1,1,2]="r"; names[1,1,3]=" ";
 names[1,1,4]="t"; names[1,1,5]="h";
 names[1,2,0]="e"; names[1,2,1]=" ";
 names[1,2,2]="n"; names[1,2,3]="e";
 names[1,2,4]="x"; names[1,2,5]="t";
 names[1,3,0]=" "; names[1,3,1]="m";
 names[1,3,2]="i"; names[1,3,3]="n";
 names[1,3,4]="u"; names[1,3,5]="t";
 names[2,4,0]="e"; names[2,4,1]=" ";
 names[2,4,2] = "y"; names[2,4,3] = "o";
 names[2,4,4] = "u"; names[2,4,5] = "r";
 names[3,0,0] = " "; names[3,0,1] = "c";
 names[3,0,2] = "o"; names[3,0,3] = "m";
 names[3,0,4] = "p"; names[3,0,5] = "u";
 names[3,1,0] = "t"; names[3,1,1] = "e";
 names[3,1,2] = "r"; names[3,1,3] = " ";
 names[3,1,4] = "w"; names[3,1,5] = "i";
 names[3,2,0] = "l"; names[3,2,1] = "l";
 names[3,2,2] = " "; names[3,2,3] = "b";
 names[3,2,4] = "e"; names[3,2,5] = " ";
 names[3,3,0] = "c"; names[3,3,1] = "o";
 names[3,3,2] = "n"; names[3,3,3] = "d";
 names[3,3,4] = "u"; names[3,3,5] = "c";
 names[3,4,0] = "t"; names[3,4,1] = "i";
```

```
names[3,4,2] = "n"; names[3,4,3] = "g";
names[3,4,4] = "\n"; names[3,4,5] = "a";
names[4,0,0] = " "; names[4,0,1] = "t";
names[4,0,2] = "e"; names[4,0,3] = "s";
names[4,0,4] = "t"; names[4,0,5] = " ";
names[4,1,0] = "o"; names[4,1,1] = "f";
names[4,1,2] = " "; names[4,1,3] = "t";
names[4,1,4] = "h"; names[4,1,5] = "e";
names[4,2,0] = " "; names[4,2,1] = "m";
names[4,2,2] = "u"; names[4,2,3] = "l";
names[4,2,4] = "t"; names[4,2,5] = "i";
names[4,3,0] = "d"; names[4,3,1] = "i";
names[4,3,2] = "m"; names[4,3,3] = "e";
names[4,3,4] = "n"; names[4,3,5] = "s";
names[4,4,0] = "i"; names[4,4,1] = "o";
names[4,4,2] = "n"; names[4,4,3] = "a";
names[4,4,4] = "l"; names[4,4,5] = " ";
names[5,0,0] = "a"; names[5,0,1] = "r";
names[5,0,2] = "r"; names[5,0,3] = "a";
names[5,0,4] = "y"; names[5,0,5] = " ";
names[5,1,0] = "s"; names[5,1,1] = "e";
names[5,1,2] = "q"; names[5,1,3] = "u";
names[5,1,4] = "e"; names[5,1,5] = "n";
names[5,2,0] = "c"; names[5,2,1] = "e";
names[5,2,2] = "."; names[5,2,3] = "\n";
names[5,2,4] = "T"; names[5,2,5] = "H";
names[5,3,0] = "I"; names[5,3,1] = "S";
names[5,3,2] = " "; names[5,3,3] = "I";
names[5,3,4] = "S"; names[5,3,5] = " ";
names[5,4,0] = "O"; names[5,4,1] = "N";
names[5,4,2] = "L"; names[5,4,3] = "Y";
names[5,4,4] = " "; names[5,4,5] = "A";
names[6,0,0] = " "; names[6,0,1] = "T";
names[6,0,2] = "E"; names[6,0,3] = "S";
names[6,0,4] = "T"; names[6,0,5] = "!";
names[6,1,0] = "\n"; names[6,1,1] = "A";
names[6,1,2] = "B"; names[6,1,3] = "C";
names[6,1,4] = "D"; names[6,1,5] = "E";
names[6,2,0] = "F"; names[6,2,1] = "G";
names[6,2,2] = "H"; names[6,2,3] = "I";
names[6,2,4] = "J"; names[6,2,5] = "K";
names[6,3,0] = "L"; names[6,3,1] = "M";
names[6,3,2] = "N"; names[6,3,3] = "O";
names[6,3,4] = "P"; names[6,3,5] = "Q";
names[6,4,0] = "R"; names[6,4,1] = "S";
names[6,4,2] = "T"; names[6,4,3] = "U";
names[6,4,4] = "V"; names[6,4,5] = "W";
names[7,0,0] = "X"; names[7,0,1] = "Y";
names[7,0,2] = "Z"; names[7,0,3] = "a";
names[7,0,4] = "b"; names[7,0,5] = "c";
names[7,1,0] = "d"; names[7,1,1] = "e";
names[7,1,2] = "f"; names[7,1,3] = "g";
```

```
names[7,1,4] = "h"; names[7,1,5] = "i";
names[7,2,0] = "j"; names[7,2,1] = "k";
names[7,2,2] = "l"; names[7,2,3] = "m";
names[7,2,4] = "n"; names[7,2,5] = "o";
names[7,3,0] = "p"; names[7,3,1] = "q";
names[7,3,2] = "r"; names[7,3,3] = "s";
names[7,3,4] = "t"; names[7,3,5] = "u";
names[7,4,0] = "v"; names[7,4,1] = "w";
names[7,4,2] = "x"; names[7,4,3] = "y";
names[7,4,4] = "z"; names[7,4,5] = " ";
Display (names) ;
}

static void Display (String* print[,,]) {
 const short sets = 8, rows = 5, columns = 6;
 for (int i = 0; i < sets; i++) {
  for (int j = 0; j < rows; j++)
   for (int k = 0; k < columns; k++) {
    Console::Write ("\a");
    Console::Write (print[i, j, k]) ;
   }
  }
 Console::WriteLine () ;
}
```

Multidimensional arrays are also considered to be either jagged (without a constant shape) or rectangle/square (to have two or more sides with the same length).

Sorting Arrays

Sorting, as related to an array, is the action of rearranging or reorganizing the order of elements to make a particular task easier to follow. This usually involves some logical reference point such as letters placed in alphabetical order and numbers listed in a numeric order. The principle method used to displace these values involves both the comparison and reassignment of that data. The techniques used to sort these values range from the very simple to the complex, but they all do pretty much the same thing; thus, the need for alternate techniques then has more to do with the speed of the process than the result. The simplest of these is known as the *bubble sort* (also referred to as the *sinking sort*); values are listed in a single array, compared with one another and swapped as needed, until all the values are in the proper order. The word bubble is used to aid in visualizing the smaller (lighter) values rising to the top and the word sinking is used to visualize the larger (heavier) values sinking to the bottom. The coding for this type of sort is also very straightforward—see Example 5.19.

Example 5.19. Bubble sort.

```
/* bubble sort */
#include "stdafx.h"
#using <mscorlib.dll>
#include <tchar.h>
using namespace System;
```

112

```
static void BubbleSort (int my_array[], short size);

void _tmain(void) {
 const short array_size = 12;
 int simple_array[] = {31, 31, 54, 0, 60, 35, 34, 29, 18, 17, 13, 10};

 BubbleSort (simple_array, array_size);
}

static void BubbleSort (int my_array[], short size) {
 int temp = 0;
 Console::WriteLine ("\nRandom numbers inputted in this order");

 for (int i = 0; i < size; i++)
  Console::WriteLine (my_array[i]);
  for (int i = 0; i < size; i++)
   for (int j = 0; j < size-1; j++)
    if (my_array[j] > my_array [j+1]){
     temp = my_array[j];
     my_array[j] = my_array [j+1];
     my_array [j+1] = temp ;
     }

   Console::WriteLine ("\nsorting...\n \nIn ascending order");
   for (int i = 0; i < size; i++)
    Console::WriteLine (my_array[i]);

   Console::WriteLine ("\nand in descending order");
   for (int i = size-1; i > -1; i--)
    Console::WriteLine (my_array[i]) ;
}
```

Searching Arrays

There are two basic types of searches that are useful and relate directly to data stored in an array. The first is the *linear search*, which, as its name implies, is a consecutive comparison that tests each element until the correct information is found. This is a very common and particularly useful search algorithm, especially when dealing with random or unrelated data that cannot be sorted. The second, also considered the more efficient search, is the *binary search*. This search divides and compares two criteria, where the total value is divided into two sets and the irrelevant set is discarded. This process is repeated as many times as possible before reverting back to a basic linear search. Both searches are considered effective, but the binary search is preferred when dealing with longer, sortable data streams that require repeated searches (see Examples 5.20 and 5.21). The binary search also requires that the data be presorted; the presorted data can also be stored as a secondary file, thus, eliminating the need for continuous resorting.

Example 5.20. Linear search (finding a number in an array).

```
/* This program depicts the linear search */
#include "stdafx.h"
#using <mscorlib.dll>
```

```
#include <tchar.h>
using namespace System;

static void CreateArray (int random_array __gc[], int size);
static int Comparison (int array __gc[], int input, int size);

void _tmain(void) {
 String* input;
 const int array_size = 100;
 int our_array __gc[] = new int __gc[array_size];
 int number, total;

 CreateArray (our_array, array_size);

 Console::WriteLine ("Enter a number between 1-100:");
 input = Console::ReadLine ();
 number = input->ToInt32(0);

 total = Comparison (our_array, number, array_size);
 Console::Write ("That number occurred ");
 Console::Write (total);
 Console::WriteLine (" time(s)") ;
}

// creates a random array with values between 1 and 100
static void CreateArray (int random_array __gc[], int size)  {
 Random* rnd = new Random ();

 for (int index = 0; index < size; index++)
 random_array [index] = (int) Math::Round (rnd->NextDouble () * 100) ;
}

// searches that array with a linear search
static int Comparison (int array __gc[], int input, int size)  {
 int count = 0;
 for (int index = 0; index < size; index++)
  if (array[index] == input)
    count++;

 return count;
}
```

Example 5.21. Bubble sort and binary search (finding a number in an array).

```
/* bubble sort & binary search */
#include "stdafx.h"
#using <mscorlib.dll>
#include <tchar.h>
using namespace System;

static void CreateArray (long random_array __gc[]);
static void BubbleSort (long my_array __gc[]);
```

```
static void BubbleSort (long my_array __gc[]);
static void BinarySearch (long array __gc[], long size, long input, long
high, long low, bool* found);

void _tmain(void) {
 String* ScreenInput;
 const long array_size = 100;
 long our_array __gc[] = new long __gc[array_size];
 long input;
 bool found = false;

 CreateArray (our_array);
 BubbleSort (our_array);

 while (true) {
  Console::WriteLine ("Enter a number between 1-100:");
  ScreenInput = Console::ReadLine ();
  input = (long)ScreenInput->ToInt64(0);

  BinarySearch (our_array, array_size, input, array_size, 0, &found);

  if (found)
   Console::WriteLine ("Value found!");
  else
   Console::WriteLine ("Value not found!");

  found = false;
 }
}

// This function creates a random array of numbers
// with values between 1 and 100
static void CreateArray (long random_array __gc[])  {
 Random* rnd = new Random ();

 for (int index = 0; index < random_array.Length; index++)
  random_array [index] = (long) (rnd->NextDouble () * 100+1);
}

static void BubbleSort (long my_array __gc[]) {
 long temp = 0;
 Console::WriteLine ("\nRandom numbers inputted in this order");

 for (int i = 0; i < my_array.Length; i++) {
  Console::WriteLine (my_array[i]);
 }
// sort
 for (int i = 0; i < my_array.Length; i++) {
  for (int j = 0; j < my_array.Length-1; j++) {
   if (my_array[j] > my_array [j+1]) {
    temp = my_array[j];
    my_array[j] = my_array [j+1];
```

```
  my_array [j+1] = temp ;}
  }
 }
 Console::WriteLine ("\nsorting...\n \nIn ascending order");

 for (int index = 0; index < my_array.Length; index++) {
  Console::WriteLine (my_array [index]) ;
 }

 Console::WriteLine () ;
 }

// this function searches and compares
// data using a binary search pattern.
static void BinarySearch (long array __gc[], long size, long input,
long high, long low, bool* found) {
 if (input < array [(size/2)-1]) {
  if (input == array [high -1])
   *found = true;
  else if (input < array [(high/2)-1])
   BinarySearch (array, size, input, high/2, low, found);
  else if (high > low)
   BinarySearch (array, size, input, (high-1), low, found) ;}
  else if (input > array [(size/2)-1]) {
   if (low < 0 && input == array [low])
    *found = true;
   else if (input > array [((high+low)/2) - 1] && (high-low) >= 2)
    BinarySearch (array, size, input, high, (high+low)/2, found);
   else if (low < high)
    BinarySearch (array, size, input, high, (low+1), found) ;
  }
 }
}
```

Dynamic Arrays in Managed C++

The word dynamic is defined as the ability to adapt or alter an otherwise restricted set of coding. The most prominent example of this is the dynamic variable (what we think of as the standard variable). This variable, unlike a "constant," can be adjusted to virtually any value both at compile time and during execution. While the definition of the managed C++ array is a bit more dynamic then that of the Native C++ or C version, it is still a constant parameter that cannot be changed while the program is in motion. We can, however, set up arrays to include dynamically calculated assessments that occur at runtime using a nonconstant integer variable type.

 The most inconvenient aspect of declaring an array is in its requirement of a constant variable, or literal constant, which always forces the programmer to make a guestimation that can lead to arrays that are either too small (making them incapable of the task) or oversized (unnecessarily tying up much needed system resources). The solution to both of these problems lies in the use of *dynamic arrays*. Dynamic arrays, as the term implies, are arrays that do not require predetermined constants at declaration, but they do require a constant size once that value is assigned, which is almost the same thing, but it does offer a few new options.

Since Managed C++ also uses the **new** keyword to declare its arrays, we won't actually have to change the way we reference those values to make them dynamic. In addition, since the .NET structure offers a managed heap, we won't need to refer to a deallocating method (as was done with the word delete). We should, however, at least formally define the word **new**. The keyword **new** allows us to declare dynamic arrays using standard variables, which are then referenced from inside the heap. The heap is a special area of memory reserved for dynamic arrays, reference variables, etc. To assign an array's parameters, simply follow the format listed in Example 5.22.

Example 5.22. Dynamic arrays.

```
/* Dynamic Arrays */
#include "stdafx.h"
#using <mscorlib.dll>
#include <tchar.h>
using namespace System;

void _tmain(void) {
 String* input;
 int array_size;

 Console::Write ("How many students in the classroom? ");
 input = Console::ReadLine ();
 array_size = input->ToInt32(0);

 String* students_grades __gc[] = new String* __gc[array_size];

 for (int index = 0; index < students_grades.Length; index++) {
  Console::Write ("Enter the ");
  Console::Write (index+1);
  Console::Write ("'s student's grade:");
  input = Console::ReadLine ();
  students_grades [index] = input ;
 }

 Console::Write ("Their grades were ");
 for(int index = 0; index < students_grades.Length; index++)
  Console::Write (students_grades [index]);

 Console::WriteLine () ;
}
```

Enumerating Constant Integers

Another limited version of a collective set of values is the integer data type known as the *enumerator*. This constant integer type (as in **signed** and **unsigned**, **short**, **integer**, and **long** values) is a basic aggregated type that promotes simple reference manipulations. It also allows for some unique references such as user-defined data structures and lists of assignments to those declarations. Initial structures are declared using the keyword **enum** with instances of those values declared and assigned as if they were class references. If no values are assigned to these references, then the initial point would be zero, and each new component would automatically increment by one. However, we can also short step this process by beginning at some arbitrary point (such as 2000), or we could individually declare each value (see Example 5.24).

Example 5.24. Enumerating integers.

```
/* Enumerating Integers */
#include "stdafx.h"
#using <mscorlib.dll>
#include <tchar.h>
using namespace System;

public __value enum Months {
 Jan = 1, Feb, Mar, Apr, May, Jun, Jul, Aug, Sep, Oct, Nov, Dec
};

public __value enum Day {
 AprilFools = 1, Birthday = 16,
 XMas = 25, Feb29 = 29, NYeve = 31
};

public __value enum Year {
 Year2 = 2002, Year3, LeapYear
};

int _tmain(void) {
 String* input;
 int TheMonth, TheDay, TheYear;

 while (true) {
  Console::Write ("Enter the current Month (Example: \"Jan\" = 1): ");
  input = Console::ReadLine ();
  TheMonth = input->ToInt32(0);

  Console::Write ("What day of the Month is it? ");
  input = Console::ReadLine ();
  TheDay = input->ToInt32(0);

  Console::Write ("What year is it 2002, 2003... ");
  input = Console::ReadLine ();
  TheYear = input->ToInt32(0);

  if (TheMonth == (int)Months::Feb && TheDay == (int)Day::Feb29 &&
  TheYear == (int) Year::LeapYear)
   Console::WriteLine ("Happy Leap Year!");

  if (TheMonth == (int)Months::Apr && TheDay == (int)Day::AprilFools)
   Console::WriteLine ("April Fool's");

  if (TheMonth == (int)Months::Sep && TheDay == (int)Day::Birthday)
   Console::WriteLine ("Happy Birthday!");
```

```
    if (TheMonth == (int)Months::Dec){
     if (TheDay == (int)Day::XMas)
      Console::WriteLine ("Mary Christmas!");
      if (TheDay == (int)Day::NYeve)
       Console::WriteLine ("Happy New Year!") ;
    }
   }
}
```

Pointers

A *pointer* is a special type of variable used to access the space in memory occupied by traditional variables. They point at the values held inside of those locations, and although they are capable of assessing and even changing that information, they remain only links to the address. This should remind you of the call-by-reference in Chapter 4. These were, for the most part, limited pointers, which as you'll recall, enabled us to both access and alter the passed variables from inside our subprograms. This gave us the power to use those values as if they were global variables, but with the increased plug-n-play ability of local variables, which makes pointers very useful, but also potentially dangerous. Thus, languages like C# allow pointer manipulations, but only under *unsafe* mode.

Pointer Variables

Pointer variables, like all other types of variables, need to be declared, but because they require a location to point to, they also need to be assigned before they can be referenced. Pointers are also limited, like standard variables, by their data types and rules of naming. Thus, it stands to reason that pointers declared as integers can only point to standard variables that were also declared as integers, doubles with doubles, floats to floats, and characters to characters. The one key visual difference when declaring pointers is the insertion of the asterisk symbol (*), which is placed in front of the data type's reference. This asterisk tells the compiler that this data type is actually intended to declare pointer variables. The asterisk, in this case, is referred to as the *dereferencing operator*, and the variable is referred to as the *dereferenced variable*. The second step is to assign the pointer; this is done by making the pointer equal to the standard variable. An ampersand symbol (&) must precede the standard variable (ampersands are referred to as *address operators*). Remember, a pointer that has not been assigned has nothing to point to, and cannot be used (see Example 5.25). Note: There is also a void data type pointer, which is a generalized pointer that can be linked to any of the other data types. Void pointer data types are discussed later in this chapter.

> Note:
> The asterisks signify to the compiler that these values are pointers. The unmarked variables remain as standard variables, with the ampersands used to denote the pointers address. The cout command must include a asterisk identifier (as in cout << *pointer1;).

Example 5.25. Pointer variables.

```
/* pointers */
#include "stdafx.h"
#using <mscorlib.dll>
```

```
#include <tchar.h>
using namespace System;

void _tmain(void) {
 int* pointer1;
 int variable1 = 1;
 float* pointer2;
 float variable2 = 2.0f;
 double *pointer3;
 double variable3 = 3.01;
 char *pointer4;
 char variable4 = 'A';

 pointer1 = &variable1;
 pointer2 = &variable2;
 pointer3 = &variable3;
 pointer4 = &variable4;

 Console::WriteLine (variable1);
 Console::WriteLine (*pointer1);
 Console::WriteLine (variable2);
 Console::WriteLine (*pointer2);
 Console::WriteLine (variable3);
 Console::WriteLine (*pointer3);
 Console::WriteLine (variable4);
 Console::WriteLine (*pointer4);
}
```

We can also assign numeric values to pointers, but only after they have been assigned memory locations. Again, we'll use the equal sign to assign the values and the asterisk symbol to reference the pointer. You should note that since pointers place their new values in the memory locations used by standard variables, any previous information is overwritten.

I just got this new pointer VISA–it has my name on it,
but apparently all my purchase are sent of someone else.

Pointers can also be used to assign locations to other pointers –see the code in Example 5.26.

Example 5.26. Assigning numeric values to pointers.

```
/* this program demonstrates how to assign numeric values to pointers
 * And how to assign memory locations to other pointers */
#include "stdafx.h"
#using <mscorlib.dll>
#include <tchar.h>
using namespace System;
```

```
void _tmain(void) {
 int *pointer1, *pointer2;
 int variable1 = 1, pointer3;
// Warning, pointer3 is not an actual pointer!
// Assigning a pointer to a value
 pointer1 = &variable1;
// Pointer to pointer assignments DO NOT required the asterisk.
 pointer2 = pointer1;
// Pointers can also pass values to variables.
 pointer3 = *pointer2;

 Console::WriteLine (variable1);
 Console::WriteLine (*pointer1);
 Console::WriteLine (*pointer2);
 Console::WriteLine (pointer3);

// the value inside that address is now 20.
 *pointer1 = 20;

 Console::WriteLine (variable1);
 Console::WriteLine (*pointer1);
 Console::WriteLine (*pointer2);
 Console::WriteLine (pointer3);
}
```

To review declaring, displaying, and assigning values all require asterisks, but assigning pointers to a variable location and assigning pointers to other single pointer locations do not. Assigning pointer locations also requires the ampersand symbol.

> NULL pointers:
> Zero is the only integer value that can be assigned to an unassigned pointer. This can also be represented using the NULL statement, since NULL is in essence a zero value. NULL statements are sometimes useful when passing meaningless values to a generalized function.

Call-by-Reference Values with Pointer Arguments

As you'll remember from Chapter 4, we were able to write function calls as both calls-by-value and calls-by-reference, but calls-by-reference also let us change the values of the original variables. You should also recall (from our introduction to pointers) that calls-by-reference are actually limited forms of pointers. This makes it possible to rewrite those programs so that they use actual pointer notation without significantly changing those programs (see Example 5.27)

Example 5.27. Calls by reference.

```
/* Calls by reference with pointer arguments */
#include "stdafx.h"
#using <mscorlib.dll>
```

```
#include <tchar.h>
using namespace System;

static void the_race (int *number1, int *number2, int *number3) {
 Random* rnd = new Random ();

 *number1 = (int) (rnd->NextDouble () * 100);
 *number2 = (int) (rnd->NextDouble () * 100);
 *number3 = (int) (rnd->NextDouble () * 100);
 Console::Write (".");
}

static void tie_breaker (int *num1, int *num2)  {
 if (*num1 == *num2) *num2 = *num2 - 1;
  Console::Write (".");
}

static char the_winner (int *num1, int *num2, int *num3) {
 char winner;
 if (*num1 > *num2 && *num1 > *num3)
  winner = '1';
 else if (*num2 > *num1 && *num2 > *num3)
  winner = '2';
 else winner = '3';
 Console::Write (".");

 return (winner);
}

void _tmain(void) {
 String* input;
 char race = 'Y';
 int winner, number1 = 0, number2 = 0, number3 = 0;

 Console::WriteLine ("Let's have a horse race.\n ",
  "To play select one of the horses below");

 while (race != 'N') {
  Console::WriteLine ("(1) for Whitefire\n (2) ",
   "for The Train and, \n (3) for Noisy Glue");
  input = Console::ReadLine ();
  the_race (&number1, &number2, &number3);
  tie_breaker (&number1, &number2);
  tie_breaker (&number2, &number3);
  tie_breaker (&number1, &number3);

  winner = the_winner (&number1, &number2, &number3);
  Console::Write ("And the winner is ");

  if (winner == '1')
   Console::WriteLine ("Whitefire");
  else if (winner == '2')
```

```
  Console::WriteLine ("The Train");
else
  Console::WriteLine ("Noisy Glue");

Console::Write ("Would you like to play again (Y/N)?");
input = Console::ReadLine ();
input = input->ToUpper ();
race = (char)input->ToChar(0);
 }
}
```

Pointer Arithmetic

Pointer arithmetic is simply variable arithmetic as applied to pointers (note: asterisks are required). In pointer arithmetic, pointers are used like variables to add, subtract, multiply, divide, and find the remainder of stored values. Pointers can also be used with shorthand notation and the incrementing and decrementing operators (incrementing & decrementing operators also require the insertion of parentheses—see Examples 5.28 and 5.29).

Example 5.28. Arithmetic with pointers.

```
/* Arithmetic with pointers */
#include "stdafx.h"
#using <mscorlib.dll>
#include <tchar.h>
using namespace System;

void _tmain(void) {
 int number1 = 0, number2 = 0;
 int* pointer1 = &number2;

 number1 = number1 + 10;      // Addition
 *pointer1 = *pointer1 + 10;
 Console::WriteLine (number1);
 Console::WriteLine (number2);

 number1 = number1 - 1;    // Subtraction
 *pointer1 = *pointer1 - 1;
 Console::WriteLine (number1);
 Console::WriteLine (number2);

 number1 = number1*2;     // Multiplication
 *pointer1 = *pointer1*2;
 Console::WriteLine (number1);
 Console::WriteLine (number2);

 number1 = number1/2;      // Division
 *pointer1 = *pointer1/2;
 Console::WriteLine (number1);
 Console::WriteLine (number2);
```

```
 number1 = number1%3;        // Remainders
 *pointer1 = *pointer1%3;
 Console::WriteLine (number1);
 Console::WriteLine (number2);
}
```

Example 5.29. Shorthand notation.

```
/* shorthand notation and the incrementing
and decrementing operators */
#include "stdafx.h"
#using <mscorlib.dll>
#include <tchar.h>
using namespace System;

void _tmain(void) {
 int number1 = 0, number2 = 0;
 int* pointer1 = &number2;

 for (int index = 0; index < 10; index++) {
  number1 = number1++;
  *pointer1 = (*pointer1) ++ ;
 }
 Console::WriteLine (number1);
 Console::WriteLine (number2);

 number1 = number1 - 1;
 *pointer1 = (*pointer1)--;
 Console::WriteLine (number1);
 Console::WriteLine (number2);

 number1 = number1 += number1;
// number1 = number1 + number1
 *pointer1 = *pointer1 += *pointer1;
// *pointer1 = *pointer1 + *pointer1
 Console::WriteLine (number1);
 Console::WriteLine (number2);

 number1 = number1 -= number1;
// number1 = number1 - number1
 *pointer1 = *pointer1 -= *pointer1;
// *pointer1 = *pointer1 - *pointer1
 Console::WriteLine (number1);
 Console::WriteLine (number2);

 number1 = 5;
 *pointer1 = 5;
 number1 = number1*=2;
 *pointer1 = *pointer1*=2;
 Console::WriteLine (number1);
 Console::WriteLine (number2);
```

```
number1 = number1/=2;
*pointer1 = *pointer1/=2;
Console::WriteLine (number1);
Console::WriteLine (number2);
number1 = number1/=2;
*pointer1 = *pointer1/=2;
Console::WriteLine (number1);
Console::WriteLine (number2);
number1 = 5;
*pointer1 = 5;
number1 = number1%=2;
*pointer1 = *pointer1%=2;
Console::WriteLine (number1);
Console::WriteLine (number2);
}
```

String and Address Arithmetic

String arithmetic is also fairly simple, but it doesn't involve changing numeric values. Instead, we'll use arithmetic commands to move an array's index from address to address. This is possible because of the strings sequentially stored memory locations. Since we cannot know the spatial difference between any two strings, this type of memory manipulation must be limited to arrogated variables that are part of the same string (see memory mapping for further details).

Mapping Memory.

Computers allocate a certain amount of Random Access Memory (RAM) to each variable declared inside of our programs. This memory is actually part of a computer's hardware, and is reused and/or overwritten every time we run a new program. The methods used to store our variables and the exact locations in memory of those variables are irrelevant to us as programmers, and will be left to books related to computer operating systems and hardware. Our understanding of how and where our data is placed then will have to be on an abstract scale. This therefore includes an imaginary point of reference that we can then build upon to access and alter any arrays or strings of data declared in our programs.

First off, let's assume that we've just declared and initialized a character array or string to the values A, B, C, D, and E. We know that the strings positions will reflect our points (as in zero equals A, one equals B and two equals C…), but we don't know how this will relate to our computers placement of that data. If we then reason that, the computer places the first component "A" in some arbitrary location (say memory location 1000). Using the basic form of 1 byte per character we can deduce that the location 1001 would then hold the value "B," location 1002 would hold C, and so on. From this, we can also graph a map of the locations as in

Memory Location		Referencing Array		Value in Memory
[1000]	=	array[0]	=	A
[1001]	=	array[1]	=	B
[1002]	=	array[2]	=	C
[1003]	=	array[3]	=	D
[1004]	=	array[4]	=	E

[1005]	=	array[5]	=	\0

If a character were to takes up 2 bytes per element, thus their memory locations would be listed as

Memory Location		Referencing Array		Value in Memory
[1000 – 1001]	=	array[0]	=	1
[1002 – 1003]	=	array[1]	=	2
[1004 – 1005]	=	array[2]	=	3
[1006 – 1007]	=	array[3]	=	4
[1008 – 1009]	=	array[4]	=	5

In addition, if a data type were to take up 4 bytes per element it would produce a larger span or cluster of data.

Memory Location		Referencing Array		Value in Memory
[1000 – 1003]	=	array[0]	=	1
[1004 – 1007]	=	array[1]	=	2
[1008 – 1011]	=	array[2]	=	3
[1012 – 1015]	=	array[3]	=	4
[1016 – 1019]	=	array[4]	=	5

Further, this could continue on and on at least up to 64bit (the 128-bit machines are quite ready yet). 8 bytes are equivalent to…

Memory Location		Referencing Array		Value in Memory
[1000 – 1007]	=	array[0]	=	1
[1008 – 1015]	=	array[1]	=	2
[1016 – 1023]	=	array[2]	=	3
[1024 – 1031]	=	array[3]	=	4
[1032 – 1039]	=	array[4]	=	5

Manipulating pointers using arithmetic is fairly straightforward, as shown is Example 5.30.

Table 5.1. Incrementing Operators.

Incrementing Operators: For Pointers	Equivalent Array Manipulation:
for(; *pointer != '\0'; pointer++) Console::WriteLine(*pointer);	for(int index = 0; alpha[index] != '\0'; index++) Console::WriteLine(alpha[index]);
Decrementing Operators:	
for(; *pointer != 'a' pointer--) Console::WriteLine(*pointer);	for(index = 51; alpha[index] != 'a'; index++) Console::WriteLine(alpha[index]);
Addition:	

for(int index = 0; index < 26; index++)
if(input == *(pointer + index)))
input = *(pointer + (index+26));
	for(int index = 26; index < 52; index++)
	if(input == alpha[index])
	input = alpha[index+26];

Subtraction:	

for(int index = 26; index < 52; index++)
if(input == *(pointer + index))
input = *(pointer + (index-26));
	for(int index = 26; index < 52; index++)
	if(input == alpha[index])
	input = alpha[index-26];

Shorthand Addition:	

Console::WriteLine(*pointer); for(int index = 0; index < 52; index++) Console::WriteLine(*pointer += 1);	See Example 5.30
Shorthand Subtraction:	
for(int index = 0; index < 52; index++) Console::WriteLine(*pointer -= 1);	See Example 5.30

Special Note: You can also subtract one pointer location from another as long as they're referencing the same string. This special situation gives us an integer value equal to the distance between the two.

This program converts letters from uppercase to lowercase and back from lowercase to uppercase using string (address) arithmetic rather than the ToUpper and ToLower functions.

Example 5.30. Address arithmetic.

```
/* Address arithmetic */
#include "stdafx.h"
#using <mscorlib.dll>
#include <tchar.h>
using namespace System;
char MyToupper(char);
char MyTolower(char);

void _tmain(void) {
char input = ' ';

do { // begin do-while loop
input = Console::ReadLine()->ToChar(0);
// return uppercase letter(s) to our variable
input = MyToupper(input);
Console::WriteLine("{0}", __box(__box(input)->ToChar(0)));
// return lowercase letter(s) to our variable
input = MyTolower(input);
Console::WriteLine("{0}", __box(__box(input)->ToChar(0)));
} while(input != ' '); }

char MyToupper(char input) {
char *pointer,
alpha[] = "abcdefghijklmnopqrstuvwxyzABCDEFGHIJKLMNOPQRSTUVWXYZ";
pointer = alpha;
for(int index = 0; index < 26; index++)
 if(input == *(pointer + index))
   input = *(pointer + (index+26));
return(input); }

char MyTolower(char input) {
char *pointer,
alpha[] = "abcdefghijklmnopqrstuvwxyzABCDEFGHIJKLMNOPQRSTUVWXYZ";
pointer = alpha;
for(int index = 26; index < 52; index++)
 if(input == *(pointer + index))
   input = *(pointer + index-26);
```

```
return(input); }
```

The Void Pointer

The void data type can be used to declare generalized pointers, that is, pointers that do not, as yet, have a set data type. These all-purpose pointers can be reassigned to different data types with each function call or as part of an abstract subroutine. Void pointers can be converted to any of the other data types and can be used as a sort of template, always changing to fit the needs of a program (see Example 5.31).

Example 5.31. The void data type.
```
/* the void data Type */
#include "stdafx.h"
#using <mscorlib.dll>
#include <tchar.h>
using namespace System;

static void MyFunction (void *values, char data_type);

void _tmain(void) {
short variable1 = 20;
int variable2 = 20;
long variable3 = 100000;
float variable4 = 6.0F;
double variable5 = 123.456789;

Console::WriteLine (variable1);
Console::WriteLine (variable2);
Console::WriteLine (variable3);
Console::WriteLine (variable4);
Console::WriteLine (variable5);

MyFunction (&variable1,'s');       // s for short
MyFunction (&variable2, 'i');      // i for integer
MyFunction (&variable3, 'l');      // l for long
MyFunction (&variable4, 'f');      // f for float
MyFunction (&variable5,'d');     // d for double

Console::WriteLine (variable1);
Console::WriteLine (variable2);
Console::WriteLine (variable3);
Console::WriteLine (variable4);
Console::WriteLine (variable5);}

static void MyFunction (void *values, char data_type){
switch (data_type) {
case 's':
{*((short *) values) += 1;
break; }

case 'i':
```

```
{*((int *) values) -= 1;
break; }

case 'l':
{*((long *) values) *= 2;
break; }

case 'f':
{*((float *) values) /= 2;
break; }

case 'd':
{*((double *) values) = *((double *) values) + 2;
break; }

case 'e':
{*((double *) values) = *((double *) values) - 2;
break; }

default:
{Console::WriteLine ("ERROR");
break;} } }
```

Finding the Mean, Median, Mode, and Range

Another important exercise that we can illustrate with pointers and/or arrays is to use them to find the mean, median, mode, and range of data. These can be very important tasks when the need arises, but for now let's just look at them as exercises we can do to improve our skills. All four tasks will be wrapped into one large program, and the coding will be left for you to go through as needed (see Example 5.33). Note: multiple modes mean that there was a tie when calculating the most frequently referenced variable.

Example 5.32. Mean, median, mode, and range.
```
/* mean, median, mode, and range. */
#include "stdafx.h"
#using <mscorlib.dll>
#include <tchar.h>
using namespace System;

static void Display (short my_array __gc[]);
static void Range (short array __gc[]);
static void Mode (short array __gc[]);
static void Median (short array __gc[]);
static void Mean (short array __gc[]);

void _tmain(void) {
Random* rnd = new Random ();
short   random_array __gc[] = {
(short)(rnd->NextDouble () * 100),
(short)(rnd->NextDouble () * 100),
(short) (rnd->NextDouble () * 100),
```

```
(short) (rnd->NextDouble () * 100),
(short) (rnd->NextDouble () * 100),
(short) (rnd->NextDouble () * 100),
(short) (rnd->NextDouble () * 100),
(short) (rnd->NextDouble () * 100),
(short) (rnd->NextDouble () * 100),
(short) (rnd->NextDouble () * 100),
(short) (rnd->NextDouble () * 100),
(short) (rnd->NextDouble () * 100),
(short) (rnd->NextDouble () * 100),
(short) (rnd->NextDouble () * 100),
(short) (rnd->NextDouble () * 100),
(short) (rnd->NextDouble () * 100),
(short) (rnd->NextDouble () * 100),
(short) (rnd->NextDouble () * 100),
(short) (rnd->NextDouble () * 100),
(short) (rnd->NextDouble () * 100),
(short) (rnd->NextDouble () * 100),
(short) (rnd->NextDouble () * 100),
(short) (rnd->NextDouble () * 100),
(short) (rnd->NextDouble () * 100),
(short) (rnd->NextDouble () * 100)};

Display (random_array);
Mean (random_array);
Median (random_array);
Mode (random_array);
Range (random_array);}

// The mean is the average of the sum of the
// values placed inside the array.
static void Mean (short array __gc[]) {
short average = 0, array_sum = 0;
for (int index = 0; index < array.Length; index++)
array_sum += array [index];

average = (short) (array_sum/array.Length);
Console::WriteLine ("\nThe mean is ");
Console::WriteLine (average); }

// The median is the number that sits in the middle of the list
// take the middle two numbers, add them and divide by two.
static void Median (short array __gc[]) {
      if (array.Length%2 > 0) {
Console::WriteLine ("The median is ");
Console::WriteLine (array[(array.Length/2)]);}
else
Console::WriteLine ("The median value is ");
Console::WriteLine ((array [array.Length/2 - 1] + array
[array.Length/2])/2) ;}

// The mode is the most frequent number in the list.
```

```
// Note: If there's a tie multiple modes will appear
static void Mode (short array __gc[]) {
short counter __gc[] = new short __gc[25];
short temp __gc[] = new short __gc[25];

for (int index = 0; index < array.Length; index++) {
for (int index2 = 0; index2 < array.Length; index2++) {
if (array [index] == array [index2])
counter [index] += 1;} }

for (int index = 0; index < array.Length; index++)
temp [index] = counter [index];

Array::Sort (array);

for (int index = 0; index < array.Length; index++) {
if (counter [index] == temp [array.Length-1]) {
if (index != 0 && array[index] != array[index-1]) {
Console::Write ("The mode is ");
Console::WriteLine (array [index]); }}}}

// Range- the difference between the
// highest number and the lowest number.
static void Range (short array __gc[]) {
Console::Write ("The range spans from ");
Console::Write (array[0]);
Console::Write (" to ");
Console::WriteLine (array [array.Length-1]);}

static void Display (short my_array __gc[]) {
Console::WriteLine ("\nRandom numbers inputted in this order\n");
for (int i = 0; i < my_array.Length; i++)
Console::WriteLine (my_array[i]);

Array::Sort (my_array);
Console::WriteLine ("\nsorting...\n \nIn ascending order\n");

for (int i = 0; i < my_array.Length; i++)
Console::WriteLine (my_array[i]);
Console::WriteLine ("\nand in descending order\n");
Array::Reverse (my_array);

for (int i = 0; i < my_array.Length; i++)
Console::WriteLine (my_array[i]) ;}
```

Arrays as Pointers

When arrays are pasted between functions it's not the elements that are past, but instead only their locations. These locations (as determined by the first element) are accompanied by constant values (numeric values that contain their predetermined size) that are used to represent those arrays and are all that's required to access those aggregate sets. Pointers, by description, are based on the linking of memory locations and thus by that description can also be made equal to the first elements location. This will then enable us to use a combination of pointer variables and pointer arithmetic to access and alter an array in its entirety. The first place to begin is with the notation for a simple assignment (see Example 5.33).

Example 5.33. Arrays as pointers -1.
int our_array[10], *our_pointer;
our_pointer = our_array;

A practical use for assigning pointers to array locations would be in the calling of functions. This combined with pointer arithmetic creates a fun alternative to standard array manipulation (see Example 5.34).

Example 5.34. Arrays as pointers -2.
```
/* Arrays as Pointers */
#include "stdafx.h"
#using <mscorlib.dll>
#include <tchar.h>
#include <iostream>
using namespace System;
using namespace std;

static void Ageism (int array[], int, int);

void _tmain(void) {
int const array_size = 10;
int childrens_ages[array_size], *our_pointer;
our_pointer = childrens_ages;

for(int counter = 0; counter < array_size; counter++) {
Console::WriteLine("Enter student {0}'s age:", __box(counter+1));
// *(array + n0) to *(array + n∞)
std::cin >> *(childrens_ages+counter);
Ageism(our_pointer, array_size, counter); }}

void Ageism(int tester[], int size, int index) {
if(*(tester + index) > 6)
 Console::WriteLine("Your child is to old.");
else
 Console::WriteLine("Okay.\n"); }
```

Pointer Subscript Notation:
$*(array + n_0) == array[n_0]$ // $*(array + 0) == array[0];$
$*(array + n_1) == array[n_1]$ // $*(array + 1) == array[1];$
...
$*(array + n_\infty) == array[n_\infty]$ // $*(array + 2) == array[2];$

We can also use pointers in assigning and passing multiple arrays (see Example 5.35).

Example 5.35. Multiple arrays as pointers.

```
/* Multiple Arrays as Pointers */
#include "stdafx.h"
#using <mscorlib.dll>
#include <tchar.h>
#include <iostream>
using namespace System;
using namespace std;

static void Initials(char (*array)[10]);

void _tmain(void) {
int const array_size = 10;
char my_initials[array_size][array_size] = {{32}, {32}},
  (*our_pointer)[array_size];
our_pointer = my_initials;

Console::WriteLine("Hello, what is your name? ");
std::cin >> *my_initials;
Initials(our_pointer);}

void Initials(char (*array)[10]) {
std::cout << "Hello " << *array << std::endl;}
```

void Initials(char array[][10], int); is equivalent to	void Initials(char(*array)[10], int);
void Initials(char array[][20], int size)	void Initials(char(*array)[10], int size);
Console::Write("Hello {0}", __box(array[0]);	Console::Write("Hello {0}", __box(*array));

Example 5.36. Pointers as arrays.
```
/* Pointers as Arrays */
#include "stdafx.h"
#using <mscorlib.dll>
#include <tchar.h>
using namespace System;

static void Ageism (int* tester, int size);

void _tmain(void) {
const int array_size = 5;
int* kids = new int [array_size];
int* our_pointer = new int [array_size];

for (int counter = 0; counter < array_size; counter++) {
Console::Write ("Enter student ");
Console::Write (counter+1);
Console::WriteLine ("'s age");

kids [counter] = (Console::ReadLine ())->ToInt32(0);
our_pointer [counter] = kids [counter];}

Ageism (our_pointer, array_size); }
```

```
static void Ageism (int* tester, int size) {
for (int counter = 0; counter < size; counter++) {
if ((int)*(tester + counter) > 6)
     Console::WriteLine ("Your child is to old.");
else {
Console::WriteLine("{0}the kid is okay",
__box(counter+1));}}}
```

Double Asterisk and __based Pointers

In addition to being able to pass pointer values to other pointers, you can also set up special double asterisk and based pointers (pointers to pointers). These secondary pointers are as versatile as regular pointers, except that they require some additional notation (see Examples 5.37-5.39).

Example 5.37. Pointers to pointers.
```
/* pointers to pointers */
#include "stdafx.h"
#using <mscorlib.dll>
#include <tchar.h>
using namespace System;

void _tmain(void) {
int* pointer1, *pointer2;
int** pointer3;
int variable1 = 1;

pointer1 = &variable1;    // variable to pointer
pointer2 = pointer1;      // pointer to pointer
pointer3 = &pointer1;     // pointer to double-pointer.

Console::WriteLine (variable1);
Console::WriteLine (*pointer1);
Console::WriteLine (*pointer2);
Console::WriteLine (**pointer3);

**pointer3 = 20;
// the value inside that variable1 is now 20.

Console::WriteLine (variable1);
Console::WriteLine (*pointer1);
Console::WriteLine (*pointer2);
Console::WriteLine (**pointer3);}
```

Note: Pointers can normally be assigned to other pointers without this special notation (as in pointer1 = pointer2 ;).

Example 5.38. Passing double asterisk pointers.

```
/* passing double asterisk pointers */
#include "stdafx.h"
#using <mscorlib.dll>
#include <tchar.h>
using namespace System;

static int pointers (int local_number);

void _tmain(void) {
int variable1 = 1;
int *pointer1 = &variable1, *pointer2 = pointer1;
int** pointer3 = &pointer1;

Console::WriteLine (variable1);
Console::WriteLine (*pointer1);
Console::WriteLine (*pointer2);
Console::WriteLine (**pointer3);

**pointer3 = pointers (**pointer3);

Console::WriteLine (variable1);
Console::WriteLine (*pointer1);
Console::WriteLine (*pointer2);
Console::WriteLine (**pointer3);}

static int pointers (int local_number) {
return (local_number = local_number + 20);}
```

Note: __based is a synonym for _based.

Example 5.39. __based.
```
/* __based pointers */
#include "stdafx.h"
#using <mscorlib.dll>
#include <tchar.h>
using namespace System;

void _tmain(void) {
int variable1 = 1, *pointer2 = &variable1, *pointer3 = &variable1;

int _based (pointer3)*pointer;
int __based(pointer3)*pointer1;

Console::WriteLine(*pointer);
Console::WriteLine (*pointer1);
Console::WriteLine (*pointer2);
Console::WriteLine (*pointer3);}
```

Assigning Pointers to Functions

The standard nonvoid, user-defined function typically returns a value that is a variable of one of the four basic data types. This value is then reassigned to a matching/receiving variable and the program continues. This procedure is only slightly altered when dealing with functions that return pointers. The key changes are based on the returning and receiving values, which are both converted into pointers. We'll also need to alter the notation when declaring those functions, but this is done by simply attaching an asterisk to the function's name. Be careful not to confuse this notation with the one used to declare a pointer function (see Examples 5.40 and 5.41).

Example 5.40. Assigning pointers to functions -1.
```
int (*pointer)(int) // int Function(int);
int (*pointer)(int, int); // int Functions(int, int);
int (*pointer)(double, float); // int Function(double, float);
float (*pointer)(double, char); // float Function(double, char);
void (*pointer)(double, char); // void Function(double, char);
```

Example 5.41. Assigning pointers to functions -2.
```
/* This program demonstrates a pointer to function */
#include "stdafx.h"
#using <mscorlib.dll>
#include <tchar.h>
using namespace System;

int function(int);

void _tmain(void) {
int (*pointer_to_function)(int), variable1 = 1;
pointer_to_function = function; // pointer = function
Console::WriteLine(variable1);
Console::WriteLine(pointer_to_function(variable1)); }

int function(int local_number) {
return(local_number += 20); }
```

Functions Returning Pointers

The standard nonvoid, user-defined function typically returns a value that is a variable of one of the four basic data types. This value is then reassigned to a matching/receiving variable and the program continues. This procedure is only slightly altered when dealing with functions that return pointers. The key changes are based on the returning and receiving values, which are both converted into pointers. We'll also need to alter the notation when declaring those functions, but this is done by simply attaching an asterisk to the function's name. Be careful not to confuse this notation with the one used to declare a pointer function (see Example 5.42).

Example 5.42. Functions returning pointers.
```
/* returning functions as pointers */
#include "stdafx.h"
```

```
#using <mscorlib.dll>
#include <tchar.h>
using namespace System;

static int *function1 (int variable, int *pointer);
static int *function2 (int *pointer, int variable);
static int function3 (int *point);

int _tmain(void) {
int variable;
int* pointer = &variable;

Console::WriteLine ("Enter a number: ");
variable = (Console::ReadLine ())->ToInt32(0);
pointer = function1 (variable, pointer);

Console::WriteLine (variable);
pointer = function2 (&variable, *pointer);

Console::WriteLine (variable);
Console::WriteLine (function3 (pointer)); }

static int *function1 (int variable, int *pointer){
*pointer = variable*(*pointer);
return (pointer);}

static int *function2 (int *pointer, int variable) {
*pointer = variable/ (*pointer);
return (pointer);}

static int function3 (int *point) {
return (*point = 20);}
```

Storage Class Specifiers

C++ offers two storage class specifiers—extern and static. The first storage class specifier, extern, which is short for the word external, is primarily used to transcend the limitations caused by moving between files. This keyword is primarily used to convey global references, and are usually of the object data types (as are structures and classes). Static variables are specialized local variables that are not physically discarded with their function's termination, but instead are stored and reapplied to those functions if and when they are recalled. There are many practical instances when this added flexibility becomes important, and it helps us to remove any further need for global variables.

String Basics

The principles behind arrays and pointers should reveal that characters can be combined to total much more than the sum of their parts. One simple use of this collection is simply to make a sentence such as:

char array[ ] = {'T', 'h', 'I', 's', ' ', 'i', 's', ' ', 'a', ' ', 's', 't', 'r', 'i', 'n', 'g', ' ', 'o', 'f', ' ', 'd', 'a', 't', 'a', ' ', 's', 't', 'o', 'r', 'e', 'd', ' ', 'a', 's', ' ', 'a', 'n', ' ', 'a', 'r', 'r', 'a', 'y'}

A slightly less obvious choice would be to include that string as an array of characters, i.e., "This is a string of data." Of course, we've already seen that either of these cases can be used as output (Console::Write (String1); and Console::Write (Array1 [index]);). However, it might not be as obvious to think of modifying these processes to include the passing of arguments and/or the ability to store data. A literal collection of characters, or a string, can be passed to a function using the same process as a standard array. This string argument requires a defined parameter (formally referred to as a *string parameter*), which is equivalent to an array's parameter. The string will be listed in quotations, e.g., MyString ("This is a string of data"). The literal string will be stored as a string value: static void MyString (string String1) {/* our string function */}. In addition, since strings handle literal constants differently than arrays, we will not suffer the effects of automatic truncation when attempting to add characters that include whitespaces. This should also remind us of the getline function used in native C++, as in cin.getline (array, array_size), wherein we were able to avoid such truncations.

Manipulating String Data

Another significant aspect of manipulating string data comes from the use of the *string extensions*. These are methods included in the Base Class Library that make many of the older string manipulations obsolete. A few of the basic references include commands that test, alter, and apply to both strings and their literal counterparts. The use of these string manipulators has found its way through both C "string.h" and Native C++ "cstring", with these newly defined methods giving the clearest representation yet (see Table 5.1).

Table 5.1. Manipulating String Data.

Managed C++	Native C++	Older C/C++
Copies the value of our original string into that of the new string		
#include "stdafx.h" #using <mscorlib.dll> #include <tchar.h> using namespace System; void _tmain(void) { String* S = "This is a string\n", *S1, *S2; S1 = S; S2 = String::Copy(S); Console::WriteLine("{0}\n{1}", S1, S2); }	#include <iostream> #include <string> using namespace std; void main(void) {string S("This is a string\n"), S1, S2; S1 = S; S2.assign(S); std::cout << S1 << std::endl << S2 << std::endl; }	#include <iostream> #include <cstring> using namespace std; void main(void) {char S[ ] = "This is a string\n", *S1; S1 = (char*)malloc(strlen(S)+1); strcpy(S1, S); std::cout << S1; }
Copies a limited portion of our longer string to that of the shorter string		

``
#include "stdafx.h"
#using <mscorlib.dll>
#include <tchar.h>
using namespace System;
 	
void _tmain(void) {
String* S = "This is a string\n", *S1;
S1 = S->Substring(0, 4);
Console::WriteLine("{0}",
S1);}
``
	``
	#include <iostream>
	#include <string>
	using namespace std;
	void main(void)
	{string S("This is a
	string\n"), S1;
	S1.assign(S, 0, 4);
	std::cout << S1 <<
	std::endl;}
	``
		``
		#include <iostream>
		#include <cstring>
		using namespace std;
		void main(void)
		{char S[ ] = "This is a string of
		data\n", S1[ ] = " ";
		strncpy(S1, S, 3);
		std::cout << S1 << std::endl;}
		``

Appends the original string with that of the additional string

``
#include "stdafx.h"
#using <mscorlib.dll>
#include <tchar.h>
using namespace System;
 	
void _tmain(void) {
String* S = "This is a string\n",
*Extra = "Good bye";
S = S->Insert(17, Extra);
Console::WriteLine("{0}", S);}
``
	``
	#include <iostream>
	#include <string>
	using namespace std;
	void main(void)
	{string
	S("This is a string\n"),
	Extra("Good Bye\n");
	S.append(Extra);
	std::cout << S <<
	std::endl;}
	``
		``
		#include <iostream>
		#include <cstring>
		using namespace std;
		void main(void)
		{char S[50] = "This is a string of
		data\n",
		Extra[] = "Good Bye\n";
		strcat(S, Extra);
		std::cout <<S; }
		``

Appends the original string with a limited portion of the additional string

``
#include "stdafx.h"
#using <mscorlib.dll>
#include <tchar.h>
using namespace System;
 	
void _tmain(void) {
String* S = "This is a string\n",
 *Extra = "Good bye";
 S = S->Insert(17, Extra-
>Substring(0, 4));
 Console::WriteLine("{0}", S); }
``
	``
	#include <iostream>
	#include <string>
	using namespace std;
	void main(void)
	{string S("This is a
	string\n"),
	Extra("Good Bye\n");
	S.append(Extra, 0, 4);
	std::cout << S <<
	std::endl;}
	``
	Where 0 is the starting point and 4 is the length of the attachment.
		``
		#include <iostream>
		#include <cstring>
		using namespace std;
		void main(void)
		{char OurArray[50] = "This is a
		string of data\n",
		Extra[] = "Good Bye\n This
		string is too long and would
		cause an error.";
		strncat(OurArray, Extra, 10);
		std::cout << OurArray <<
		std::endl; }
		``

Compares two strings

``
#include "stdafx.h"
#using <mscorlib.dll>
#include <tchar.h>
using namespace System;
 	
void _tmain(void) {
String* S = "This is a string\n",
*Extra = "Good bye";
if(Extra->CompareTo(S) == 0)
Console::WriteLine("They match!");
else
Console::WriteLine("They don't match!");
if(String::Equals(S, S))
``
	``
	#include <iostream>
	#include <string>
	using namespace std;
	void main(void)
	{string S("This is a
	string\n"),
	S1("This is a string\n"),
	S2("Is this string larger?
	\n");
	if(S == S1)
	std::cout <<
	"I can't tell them a part
	\n";
	int test =
	``
		``
		#include <iostream>
		#include <cstring>
		using namespace std;
		void main(void)
		{char S[ ] = "This is a string\n",
		S1[ ] = "This is a string\n",
		S2[ ] = "Is this string larger? \n";
		if(!strcmp(S, S1))
		std::cout <<
		"I can't tell them a part \n";
		if(strcmp(S, S2) > 0) // T > S
		std::cout <<
		"I think I was cheated \n"; }
		``

Console::WriteLine("Found!"); if(String::ReferenceEquals(S, S)) Console::WriteLine("Found!"); }	S1.compare(S2); if(test == 0) std::cout << "There equal"; else if(test > 0) std::cout << "S2 is greater"; else if(test < 0) std::cout << "S1 is greater"; std::cout << std::endl; }	
Compares a limited portion of string1 with that of string2		

#include "stdafx.h"
#using <mscorlib.dll>
#include <tchar.h>
using namespace System;
 	
void _tmain(void) {
String* S = "This is a string\n",
*Extra = "This is good bye";
if(Extra->Substring(0, 4)-
>CompareTo(S->Substring(0, 4)) = =
0)
 Console::WriteLine("They match!");
else
Console::WriteLine("They don't
match!");}
	#include <iostream>
	#include <string>
	using namespace std;
	void main(void)
	{int T;
	string S("This is a
	string\n"),
	S1("This is a string\n"),
	S2("Is this string larger?
	\n");
	T = S1.compare(0,
	S1.size(), S2, 0,
	S2.size());
	if(T > 0)
	 cout << "S2 is greater"
	<< endl; }
	Where 0 to S1.size()
	equals the length of S1,
	and 0 to S2 equals the
	length of the comparison.
		#include <iostream>
		#include <cstring>
		using namespace std;
		void main(void)
		{char S[ ] = "This is a string\n",
		S1[ ] = "This is a string\n",
		S2[ ] = "This is a string of
		data\n";
		if(strcmp(S1, S2) < 0)
		std::cout << "Super array is
		better \n";
		if(strncmp(S1, SuperArray, 4)
		= = 0)
		std::cout << "Are first 4 letter
		are equal \n"; }

Determines the length of our string		

#include "stdafx.h"
#using <mscorlib.dll>
#include <tchar.h>
using namespace System;
 	
void _tmain(void) {
String* S = "This is a string\n";
int ArrayLength = S->Length;
Console::WriteLine(S->Length);}
	#include <iostream>
	#include <string>
	using namespace std;
	void main(void)
	{string String1;
	 std::cout << "Enter a test
	sentence. \n";
	std::getline(cin, String1);
	int Length =
	String1.length();
	std::cout << "\nThe
	arrays length is "
	 << Length <<
	std::endl; }
		#include <iostream>
		#include <cstring>
		using namespace std;
		void main(void)
		{const int array_size = 100;
		int length;
		char Array[array_size];
		std::cout <<
		"Enter a test sentence. \n";
		std::cin.getline(Array,
		array_size);
		length = strlen(Array);
		std::cout <<
		"\nThe arrays length is "
		 << length << std::endl; }

Note: There are dozens more, all quickly accessible from our visual compilers pop-up menu.

Converting and Safeguarding Data

In addition to inputting and manipulating data, we can also convert and safeguard against data input errors. For example, when our users need to input numeric data, we can use the broader string data type and then test and convert that data as necessary. The data comparison functions are quite numerous, as shown in Table 5.2.

Table 5.2. Converting and Safeguarding Data.

Commands/ Examples:	Description:
Char::IsLetterOrDigit	Returns true when an alphanumeric character (A-Z, a-z, or 0-9) is found.
Char::IsLetter	Returns true when an alphabetic character (A-Z or a-z) is found.
Char::IsSymbol	Returns true when a character is found to be a symbol.
Char::IsControl	Returns true when a control character (0x00-0x1F or 0x7F) is found
Char::IsSeparator	Returns true when a separator character is found
Char::IsSurrogate	Returns true when a surrogate character is found
Char::IsDigit, Char::IsNumber	Returns a non-zero value when a decimal value (0-9) is found
Char::IsLower:	Returns true when a alphanumeric character is found
Char::IsPunctuation	Returns true when a alphanumeric character is found
Char::WhiteSpace	Returns true when an alphanumeric character is found (0x09-0x0D or 0x20).
Char::IsUpper	Returns true when an alphanumeric character is found Uppercase letters (A-Z).

In the ancient times, many of the primitive C programmers fell victim too an unspeakable evil known as the Malloc.

From Strings to Streams: System::IO

In addition to storing and retrieving simple character strings, we can also widen our perspective by beginning to access and write to files via our floppy and hard drives. The use of file manipulations also includes the addition of a second reference, System::IO, which enables the use of two key file related methods: StreamReader and StreamWriter. These methods, as their names imply, allow us to read and write to those files. The files in question need to be opened and closed separately, that is, one reference is used to identify the file as a storage device and one to retrieve that data. As with many of the object-based functions, our data streams also offer a host of member accessible functions that will be explored as we uncover the Base Class Library. The correct procedure for accessing these methods always includes an opening statement, a reading or writing to statement, and the closing method (see Table 5.5). Note that forgetting to close these files will produce a runtime error.

Table 5.5. From Strings to Streams

Managed C++	Native C++

#include "stdafx.h"
#using <mscorlib.dll>
#include <tchar.h>
#include <fstream>
#include <iostream>
using namespace System;
using namespace std;
using namespace System::IO;
 	
void main(void)
{char output[80];
ofstream save;
save.open("File.dat");
save << "This is a test!";
save.close();
ifstream read;
read.open("File.dat");
if(read.fail( ))
{cout << "File not found!"
    << endl;
return; }
while(!read.eof())
{read >> output;
cout << output << " "; }
cout << endl;
read.close(); }
	#include <fstream.h>
	void main(void)
	{char output[80];
	ofstream save;
	save.open("File.dat");
	save << "This is a test!";
	save.close();
	ifstream read;
	read.open("File.dat");
	if(read.fail( ))
	{cout << "File not found!"
	    << endl;
	return; }
	while(!read.eof())
	{read >> output;
	cout << output << " "; }
	cout << endl;
	read.close(); }

Exampling Object Types

Another important point when working with object types involves the use of extensions, which are methods that allow us to manipulate objects, including Equals ( ), GetHashCode ( ), GetType ( ), and ToString ( ). The use of extensions can determine a host of information and thus simplify our tasks (see Table 5.6).

Table 5.6. Exampling Object Types.

CTS Type	Description
Boolean bool Object.Equals(object obj)	Determines whether the specified Object is equal to the current Object
Boolean bool Object.GetHashCode (object obj)	Serves as a hash function for a particular type, suitable for use in hashing algorithms and data structures like a hash

	table
Boolean bool Object.GetType(object obj)	Gets the type of the current instance
Boolean bool Object.ToString(object obj)	Returns a string that represents the current object

The *goto* Statement

The goto statement is probably the most picked-on of all the keywords. Its use is considered a poor programming habit, yet somehow it manages to endure. Its fault lies in its ability to transgress order. Of course, there is a few practical reason for using such a maneuver, so I'll leave it to your discretion. C++'s goto also has some limitations, including not being able to jump into localized blocks, between classes, and it can't (and shouldn't) be used to alter try-catch blocks, as explained in Chapter 6 (see Example 5.43).

Example 5.43. The goto statement.

```
/* The goto statement */
#include "stdafx.h"
#using <mscorlib.dll>
#include <tchar.h>
using namespace System;

int _tmain(void) {
char Character = '1';

switch (Character) {
case '1':
Console::WriteLine ("1 and a");
goto case2;
break;

case '2':
case2:
Console::WriteLine ("2");
goto case3;
break;

case '3':
case3:
Console::WriteLine ("and a 3");
break; }

Console::WriteLine ("Program Terminated"); }
```

Trouble Shooting

The last three chapters should cover virtually everything you'll need to solve any compiler or Windows errors. If your getting syntax errors involving pointers or array notations, you'll have to go back and make sure everything's been entered correctly also try loading that coding from the CD-ROM.

Common Errors, Problems and Pits:

1. If the games are compiling, but your getting a runtime error and/or your only detecting the default sound. This would indicate that your references are not to the appropriate director. For example, if you've copied the games to your D drive then the C:\ listings would all be in error. Make sure all the bitmaps, wav files and classes are not only included as part of your project, but also referenced at the appropriate locations.
2. Attempting to access elements that go beyond an arrays size will result in a systems error.
3. Attempting to alter the size of an array inside of a user-defined function will result in a systems error.
4. Attempting to use floating point numbers or integers that are negative as array elements will result in a systems error.
5. Attempting to assign pointers to variables and/or pointers to other pointers of different data types will result in a systems error.
6. You <u>can not</u> allocate more systems memory than what is available to your system. (Note: If you do not test for successful allocation of that memory, your system may act incorrectly or crash).
7. Attempting to access a pointer that has not been assigned an address is a program error.
8. Attempting to copy array larger array into one of a smaller declared size will result in a program error.

Things to Remember

1. An array is an aggregated set of variables that are of the same data type. They are linked by their location in memory and can be accessed either individually (by their subscripts) or as a whole (when a terminating value "\0" is assigned).
2. Array subscripts can be either literal constants or variables declared as constants. Dynamic arrays allow for standard variables, but once declared the arrays size must not be altered.
3. Arrays can be passed as elements (as in array[x]) or as whole arrays (as in array).
4. Multidimensional arrays are said to list their rows first and then there columns.
5. Linear searches compare data in a consecutive order beginning with one element and moving to the next… while binary searches short cut that process by repeatedly dividing the total by two and then searching the final non-divisible portion.
6. Binary searches tend to be faster when working with longer lists of data and they are the preferred when working with longer listed that require repeated searches. (Note: Binary searches must be sorted before they can be tested).
7. Pointers are usually assigned to variables, but they can also be assigned to the values zero and NULL.
8. The ampersand symbol is required when assigning pointers to variables, but they are not required when assigning pointers to pointers or when passing array.
9. An array is a constant equivalent to a pointer address.

Questions

1. Describe an array.
2. Declare and assign an array of 5 real numbers using the values 3.5, 2.34, 25.4, 2.002, 1.0.
3. Write a program that uses an array to print the word hello. (Hint array[4] = "hello").
4. Revise the last program so that the word hello is passed to a secondary function before being displayed.
5. Write a program that displays the values 1, 2, 3, 4, 5, 6, 7, 8, 9.
6. Revise the last program so as to use a multidimensional array.
7. Write a simple bubble sort program using letters rather than numbers.
8. Write a simple linear search program use it to count the total number of lower case letters.
9. Write a simple binary search program that attempts to find a number between 1 and 100. Allow the user to enter a searchable number.
10. Write a program to find the mode, mean, median, and range.
11. Declare and assign a dynamic array.
12. Declare and assign a pointer variable.
13. Write a program that displays the word "World," using a pointer string.
14. Revise that last program, allowing the pointer to be passed before the word is displayed.
15. Write a program that allows the user to add, subtract, multiply, divide, and find the remainder of two integers.
16. Use pointer arithmetic to move from one point in an array to an other.
17. Write a program that begins with a void pointer, but than assigns that pointer to the four basic data types.
18. Write a function that returns a value as a pointer.

Chapter Six

"If I have seen farther than others, it is because I was standing on the shoulders of giants."
Isaac Newton

Object-Oriented Design

This chapter begins with several sections that define and detail the many attributes of the collective data type known as the structure. This aggregated data type includes several options that aid in the removal of literal limitations, and thus help us to further our move into object-oriented programming. Once the basics of these simpler concepts are committed to memory, we'll want to progress onto the extended topics using classes. Classes, while not meant to totally replace structures, do allow for a greater level of control, which includes the use of reference types. The second portion of this chapter will also offer several new keywords and operators whose potential can only be reached through class manipulations.

What are Structures?

Structures are user-defined data types that allow for groupings of similar or related data that do not have a single base data type. These groups can include all the basic value data types, as well as a list of methods used to manipulate those values. The data types declared inside a structure are referred to as the structure's members (or fields), while their declarations are referred to as its instances. The correlations between these internal values and our structures are usually guided by some common theme or purpose. A structure is made up of the keyword struct, the structure's tag (or name), a list of the fields (written as declared members), and a list of possible methods used to manipulate that data. Structures are generally contained within a single block placed inside our referencing namespace, but as shown below, they can also be used to invoke our main method (see Example 6.1).

Example 6.1. A simple structure.
```
/* A Simple Structure */
#include "stdafx.h"
#using <mscorlib.dll>
#include <tchar.h>
using namespace System;

__gc struct BankAccount {
String* first_name;
String* last_name;
long account_number;
double Checking;
double Savings;
short pin_number; };

void _tmain(void) {
BankAccount* Balance = new BankAccount();
Balance->account_number = 1234;

Console::WriteLine (Balance->account_number); }
```

Declaring and Assigning Fields

Fields are not declared and assigned values directly, rather, they are declared as objects through the use of instances and are assigned as a combination of those instances and their referencing points. The combination of terms is marked by a connecting dot as the member selection operator (.), which is necessary because fields are essentially generalized variables that can be used for multiple purposes. Thus, the use of assignment statements is also restricted from within those structures. Once a structure is listed, the proper declaration and assignment includes both a declaring structure's instance and an assignment to that field (see Examples 6.2 and 6.3).

Example 6.2. Declaring and Assigning Structures.

```
/* Declaring and Assigning Structures */
#include "stdafx.h"
#using <mscorlib.dll>
#include <tchar.h>
using namespace System;

__gc struct BankAccount {
public:
String* first_name;
String* last_name;
long account_number;
double Checking;
double Savings;
int pin_number; };

void _tmain(void) {
BankAccount* account = new BankAccount();
Console::Write ("Enter your pin number here (2001): ");
account->pin_number = (Console::ReadLine ())->ToInt32(0);

if (account->pin_number == 2001)        {
account->account_number = 43297;
account->first_name = "John";
account->last_name = "Doe";
account->Checking = 0;
account->Savings = 112.53;
Console::Write ("Account Number: ");
Console::WriteLine (account->account_number);
Console::Write ("Identity: ");
Console::Write (account->first_name);
Console::Write (" ");
Console::WriteLine (account->last_name);
Console::Write ("Savings Account Balance: ");
Console::WriteLine (account->Savings);
Console::Write ("Checking Account Balance: ");
Console::WriteLine (account->Checking);}}
```

Screen Shot 6.1:

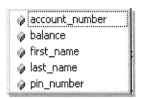

Note: When inserting the dot operator, visual compiler users may encounter a popup window resembling Screen Shot 6.1. This window is generally used as a reminder indicating to the programmer that certain fields are available. If a certain item is not present, this may indicate that it was coded incorrectly or that a certain reference is missing or incomplete. A padlock symbol indicates a protected or private member/field.

Example 6.3. Declaring and assigning multiple instances.

```
/* Declaring and assigning multiple instances */
#include "stdafx.h"
#using <mscorlib.dll>
#include <tchar.h>
using namespace System;

__gc struct BankAccount {
public:
String* first_name;
String* last_name;
long account_number;
double Checking;
double Savings;
short pin_number;};

void _tmain(void) {
BankAccount *account1 = new BankAccount();
BankAccount *account2 = new BankAccount();

short input;
account1->pin_number = 2001;
account1->account_number = 43297;
account1->first_name = "John";
account1->last_name = "Doe";
account1->Savings = 0;
account1->Checking = 112.53;

account2->pin_number = 2002;
account2->account_number = 78978;
account2->first_name = "Jane";
account2->last_name = "Happy";
account2->Savings = 312.43;
account2->Checking = 2134.65;

Console::Write ("\nEnter your pin number here: ");
input = (Console::ReadLine ())->ToInt32(0);
```

```
if (input == account1->pin_number) {
Console::Write ("Account Number: ");
Console::WriteLine (account1->account_number);
Console::Write ("Identity: ");
Console::Write (account1->first_name);
Console::Write (" ");
Console::WriteLine (account1->last_name);
Console::Write ("Savings Account Balance: ");
Console::WriteLine (account1->Savings);
Console::Write ("Checking Account Balance: ");
Console::WriteLine(account1->Checking) ;}
else if (input == account2->pin_number) {
Console::Write ("Account Number: ");
Console::WriteLine (account2->account_number);
Console::Write ("Identity: ");
Console::Write (account2->first_name);
Console::Write (" ");
Console::WriteLine(account2->last_name);
Console::Write ("Savings Account Balance: ");
Console::WriteLine (account2->Savings);
Console::Write ("Checking Account Balance: ");
Console::WriteLine (account2->Checking); }}/* Declaring and assigning
multiple instances */
#include "stdafx.h"
#using <mscorlib.dll>
#include <tchar.h>
using namespace System;

__gc struct BankAccount {
public:
String* first_name;
String* last_name;
long account_number;
double Checking;
double Savings;
short pin_number;};

void _tmain(void) {
BankAccount *account1 = new BankAccount();
BankAccount *account2 = new BankAccount();

short input;
account1->pin_number = 2001;
account1->account_number = 43297;
account1->first_name = "John";
account1->last_name = "Doe";
account1->Savings = 0;
account1->Checking = 112.53;

account2->pin_number = 2002;
account2->account_number = 78978;
account2->first_name = "Jane";
```

```
account2->last_name = "Happy";
account2->Savings = 312.43;
account2->Checking = 2134.65;

Console::Write ("\nEnter your pin number here: ");
input = (Console::ReadLine ())->ToInt32(0);

if (input == account1->pin_number) {
Console::Write ("Account Number: ");
Console::WriteLine (account1->account_number);
Console::Write ("Identity: ");
Console::Write (account1->first_name);
Console::Write (" ");
Console::WriteLine (account1->last_name);
Console::Write ("Savings Account Balance: ");
Console::WriteLine (account1->Savings);
Console::Write ("Checking Account Balance: ");
Console::WriteLine(account1->Checking) ;}
else if (input == account2->pin_number) {
Console::Write ("Account Number: ");
Console::WriteLine (account2->account_number);
Console::Write ("Identity: ");
Console::Write (account2->first_name);
Console::Write (" ");
Console::WriteLine(account2->last_name);
Console::Write ("Savings Account Balance: ");
Console::WriteLine (account2->Savings);
Console::Write ("Checking Account Balance: ");
Console::WriteLine (account2->Checking); }}
```

Multiple Structures

Another useful trick when dealing with structures is the use of an array of structures. This can quickly become a necessity when dealing with large groups of instances that also share a common set of comparisons. Notice how the structure's name is used in place of the basic data type, and how its format emulates that of a basic array style reference. This array is also subject to the limitation of size, but it also inherently takes on some of the capabilities of a multidimensional array (see Examples 6.4). While arrays of structures are allowed, internal structural arrays are not. This is because structures by definition are value based, while filed style arrays rely on a reference basic structure.

> Note:
>   The keyword new is used as both an operator and a modifier. As an
> operator, it is used to declare instances and to create objects. As a modifier,
> it is used to hide members inherited from a base class. The new operator
> cannot be overloaded or used with override statement.

Example 6.4. Arrays of structures.
```
/* Arrays of Structures */
#include "stdafx.h"
#using <mscorlib.dll>
#include <tchar.h>
using namespace System;

__gc struct BankAccount {
public :
String* first_name;
String* last_name;
long account_number;
double Checking;
double Savings;
short pin_number; };

int _tmain(void) {
BankAccount* account __gc[] = new BankAccount* __gc[3];
for(int i = 0; i < 3; i++)
account [i] = new BankAccount();

account [0]->pin_number = 2000;
account [0]->account_number = 78434;
account [0]->first_name = "Bad";
account [0]->last_name = "Dog";
account [0]->Savings = 1000.15;
account [0]->Checking = 43.12;
account [1]->pin_number = 2001;
account [1]->account_number = 43297;
account [1]->first_name = "John";
account [1]->last_name = "Doe";
account [1]->Savings = 0;
account [1]->Checking = 112.53;
account [2]->pin_number = 2002;
account [2]->account_number = 78978;
account [2]->first_name = "Jane";
account [2]->last_name = "Happy";
account [2]->Savings = 2134.65;
account [2]->Checking = 312.43;

while (true) {
Console::Write ("Enter your pin number here: ");
int input = (Console::ReadLine ())->ToInt32(0);
for (int index = 0; index < 3; index++) {
if (input == account [index]->pin_number) {
Console::Write ("Account Number: ");
Console::WriteLine (account [index]->account_number);
Console::Write ("Identity: ");
Console::Write (account [index]->first_name);
Console::Write (" ");
Console::WriteLine (account [index]->last_name);
Console::Write ("Savings Account Balance: ");
```

```
Console::WriteLine (account [index]->Savings);
Console::Write ("Checking Account Balance: ");
Console::WriteLine (account [index]->Checking) ;}}}}
```

Complex Structures

Complex structures are nothing more than structures that contain references to other structures. These
secondary structures are accessed in much the same manner as standard structures, with the addition of a
secondary dot operator and an additional member's name. The inclusion of one structure inside another is
also referred too as composition and/or nesting (see Example 6.5).

Example 6.5. Nested structures.
```
/* Nested Structures */
#include "stdafx.h"
#using <mscorlib.dll>
#include <tchar.h>
using namespace System;

__gc struct BankAccount {
public:
String* first_name;

__gc struct NestedStruct {
public:
double swiss_account;}; };

void _tmain(void) {
BankAccount* Account = new BankAccount();
BankAccount::NestedStruct* HiddenAccount = new
BankAccount::NestedStruct();

Account->first_name = "MR.RICH";
HiddenAccount->swiss_account = 5000000.00 ; }
```

Structures as Function Arguments: Calls-by-Mechanism

In addition to being able to pass our standard variables as both call-by-mechanism and call-by-reference
values, we can also pass fields using either of these techniques. In this section, we'll apply the simpler of the
two, the call-by-mechanism procedure, for which we've already defined the self-contained nature of those
values. Remember, calls-by-mechanism are used to pass data that is mutable from within that referencing
method, but which ultimately does not affect the source values (see Example 6.6).

Example 6.6. Calls-by-mechanism with structures.
```
/* calls-by-mechanism */
#include "stdafx.h"
#using <mscorlib.dll>
#include <tchar.h>
using namespace System;
```

```
static double function (double balance);

__gc struct BankAccount {
public:
String* first_name;
String* last_name;
long account_number;
double Checking;
double Savings;
short pin_number; };

void _tmain(void) {
BankAccount* account = new BankAccount();

int input;
account->pin_number = 2001;
account->Savings = 0;
account->Checking = 112.53;

Console::Write ("Enter you pin number now: ");
input = (Console::ReadLine ())->ToInt32(0);

if (account->pin_number == 2001) {
Console::WriteLine ("Savings");
account->Savings = function (account->Savings);
Console::WriteLine ("Checking");
account->Checking = function (account->Checking);
Console::WriteLine ("Updating account...");
Console::WriteLine ("Savings {0}",
__box(account->Savings));
Console::WriteLine ("Checking {0}",
__box(account->Checking)) ;}}

static double function (double balance) {
double input;
Console::WriteLine ("Your current balance: {0}",
__box(balance));
Console::Write ("\nAmount to deposit: ");
input = (Console::ReadLine ())->ToDouble(0);
balance = balance + input;
return (balance); }
```

Structures as Function Arguments: Calls-by-reference

Next, we will pass fields using a call-by-reference procedure. Call-by-reference procedures are, simply put, limited pointer values. Any alterations in the passed variable's values now alter the member's stored values. These, like their variable counterparts, are also references with the keywords *ref* and *out* as shown below (see Example 6.7).

Example 6.7. Calls-by-reference with structures.

```cpp
/* Calls-by-reference */
#include "stdafx.h"
#using <mscorlib.dll>
#include <tchar.h>
using namespace System;

static void function (double __gc* balance);

__gc struct BankAccount {
public:
String* first_name;
String* last_name;
long account_number;
double Checking;
double Savings;
short pin_number; };

void _tmain(void) {
BankAccount* account = new BankAccount();

account->pin_number = 2001;
account->Savings = 10;
account->Checking = 112.53;
Console::Write ("Enter you pin number now: ");
int input = (Console::ReadLine ())->ToInt32(0);

if(account->pin_number == 2001) {
 Console::WriteLine ("Savings");
function (&account->Savings);
Console::WriteLine ("Checking\n");
function (&account->Checking);

Console::WriteLine ("Updating account...");
Console::WriteLine ("Savings {0}", __box(account->Savings));
Console::WriteLine ("Checking {0}", __box(account->Checking));} }

static void function (double __gc* balance) {
double input;
Console::WriteLine ("Your current balance: {0}", __box(*balance));
Console::WriteLine ("Amount to deposit: ");
input = (Console::ReadLine ())->ToDouble(0);
*balance += input;   }
```

Passing Entire Structures

In addition to being able to pass single structural members, we can also pass an entire structure using a call-by-mechanism or call-by-reference procedures. In both cases, the reasoning for doing so would involve the increased portability and reusability of such generalized user-defined functions (see Examples 6.8 and 6.9).

Example 6.8. Calls-by-mechanism with structures.
```cpp
/* Calls-by-mechanism */
#include "stdafx.h"
#using <mscorlib.dll>
#include <tchar.h>
using namespace System;

__gc struct BankAccount {
public:
String* first_name;
String* last_name;
long account_number;
double Checking;
double Savings;
short pin_number; };

static void function (BankAccount* acc);

int _tmain(void) {
BankAccount* account = new BankAccount();

account->pin_number = 2001;
account->account_number = 43297;
account->first_name = "John";
account->last_name = "Doe";
account->Savings = 100.00;
account->Checking = 112.53;
function (account); }

static void function (BankAccount* acc) {
Console::Write ("Enter your pin number here: ");
int input = (Console::ReadLine ())->ToInt32(0);

if (input == acc->pin_number) {
Console::WriteLine ("Account Number: {0}",
__box(acc->account_number));
Console::Write ("Identity: ");
Console::Write (acc->first_name);
Console::Write (" ");
Console::WriteLine (acc->last_name);
Console::WriteLine ("Savings Account Balance: {0}",
__box(acc->Savings)) ;}}
```

Example 6.9. Calls-by-reference for structures.
```cpp
/* Calls-by-reference */
#include "stdafx.h"
#using <mscorlib.dll>
#include <tchar.h>
using namespace System;

__gc struct BankAccount {
public:
```

```
String* first_name;
String* last_name;
long account_number;
double Checking;
double Savings;
short pin_number; };

static void function (BankAccount __gc* acc);

int _tmain(void) {
BankAccount* account = new BankAccount();

account->pin_number = 2001;
account->account_number = 43297;
account->first_name = "John";
account->last_name = "Doe";
account->Savings = 100;
account->Checking = 112.53;
function (account);
function (account); }

static void function (BankAccount __gc* acc)    {
Console::WriteLine ("Enter your pin number here: ");
int input = (Console::ReadLine ())->ToInt32(0);

if (input == acc->pin_number) {
Console::WriteLine ("Account Number: {0}",
__box(acc->account_number));
Console::Write ("Identity: ");
Console::Write (acc->first_name);
Console::Write (" ");
Console::WriteLine(acc->last_name);
Console::WriteLine ("Savings Account Balance: {0}",
__box(acc->Savings));
Console::WriteLine ("Checking Account Balance: {0}",
__box(acc->Checking));

Console::Write ("Enter a new pin number here: ");
acc->pin_number = (Console::ReadLine ())->ToInt32(0);
Console::WriteLine ("Deposit into savings account: ");
input = (Console::ReadLine ())->ToInt32(0);
acc->Savings = acc->Savings + input;   }}
```

Storing and Retrieving Data

In the last few examples, we altered our user's accounts only to have those alterations lost at the end of the program. This, of course, would be quite impractical, but it was only done to simplify the learning process. The next few examples include coding techniques that link and store our data for further reference after our programs have been terminated. The processes involved in data storage and retrieval are not actually based on the C++ language, but instead are linked to the Base Class Library. Here, we'll use the namespace reference System::IO with the instances StreamReader and StreamWriter and a list of ReadLine and WriteLine references (see Example 6.10).

Example 6.10. Storing and retrieving data.

```cpp
/* Storing and Retrieving Data */
#include "stdafx.h"
#using <mscorlib.dll>
#include <tchar.h>
using namespace System;
using namespace System::IO;

__gc struct BankAccount {
public:
String* first_name;
String* last_name;
long account_number;
double Checking;
double Savings;
short pin_number; };

static void ReadFiles (BankAccount* acc);
static void CreateFiles (BankAccount* acc);
static void SaveFiles (BankAccount* acc, short input1, short input2);

void _tmain(void) {
BankAccount* account1 = new BankAccount();

account1->pin_number = 0;
account1->first_name = "";
account1->last_name = "";
account1->account_number = 0;
account1->Checking = 0;
account1->Savings = 0;

char input;

while (true)        {
Console::WriteLine ("Enter <C> to create new file or <V> to view
account");
input = (char)((Console::ReadLine ())->ToUpper())->ToChar(0);

if(input == 'C'){
CreateFiles (account1); }
else if (input == 'V')
{ReadFiles (account1);}
else
break;

Console::WriteLine ("Pin Number: {0}",
__box(account1->pin_number));
```

```
Console::WriteLine ("Account Number: {0}",
__box(account1->account_number));
Console::Write ("Name: {0} {1}");
Console::Write (account1->first_name);
Console::Write (" ");
Console::WriteLine (account1->last_name);
Console::WriteLine ("Savings Balance: {0}",
__box(account1->Savings));
Console::WriteLine ("Checking Balance: {0}",
__box(account1->Checking));
SaveFiles (account1, 0, 0) ;} }

static void SaveFiles (BankAccount* acc, short input1, short input2) {
StreamWriter* SaveFile = new StreamWriter ("C:\\MyFile.txt");
SaveFile->WriteLine (acc->pin_number);
SaveFile->WriteLine (acc->account_number);
SaveFile->WriteLine ((acc->Savings+input1));
SaveFile->WriteLine ((acc->Checking+input2));
SaveFile->WriteLine (acc->first_name);
SaveFile->WriteLine (acc->last_name);
SaveFile->Close () ;}

static void CreateFiles (BankAccount* acc) {
Console::WriteLine ("Enter Your New Pin Number: ");
acc->pin_number = (Console::ReadLine ())->ToInt32(0);
Random* rnd = new Random ();
acc->account_number = (long) Math::Round (rnd->NextDouble () * 100) +1;

Console::WriteLine ("\nYour New Account Number is: {0}",
__box(acc->account_number));
Console::Write ("\nEnter your first name: ");
acc->first_name = Console::ReadLine ();
Console::Write ("\nEnter your last name: ");
acc->last_name = Console::ReadLine ();
Console::WriteLine ("\nEnter your Savings Balance: ");
acc->Savings = (Console::ReadLine ())->ToDouble(0);
Console::WriteLine ("\nEnter your Checking Balance: ");
acc->Checking = (Console::ReadLine ())->ToDouble(0);
SaveFiles (acc, 0, 0) ;}

static void ReadFiles (BankAccount* acc) {
StreamReader* ReadFile = new StreamReader ("C:\\MyFile.txt");
acc->pin_number = (ReadFile->ReadLine ())->ToInt32(0);
acc->account_number = (long)(ReadFile->ReadLine ())->ToInt64(0);
acc->Savings = (ReadFile->ReadLine ())->ToDouble(0);
acc->Checking = (ReadFile->ReadLine ())->ToDouble(0);
acc->first_name = ReadFile->ReadLine ();
acc->last_name = ReadFile->ReadLine ();
ReadFile->Close () ;}
```

Note: Back to Classes
   In getting back to classes, I should mention that there are many aspects that we'll now cover for classes that are just as viable within the previously discussed structure types. These, of course, include the private, protected, and public references, as well as the basic member and method references.

Introducing Classes

As we've seen through this text, the application of classes is quite vital to the manipulation of the C++ language. An immediate comparison between classes and structures can be made, and all of the previous information can be reapplied to class references. Note that classes are both capable of using reference data types as well as inheritance. Classes mimic the naming references used with structures, including tags, fields, methods, and data blocks, as well as other key reference points including public, private, and protected access (these concepts will be explained shortly). A basic class reference can also be used to implement a simple do-nothing style program, but this time we'll also need to include a dynamically linked instance (see Example 6.11).

Example 6.11. A simple class.
```
/* A Simple Class */
#include "stdafx.h"
#using <mscorlib.dll>
#include <tchar.h>
using namespace System;

__gc class BankAccount {
public:
String* first_name;
String* last_name;
long account_number;
double Checking;
double Savings;
short pin_number; };

void _tmain(void) {
BankAccount* Info = new BankAccount ();
Info->account_number = 4353;
Console::WriteLine (Info->account_number); }
```

Note:
The keyword static is used to modify constructors, fields, methods, operators, and properties. Static constructors, for example, are called automatically and are used to initialize the rest of the class before any members are referenced. Static fields, then, are not part of a specific instance and instead are referenced as a single memory address.

Replacing Structures with Classes

Since classes are declared and assigned in basically the same manner structures, and since we haven't as yet defined the other access levels, it only makes sense than that we should begin with a simple public reference. In addition, if just to avoid the monotony of repeating all of the previous examples, I thought that I'd just jump ahead to the final example given on structures and modify it just enough to represent a working model of a class (see Example 6.12).

Note: As we examine this program, we'll find that the most important modification pertains to the dynamic instance. This change was necessary because classes are, in fact, referencing data types. You should also notice that the key methods, namely SaveFiles, CreateFiles, and ReadFiles did not need to be edited for use with this altered program. This adheres to the principles behind structured programming, wherein our functions are written as generic coding that can be reused by several applications; this is also the underlying principle of object-oriented program, as will see in the next section.

Example 6.12. Storing and retrieving date with classes.
```
/* Storing and Retrieving Data with Classes */
#include "stdafx.h"
#using <mscorlib.dll>
#include <tchar.h>
using namespace System;
using namespace System::IO;

__gc class BankAccount {
public:
String* first_name;
String* last_name;
long account_number;
double Checking;
double Savings;
short pin_number; };

static void ReadFiles (BankAccount* acc);
static void CreateFiles (BankAccount* acc);
static void SaveFiles (BankAccount* acc, short input1, short input2);

int _tmain(void) {
BankAccount* account1 = new BankAccount ();
char input;

while (true)         {
Console::WriteLine ("Enter <C> to create new file or <V> to view
account");
input = (char) ((Console::ReadLine ())->ToUpper())->ToChar(0);

if(input == 'C') {
CreateFiles (account1); }
else if (input == 'V') {
ReadFiles (account1);}
else
break;
```

```
Console::WriteLine ("Pin Number: {0}",
__box(account1->pin_number));
Console::WriteLine ("Account Number: {0}",
__box(account1->account_number));
Console::Write ("Name: ");
Console::Write (account1->first_name);
Console::Write (" ");
Console::WriteLine (account1->last_name);
Console::WriteLine ("Savings Balance: {0}",
__box(account1->Savings));
Console::WriteLine ("Checking Balance: {0}",
__box(account1->Checking));
SaveFiles (account1, 0, 0); }}

static void SaveFiles (BankAccount* acc, short input1, short input2) {
StreamWriter* SaveFile = new StreamWriter ("C:\\MyFile.txt");
SaveFile->WriteLine (acc->pin_number);
SaveFile->WriteLine (acc->account_number);
SaveFile->WriteLine ((acc->Savings+input1));
SaveFile->WriteLine ((acc->Checking+input2));
SaveFile->WriteLine (acc->first_name);
SaveFile->WriteLine (acc->last_name);
SaveFile->Close ();   }

static void CreateFiles (BankAccount* acc) {
Console::WriteLine ("Enter Your New Pin Number: ");
acc->pin_number = (Console::ReadLine ())->ToInt32(0);
Random* rnd = new Random ();
acc->account_number = (long) Math::Round (rnd->NextDouble () * 100) +1;

Console::WriteLine ("\nYour New Account Number is: {0}",
__box(acc->account_number));
Console::Write ("\nEnter your first name: ");
acc->first_name = Console::ReadLine ();
Console::Write ("\nEnter your last name: ");
acc->last_name = Console::ReadLine ();
Console::WriteLine ("\nEnter Your Savings Balance: ");
acc->Savings = (Console::ReadLine ())->ToDouble(0);
Console::WriteLine ("\nEnter Your Checking Balance: ");
acc->Checking = (Console::ReadLine ())->ToInt32(0);
SaveFiles (acc, 0, 0); }

static void ReadFiles (BankAccount* acc) {
StreamReader* ReadFile = new StreamReader ("C:\\MyFile.txt");
acc->pin_number = (ReadFile->ReadLine ())->ToInt32(0);
acc->account_number = (ReadFile->ReadLine ())->ToInt32(0);
acc->Savings = (ReadFile->ReadLine ())->ToDouble(0);
acc->Checking = (ReadFile->ReadLine ())->ToDouble(0);
acc->first_name = ReadFile->ReadLine ();
acc->last_name = ReadFile->ReadLine ();
ReadFile->Close (); }
```

Private & Protected Fields

Another programming technique that can improve program portability is the use of private and/or protected member fields. These are class or structure members that allow for restricted or limited access based on user-defined methods written specifically for those values. These user-defined methods are declared as part of that class' internal structure with the option of being declared as public, protected, or private member functions.

  Methods are user-defined functions that are declared from within classes. These functions are given both standard access to our main program and special access to our now private member variables. Public member functions can be accessed through any user-defined function that is aware of that defined class. The call to that function will need to include a class identifying statement and a dot member selection operator, while these user-defined functions include the class' identity, a type qualifier (the function's name), and a connecting binary scope resolution operator. For obvious reasons, member functions are also referred to as assessor functions (see Examples 6.13 and 6.14).

Example 6.13. Private member functions.
```
/* Private Members */
#include "stdafx.h"
#using <mscorlib.dll>
#include <tchar.h>
using namespace System;
using namespace System::IO;

__gc class BankAccount {
private:
String* first_name;
String* last_name;
long account_number;
double Checking;
double Savings;
short pin_number;

public : void ReadFiles (BankAccount* acc) {
StreamReader* ReadFile = new StreamReader ("C:\\MyFile.txt");
acc->pin_number = (ReadFile->ReadLine ())->ToInt32(0);
acc->account_number = (long) (ReadFile->ReadLine ())->ToInt64(0);
acc->Savings = (ReadFile->ReadLine ())->ToDouble(0);
acc->Checking = (ReadFile->ReadLine ())->ToDouble(0);
acc->first_name = ReadFile->ReadLine ();
acc->last_name = ReadFile->ReadLine ();
ReadFile->Close (); }

public : void CreateFiles (BankAccount* acc) {
Console::WriteLine ("Enter Your New Pin Number: ");
acc->pin_number = (Console::ReadLine ())->ToInt32(0);
Random* rnd = new Random ();

acc->account_number = (long) Math::Round (rnd->NextDouble () * 100) +1;
```

```
Console::WriteLine ("\nYour New Account Number is: {0}",
__box(acc->account_number));
Console::Write ("\nEnter your first name: ");
acc->first_name = Console::ReadLine ();
Console::Write ("\nEnter your last name: ");
acc->last_name = Console::ReadLine ();
Console::WriteLine ("\nEnter Your Savings Balance: ");
acc->Savings = (Console::ReadLine ())->ToDouble(0);
Console::WriteLine ("\nEnter Your Checking Balance: ");
acc->Checking = (Console::ReadLine ())->ToDouble(0);
SaveFiles (acc, 0, 0);   }

public : void SaveFiles (BankAccount* acc,
short input1, short input2) {
StreamWriter* SaveFile = new StreamWriter ("C:\\MyFile.txt");
SaveFile->WriteLine (acc->pin_number);
SaveFile->WriteLine (acc->account_number);
SaveFile->WriteLine ((acc->Savings+input1));
SaveFile->WriteLine ((acc->Checking+input2));
SaveFile->WriteLine (acc->first_name);
SaveFile->WriteLine (acc->last_name);
SaveFile->Close ();   }

public : void ViewFiles(BankAccount* acc) {
Console::WriteLine ("Pin Number: {0}",
__box(acc->pin_number));
Console::WriteLine ("Account Number: {0}",
__box(acc->account_number));
Console::Write ("Name: ");
Console::Write (acc->first_name);
Console::Write (" ");
Console::WriteLine (acc->last_name);
Console::WriteLine ("Savings Balance: {0}",
__box(acc->Savings));
Console::WriteLine ("Checking Balance: {0}",
__box(acc->Checking));}};

void _tmain(void){
 BankAccount* account = new BankAccount ();
 char input;
while (true)        {
Console::WriteLine ("Enter <C> to create new file or <V> to view
account");
input = (char) ((Console::ReadLine ())->ToUpper())->ToChar(0);

if(input == 'C') {
account->CreateFiles (account); }
else if (input == 'V') {
account->ReadFiles (account);}
else
break;
```

```
account->ViewFiles (account);
account->SaveFiles (account, 0, 0); }}
```

Note: While *private* is the default setting, many programmers choose too explicitly restate that command thus removing any ambiguity.

> Object-Oriented Programming
> The programs in Examples 6.13 and 6.14 are especially important when dealing with the migration of thinking from the standard structured programming model to our modern day object-oriented programming principles. Notice how the previous sections user-defined functions have been modified to serve as public methods.

Example 6.14. Protected Members.
```
/* Protected Members */
#include "stdafx.h"
#using <mscorlib.dll>
#include <tchar.h>
using namespace System;
using namespace System::IO;

__gc class BankAccount {
protected:
String* first_name;
String* last_name;
long account_number;
double Checking;
double Savings;
short pin_number;

public : void ReadFiles (BankAccount* acc) {
StreamReader* ReadFile = new StreamReader ("C:\\MyFile.txt");
acc->pin_number = (ReadFile->ReadLine ())->ToInt32(0);
acc->account_number = (long) (ReadFile->ReadLine ())->ToInt64(0);
acc->Savings = (ReadFile->ReadLine ())->ToDouble(0);
acc->Checking = (ReadFile->ReadLine ())->ToDouble(0);
acc->first_name = ReadFile->ReadLine ();
acc->last_name = ReadFile->ReadLine ();
ReadFile->Close (); }

public : void CreateFiles (BankAccount* acc) {
Console::WriteLine ("Enter Your New Pin Number: ");
acc->pin_number = (Console::ReadLine ())->ToInt32(0);
Random* rnd = new Random ();
acc->account_number = (long) Math::Round (rnd->NextDouble () * 100) +1;

Console::WriteLine ("\nYour New Account Number is: {0}",
__box(acc->account_number));
Console::Write ("\nEnter your first name: ");
acc->first_name = Console::ReadLine ();
Console::Write ("\nEnter your last name: ");
acc->last_name = Console::ReadLine ();
```

```
Console::WriteLine ("\nEnter Your Savings Balance: ");
acc->Savings = (Console::ReadLine ())->ToDouble(0);
Console::WriteLine ("\nEnter Your Checking Balance: ");
acc->Checking = (Console::ReadLine ())->ToDouble(0);
SaveFiles (acc, 0, 0);   }

Public : void SaveFiles (BankAccount* acc,
short input1, short input2) {
StreamWriter* SaveFile = new StreamWriter ("C:\\MyFile.txt");
SaveFile->WriteLine (acc->pin_number);
SaveFile->WriteLine (acc->account_number);
SaveFile->WriteLine ((acc->Savings+input1));
SaveFile->WriteLine ((acc->Checking+input2));
SaveFile->WriteLine (acc->first_name);
SaveFile->WriteLine (acc->last_name);
SaveFile->Close ();   }

public : void ViewFiles(BankAccount* acc) {
Console::WriteLine ("Pin Number: {0}",
__box(acc->pin_number));
Console::WriteLine ("Account Number: {0}",
__box(acc->account_number));
Console::Write ("Name: ");
Console::Write (acc->first_name);
Console::Write (" ");
Console::WriteLine (acc->last_name);
Console::WriteLine ("Savings Balance: {0}",
__box(acc->Savings));
Console::WriteLine ("Checking Balance: {0}",
__box(acc->Checking));}};

void _tmain(void) {
BankAccount* account = new BankAccount ();

char input;
while (true)        {
Console::WriteLine ("Enter <C> to create new file or <V> to view
account");
input = (char) ((Console::ReadLine ())->ToUpper())->ToChar(0);

if(input == 'C') {
account->CreateFiles (account); }
else if (input == 'V') {
account->ReadFiles (account);}
else
break;

account->ViewFiles (account);
account->SaveFiles (account, 0, 0); }}
```

The Internal Access Modifier

An internal access modifier is a type member used to access class components. The advantage of the internal modifier is that it allows for limited access from within a single assembly. A key disadvantage is that it is only accessible from within that assembly. In addition to the basic internal modifier, we can also use the keyword internal in combination with protected to create a internal protected modifier (see Example 6.15).

Example 6.15. Internals.
```
/* Internals */
#include "stdafx.h"
#using <mscorlib.dll>
#include <tchar.h>
using namespace System;

__gc class DynamicVariables {
public:
static short Array1 __gc[] = new short __gc[10];

public:
DynamicVariables (int n) {
Array1 = new short __gc[n];}
void SetElement (short i) {
Array1 [i] = i;}
short ReadElement (short i) {
return (Array1 [i]);} };

void _tmain(void) {
DynamicVariables* Instance = new DynamicVariables (10);
for(short i = 0; i < Instance->Array1.Length; i++) {
Instance->SetElement (i);
Console::Write ("{0} ",
__box(Instance->ReadElement (i)));}
Console::WriteLine (); }
```

Overloading Member Functions

Overloading occurs whenever two or more user-defined functions are referenced using a single definition. To avoid conflicts, however these definitions must differ by at least one passing argument. Logically, if two functions were similar enough to warrant the same name and if its arguments were identical then efforts should be taken to unify functions. Here I've listed two examples, one to demonstrate how to implement to similar, but overloaded functions while the other to demonstrate how to avoid unnecessary overloads (see Examples 6.17 & 6.18).

Example 6.18. Private member methods.
```
/* Private Member functions (Methods) */
#include "stdafx.h"
#using <mscorlib.dll>
#include <tchar.h>
using namespace System;
```

```
using namespace System::IO;

__gc class BankAccount {
protected:
String* first_name;
String* last_name;
long account_number;
double Checking;
double Savings;
short pin_number;

private : void ReadFiles (BankAccount* acc) {
StreamReader* ReadFile = new StreamReader ("C:\\MyFile.txt");
acc->pin_number = (ReadFile->ReadLine ())->ToInt32(0);
acc->account_number = (long) (ReadFile->ReadLine ())->ToInt64(0);
acc->Savings = (ReadFile->ReadLine ())->ToDouble(0);
acc->Checking = (ReadFile->ReadLine ())->ToDouble(0);
acc->first_name = ReadFile->ReadLine ();
acc->last_name = ReadFile->ReadLine ();
ReadFile->Close (); }

public : void CreateFiles (BankAccount* acc) {
Console::WriteLine ("Enter Your New Pin Number: ");
acc->pin_number = (Console::ReadLine ())->ToInt32(0);
Random* rnd = new Random ();
acc->account_number = (long) Math::Round (rnd->NextDouble () * 100) +1;
Console::WriteLine ("\nYour New Account Number is: {0}",
__box(acc->account_number));
Console::Write ("\nEnter your first name: ");
acc->first_name = Console::ReadLine ();
Console::Write ("\nEnter your last name: ");
acc->last_name = Console::ReadLine ();
Console::WriteLine ("\nEnter Your Savings Balance: ");
acc->Savings = (Console::ReadLine ())->ToDouble(0);
Console::WriteLine ("\nEnter Your Checking Balance: ");
acc->Checking = (Console::ReadLine ())->ToDouble(0);
acc->SaveFiles (acc, 0, 0); }

private : void SaveFiles (BankAccount* acc,
short input1, short input2) {
StreamWriter* SaveFile = new StreamWriter ("C:\\MyFile.txt");
SaveFile->WriteLine (acc->pin_number);
SaveFile->WriteLine (acc->account_number);
SaveFile->WriteLine ((acc->Savings+input1));
SaveFile->WriteLine ((acc->Checking+input2));
SaveFile->WriteLine (acc->first_name);
SaveFile->WriteLine (acc->last_name);
SaveFile->Close ();   }

public : void ViewFiles(BankAccount* acc) {
acc->ReadFiles(acc);
Console::WriteLine ("Pin Number: {0}",
```

```
__box(acc->pin_number));
Console::WriteLine ("Account Number: {0}",
__box(acc->account_number));
Console::Write ("Name: ");
Console::Write (acc->first_name);
Console::Write (" ");
Console::WriteLine (acc->last_name);
Console::WriteLine ("Savings Balance: {0}",
__box(acc->Savings));
Console::WriteLine ("Checking Balance: {0}",
__box(acc->Checking));}};

void _tmain(void) {
BankAccount* account = new BankAccount ();

char input;
while (true)        {
Console::WriteLine ("Enter <C> to create new file or <V> to view
account");
input = (char) ((Console::ReadLine ())->ToUpper())->ToChar(0);

if(input == 'C') {
account->CreateFiles (account); }
else if (input == 'V') {
account->ViewFiles (account);}
else
break;
account->ViewFiles (account);}}
```

As you can see this function could have been separated to include two overloading functions, but with a simple adjustment using the zero input our two functions become one.

Constructors

Constructors are member functions that are automatically implemented with the declaration of that classes instance. Each new instance tigers this execution and generally those values are made specific to that instance's reference. Constructors, like standard member functions, are declared from within those classes, but constructors do not require a base data type. Constructors are defined using the same definition as their declaring class, while their actual functions are expressed as a combination of both definitions and a connecting binary scope resolution operator. Since constructors <u>do not</u> declare a data type, they are also incapable of returning values (see example 6.21). Note: Each declared instance is allocated a portion of system memory (commonly referred to as the heap). In native C++ it is also important to define the restoration of that memory (normally referenced by that classes destructor –see this chapters section on destructors)[6].

---

[6] While destructors are an important part of native C++, their importance is minimized when referring to C#. In this modernized language, the process of destructing an object has become the primary concern of the compiler, normally occurring when the object is no longer referenced.

Example 6.21. Constructors.
```
/* Constructors */
#include "stdafx.h"
#using <mscorlib.dll>
#include <tchar.h>
using namespace System;

__gc class BankAccount {
public:
double InterestRate;
double LoanRate;

BankAccount() { // Default Constructor
InterestRate = .03; LoanRate = .13;}};

int _tmain(void) {
BankAccount* account = new BankAccount ();
}
```

Overloading Constructors

  In addition to being able to overload our standard and member type functions, we can also overload our constructors to include a plethora of possibilities. Again, these functions will be automatically referenced when the appropriate instances are declared and again their arguments will determine the accessible function. One such class revision might include a secondary constructor that gives a special rate to some depositors and a third that determines an alternate rate for both their savings and loans (see Example 6.22).

Example 6.22. Overloading Constructors.
```
/* Overloading Constructors */
#include "stdafx.h"
#using <mscorlib.dll>
#include <tchar.h>
using namespace System;

__gc class BankAccount {
public:
double InterestRate;
double LoanRate;

BankAccount() {// Default Constructor
InterestRate = .03; LoanRate = .13;}

BankAccount(double IRate) { // Overloaded Constructor
InterestRate = .03; LoanRate = .13;}

BankAccount(double IRate, double LoanRate) { // Overloaded Constructor
InterestRate = .03; LoanRate = .13;} };

int _tmain(void) {
BankAccount* account = new BankAccount (); }
```

Assigning Instances

Once two or more instances are declared by the same class the values of those instances can be passed using the assignment statement as in (account1 = account2; // *where BankAccount account1, account2;*). In this example the values from account2 are passed to account1 (this process is commonly referred to as a memberwise copy). Note: Restrictions in systems implementations may potentially cause errors when dealing with dynamically allocated storage (see Example 6.23).

Example 6.23. Memberwise Copy.
```
/* Memberwise Copy */
#include "stdafx.h"
#using <mscorlib.dll>
#include <tchar.h>
using namespace System;

__gc class BankAccount {
public:
double InterestRate;
double LoanRate;

BankAccount() {
InterestRate = .03; LoanRate = .13;}

BankAccount(double IRate) {
InterestRate = .03; LoanRate = .13;}

BankAccount(double IRate, double LoanRate) {
InterestRate = .03; LoanRate = .13;} };

int _tmain(void) {
}
```

Reading and Writing to Private Members

Encapsulation is a key point when working with private members, but for varying reasons we often find that we need to gain at least limited access in order to implement changes within our programs. These changes can be facilitated with the use of specialized member functions. The practically of these functions are usually broken up into two forms. The first to read (compare, get) those values and the second to set (put, write) or alter those values. Typically the setting functions are void, while the reading functions are meant to return the implied value. Both are usually only used to access one class member, but several equivalent member functions many be written to include as many members as required (see Example 6.24).

Example 6.24. Private Members.
```
public decimal ReadInterestRate()
{return (InterestRate);}

public void SetInterestRate(decimal IRate)
```

```
{InterestRate = IRate;}
```

The Keyword *this*

The keyword "*this*" is a specialized reference signature used to indicate the referencing object of a passing class, "*this*" is then a longhand version for the otherwise abbreviated member. While the "*this*" reference is implied, its definitions can become ambiguous and should be included to prevent this error (see examples 6.25 & 6.26). Note: unlike C++, C#'s single dot reference can be used for both reference and non-reference The proper notation for a "*this*" pointer is said to depend upon the purpose of its referencing class as in the this->variable vs. the (*this).variable.

Example 6.25. With this.
```
/* Written with the this reference*/
#include "stdafx.h"
#using <mscorlib.dll>
#include <tchar.h>
using namespace System;
using namespace System::IO;

__gc class BankAccount {
protected:
String* first_name;
String* last_name;
long account_number;
double Checking;
double Savings;
short pin_number;

private : void ReadFiles () {
StreamReader* ReadFile = new StreamReader ("C:\\MyFile.txt");
this->pin_number = (ReadFile->ReadLine ())->ToInt32(0);
this->account_number = (long) (ReadFile->ReadLine ())->ToInt64(0);
this->Savings = (ReadFile->ReadLine ())->ToInt32(0);
this->Checking = (ReadFile->ReadLine ())->ToInt32(0);
this->first_name = ReadFile->ReadLine ();
this->last_name = ReadFile->ReadLine ();
ReadFile->Close (); }

public : void CreateFiles () {
Console::WriteLine ("Enter Your New Pin Number: ");
this->pin_number = (Console::ReadLine ())->ToInt32(0);
Random* rnd = new Random ();
this->account_number = (long) Math::Round (rnd->NextDouble () * 100) +1;
Console::WriteLine ("\nYour New Account Number is: {0}",
__box(this->account_number));
Console::Write ("\nEnter your first name: ");
this->first_name = Console::ReadLine ();
Console::Write ("\nEnter your last name: ");
this->last_name = Console::ReadLine ();
Console::WriteLine ("\nEnter Your Savings Balance: ");
```

```cpp
this->Savings = (Console::ReadLine ())->ToDouble(0);
Console::WriteLine ("\nEnter Your Checking Balance: ");
this->Checking = (Console::ReadLine ())->ToDouble(0);
this->SaveFiles (0, 0); }

private : void SaveFiles (short input1, short input2) {
StreamWriter* SaveFile = new StreamWriter ("C:\\MyFile.txt");
SaveFile->WriteLine (this->pin_number);
SaveFile->WriteLine (this->account_number);
SaveFile->WriteLine ((this->Savings+input1));
SaveFile->WriteLine ((this->Checking+input2));
SaveFile->WriteLine (this->first_name);
SaveFile->WriteLine (this->last_name);
SaveFile->Close ();   }

public : void ViewFiles() {
this->ReadFiles();
Console::WriteLine ("Pin Number: {0}",
__box(this->pin_number));
Console::WriteLine ("Account Number: {0}",
__box(this->account_number));
Console::Write ("Name: ");
Console::Write (this->first_name);
Console::WriteLine (this->last_name);
Console::WriteLine ("Savings Balance: {0}",
__box(this->Savings));
Console::WriteLine ("Checking Balance: {0}",
__box(this->Checking));}};

void _tmain(void) {
BankAccount* account = new BankAccount ();

char input;
while (true)       {
Console::WriteLine ("Enter <C> to create new file or <V> to view
account");
input = (char) ((Console::ReadLine ())->ToUpper())->ToChar(0);

if(input == 'C')
{account->CreateFiles (); }
else if (input == 'V')
{account->ViewFiles ();}
else
break;
account->ViewFiles ();}}
```

Example 6.26. Implying this.
```cpp
/* The keyword "this" is only implied */
#include "stdafx.h"
#using <mscorlib.dll>
#include <tchar.h>
```

172

```
using namespace System;
using namespace System::IO;

__gc class BankAccount {
protected:
String* first_name;
String* last_name;
long account_number;
double Checking;
double Savings;
short pin_number;

private : void ReadFiles () {
StreamReader* ReadFile = new StreamReader ("C:\\MyFile.txt");
pin_number = (ReadFile->ReadLine ())->ToInt32(0);
account_number = (long) (ReadFile->ReadLine ())->ToInt64(0);
Savings = (ReadFile->ReadLine ())->ToDouble(0);
Checking = (ReadFile->ReadLine ())->ToDouble(0);
first_name = ReadFile->ReadLine ();
last_name = ReadFile->ReadLine ();
ReadFile->Close (); }

public : void CreateFiles () {
Console::WriteLine ("Enter Your New Pin Number: ");
pin_number = (short) (Console::ReadLine ())->ToInt32(0);
Random* rnd = new Random ();
account_number = (long) Math::Round (rnd->NextDouble () * 100) +1;
Console::WriteLine ("\nYour New Account Number is: {0}",
__box(account_number));
Console::Write ("\nEnter your first name: ");
first_name = Console::ReadLine ();
Console::Write ("\nEnter your last name: ");
last_name = Console::ReadLine ();
Console::WriteLine ("\nEnter Your Savings Balance: ");
Savings = (Console::ReadLine ())->ToDouble(0);
Console::WriteLine ("\nEnter Your Checking Balance: ");
Checking = (Console::ReadLine ())->ToDouble(0);
SaveFiles (0, 0); }

private : void SaveFiles (short input1, short input2) {
StreamWriter* SaveFile = new StreamWriter ("C:\\MyFile.txt");
SaveFile->WriteLine (pin_number);
SaveFile->WriteLine (account_number);
SaveFile->WriteLine ((Savings+input1));
SaveFile->WriteLine ((Checking+input2));
SaveFile->WriteLine (first_name);
SaveFile->WriteLine (last_name);
SaveFile->Close ();   }

public : void ViewFiles() {
ReadFiles ();
Console::WriteLine ("Pin Number: {0}",
```

```
__box(pin_number));
Console::WriteLine ("Account Number: {0}",
__box(account_number));
Console::Write ("Name: ");
Console::Write (first_name);
Console::Write (" ");
Console::WriteLine (last_name);
Console::WriteLine ("Savings Balance: {0}",
__box(Savings));
Console::WriteLine ("Checking Balance: {0}",
__box(Checking));}};


int _tmain(void) {
BankAccount* account = new BankAccount ();

char input;
while (true)         {
Console::WriteLine ("Enter <C> to create new file or <V> to view
account");
input = (char) (((Console::ReadLine ()))->ToUpper())->ToChar(0);

if(input == 'C')
{account->CreateFiles (); }
else if (input == 'V')
{account->ViewFiles ();}
else
break;

account->ViewFiles ();}}
```

Destructors

In addition to constructors, we can also use destructors to return the allocated portions of our objects memory as in back to the heap. This destruction or de-allocation of system resources is an extremely important systems saving technique especially when dealing with thousands of class objects that continue to exist even after their no longer referenced. Again, while Managed C++ and C# do handle these instances automatically, it is still important to understand the concept of creating a destructor. Now, destructors are also automatically referenced at the termination of a set of coding, but the exact internal structure will depend on the constructors applications and thus is user-defined. The correct way to define a destructor is to reproduce the classes definition (as was done for the constructor), but with the addition of the tilde operator (~). This destructor will not contain any arguments nor will it require a data type. Classes should be written to include only one destructor. Destructors do not return values nor can they be overloaded (see example 6.27).

Example 6.27. Overloading Constructors.
```
/* Overloading Constructors */
#include "stdafx.h"
```

```
#using <mscorlib.dll>
#include <tchar.h>
using namespace System;
using namespace System::IO;

class BankAccount {
public:
double InterestRate;
double LoanRate;

BankAccount() { // Default Constructor
InterestRate = .03; LoanRate = .13;}

BankAccount(double IRate) { // Overloaded Constructor
InterestRate = .03; LoanRate = .13;}

BankAccount(double IRate, double LoanRate) { // Overloaded Constructor
InterestRate = .03; LoanRate = .13;}

~BankAccount(){} // Destructor
};

void _tmain(void) {
BankAccount* account = new BankAccount ();}
```

Introducing Operator Overloading

Another feature that becomes available to us through the use of class manipulations is the ability to overload our operators. Operator overloading is the reapplication of our operators to include class manipulations. The standard class operator overloads include object-to-object and object-to-numeric values (including variables). Traditionally C++ overloaded operators included stream-insertion (<<), stream-extraction (>>), array notation ([ ]), but C# has limited the number of operates that can be overloaded (see table 5.1). The most important point when dealing with operator overloading is the understanding that all abbreviated forms should be made implicit. That is all who reference it should inherently know any action implied by an overloaded operator. To accomplish this we need only to take note of the implied meaning before the operator is expanded. For example when working with simple addition, we might conclude that the equation $X = 4 + 2$ returns the value 6. This observation would be based on the implied understanding of the "+" symbol. If we were to abuse the overloading process to include $X = 4/2$ (equaling 6) this would not be inherently implied, thus it could potentially confuse the programmer.

To understand the reasoning behind the application of overloaded operators, we simply need to redefine the task to meet the need. For example, if we were to convert our first value "four" into a public class member as in "Class.number = 4; *and* X = Class.number + 2;" The numeric calculations would not be altered and operator overloading would not be necessary. In addition, if we were to convert that value into a private class member using a get or read function to retrieve that value as in *short* Class.ReadValue() {*return*(*this*.number); } "X = Class.ReadValue() + 2;" overloading would remain unnecessary. Still, by the same reasoning, if we were to the express the object Class to imply Class.number, but we were to replace the cumbersome operation of relaying that value through a get or read function with that of a nested class component. The same implicit reasoning would still apply as in "X = Class.ComponentNumber + 2;" but while this is mathematically sound, it is not inherently understood by the computer. Thus in order to define the action of adding an implied class member to that of a numeric value we'll have to build a secondary application for the "+" operator. Which, of course, is then an overloaded version of that operator, hence the term operator overloading

Table 5.1:

+	-	*	/	%	^
>	<	>=	<=	==	!=
>>	<<	!	++	--	~
true	false	|	&		

Again, while C# doesn't formally allow for the overloading of the assignment operator (=), classes can be copied using the built-in function. It should also be noted that whenever any of the mathematical operators (+, -, *, /) are overloaded, the companion shortcuts are implied as in +=, -=, *=, /= (see example 6.28).

Example 6.28. Operator Overloading.

```
/* Introducing Operator Overloading */
#include "stdafx.h"
#using <mscorlib.dll>
#include <tchar.h>
using namespace System;

__gc class Objects {
public:
int Number;

public : Objects(int value){this->Number = value;}
public : static Objects* op_Addition(Objects* Ob, int value)
{Ob->Number += value; return(Ob);}
public : static Objects* op_Addition(Objects* Ob, Objects* Ob2)
{Ob->Number += Ob2->Number; return(Ob);}
public : static Objects* op_Subtraction(Objects* Ob, int value)
{Ob->Number -= value; return(Ob);}
public : static Objects* op_Substraction(Objects* Ob, Objects* Ob2)
{Ob->Number -= Ob2->Number; return(Ob);}
public : static Objects* op_Multiply(Objects* Ob, int value)
{Ob->Number *= value; return(Ob);}
public : static Objects* op_Multiply(Objects* Ob, Objects* Ob2)
{Ob->Number *= Ob2->Number; return(Ob);}
public : static Objects* op_Division(Objects* Ob, int value)
{Ob->Number /= value; return(Ob);}
public : static Objects* op_Division(Objects* Ob, Objects* Ob2)
{Ob->Number /= Ob2->Number; return(Ob);}};

int _tmain(void) {
Objects* Class1 = new Objects(4);
Objects* Class2 = new Objects(2);
// Standard arithmetic
Class1->Number += 2;
Console::WriteLine(Class1->Number);
Class1->Number -= 2;
Console::WriteLine(Class1->Number);
```

```
Class1->Number *= 2;
Console::WriteLine(Class1->Number);
Class1->Number /= 2;
Console::WriteLine(Class1->Number);
// Object-to-numeric value (or variable)
Class1->op_Addition(Class1, 2);
Console::WriteLine(Class1->Number);
//Class1->op_Substraction(Class1, 2);
Console::WriteLine(Class1->Number);
Class1->op_Multiply(Class1, 2);
Console::WriteLine(Class1->Number);
Class1->op_Division(Class1, 2);
Console::WriteLine(Class1->Number);
// Object-to-Object
Class1->op_Addition(Class1, Class2);
Console::WriteLine(Class1->Number);
Class1->op_Substraction(Class1, Class2);
Console::WriteLine(Class1->Number);
Class1->op_Multiply(Class1, Class2);
Console::WriteLine(Class1->Number);
Class1->op_Division(Class1, Class2);
Console::WriteLine(Class1->Number);}
```

Overloading Comparison Operators

Another important type of overloading involves the use of the comparison operators. Here, we'll want to use the Boolean data type with our choice of constants, variables, and object references. We'll also need to include matching comparisons as in both our greater than and less than symbols for each overload (see Example 6.29).

Example 6.29. Overloading comparison operators.
```
/* Overloading comparison operators */
#include "stdafx.h"
#using <mscorlib.dll>
#include <tchar.h>
using namespace System;

__gc class Objects {
int Number;
bool Test;

public : Objects(int Value)
{this->Number = Value;} // Constructor
public : static bool op_GreaterThan(Objects* One, Objects* Two)
{return(One->Number > Two->Number);}
public : static bool op_GreaterThan(Objects* One, int Value)
{return(One->Number > Value); }
public : static bool op_LessThan(Objects* One, Objects* Two)
{return(One->Number < Two->Number);}
public : static bool op_LessThan(Objects* One, int Value)
```

```
{return(One->Number < Value); }

public : static bool op_LessThanOrEqual(Objects* One, Objects* Two)
{return(One->Number <= Two->Number);}
public : static bool op_GreaterThanOrEqual(Objects* One, Objects* Two)
{return(One->Number >= Two->Number);}
public : static bool op_LessThanOrEqual(Objects* One, int Value)
{return(One->Number <= Value);}
public : static bool op_GreaterThanOrEqual(Objects* One, int Value)
{return(One->Number >= Value);}};

int _tmain(void) {
Objects* Class1 = new Objects(4);
Objects* Class2 = new Objects(2);
// Object-to-numeric value (or variable)
if(Class1->op_GreaterThan(Class1, 2)) Console::WriteLine(true);      // 1
if(Class1->op_LessThan(Class1, 2)) Console::WriteLine(true);  // false
if(Class1->op_GreaterThanOrEqual(Class1, 2)) Console::WriteLine(true);
// 2
if(Class1->op_LessThanOrEqual(Class1, 2))
Console::WriteLine(true);//false
// Object-to-Object
if(Class1->op_GreaterThan(Class1, Class2)) Console::WriteLine(true);
// 3
if(Class1->op_LessThan(Class1, Class2)) Console::WriteLine(true); //
false
if(Class1->op_GreaterThan(Class1, Class2)) Console::WriteLine(true); //
4 true
if(Class1->op_LessThanOrEqual(Class1, Class2)) Console::WriteLine(true);
} //false
```

Nesting Overloaded Operators

   In addition to being able to nest classes, we can also nest overloading operator functions. This actually becomes a necessity when attempting to overload two distinct subclasses as part of a single overloaded reference. The need arises because of the inability of the first operator functions to access both private members values. The second operator function then includes the first component's numeric value, thus the principles of encapsulation are not broken (see Example 6.30).

Example 6.30. Nesting overloaded operators.
```
/* Nesting Overloaded Operators */
#include "stdafx.h"
#using <mscorlib.dll>
#include <tchar.h>
using namespace System;

__gc public class PeriodicTable {
public:

__gc class Atoms {
```

```
public:
String* Symbol;
int Number;
double Weight;

Atoms() {}

Atoms(String* Symbol, int Number, double Weight) {
this->Symbol = Symbol;
this->Number = Number;
this->Weight = Weight;}

static bool op_Equality(Atoms* NE, Atoms* At) {
return (NE->Weight == At->Weight);}
static bool op_Inequality(Atoms* NE, Atoms* At)
{return (NE->Weight != At->Weight);}
};};

void _tmain(void) {
PeriodicTable::Atoms* Hydrogen =
new PeriodicTable::Atoms("H", 1, 1.0079);
PeriodicTable::Atoms* Helium =
new PeriodicTable::Atoms("He", 2, 4.00260);
PeriodicTable::Atoms* Lithium =
new PeriodicTable::Atoms("Li", 3, 6.941);
PeriodicTable::Atoms* Beryllium =
new PeriodicTable::Atoms("Be", 4, 9.01218);
PeriodicTable::Atoms* Boron =
new PeriodicTable::Atoms("B", 5, 10.81);
        // ...
PeriodicTable::Atoms* Unnilhexium =
new PeriodicTable::Atoms("Unh", 106, 263);

PeriodicTable::Atoms* NewElement =
new PeriodicTable::Atoms("XXX", 10, 1.0079);

if(NewElement->Weight == Hydrogen->Weight)
Console::WriteLine("Hydrogen Match!");
else if(NewElement->Weight == Helium->Weight)
Console::WriteLine("Helium Match!");
//...
else if(NewElement->Weight == Unnilhexium->Weight)
Console::WriteLine("Unnilhexium Match!");
else
Console::WriteLine("You've discovered a new element! \n");}
```

Overloading Unary Operators

In addition to the abundance of reasons for overloading our binary type operators, we'll also find several rather practical manipulations that involve the use of our unary operators. One such example would include the use of the not operator. This unary operator could be used to simultaneously access a Boolean component while inverting its stored value. Another two useful modifiers are the incrementing and decrementing operators. Still other practical unary operator is the negative notation as would be inserted in front of a class component's value often used to indicate a reverse in direction and/or an implied mathematically reference (Example 6.31 explores the implementation of these concepts).

Example 6.31. Overloading unary operators.
```
/* Overloading unary operators */
#include "stdafx.h"
#using <mscorlib.dll>
#include <tchar.h>
using namespace System;

__gc public class Television {
public:
bool Power;
short Channel;

Television() {
this->Channel = 2;
this->Power = false;}
public : static bool op_Negation(Television* TV) {return(!TV->Power);}
public : static Television* op_Increment(Television* TV)
{TV->Channel++; return(TV);}
public : static Television* op_Decrement(Television* TV)
{TV->Channel--; return(TV);}};

void _tmain(void) {
Television* TV = new Television();

if(TV->op_Negation(TV))
  Console::Write("The TV is not turned on. \n");

TV->op_Increment(TV);
TV->op_Decrement(TV); }
```

Introducing Inheritance

It is through the use of inherited classes, their virtual functions, and the methods and fields used to construct those classes that transitions this definition from abstraction to a tangible coding methodology. The theory behind object-oriented programming embraces three key principles namely encapsulation, inheritance, and polymorphism. It becomes natural then to expand those concepts to include both a generic reusability and a hierarchical structure.

Inheritance is the ability of a specialized or derived class to appropriate the coding included in an abstract or base class. This appropriation allows for the re-administration of that base classes attributes without the cost of redevelopment and testing usually found when attempting to expand upon a previously developed component. A derived class then is both a combination of its unique coding and that of the linked coding. Once a derived class is established, it too becomes subject to other derived classes or what can be thought of as a string of inherited classes. This should not be confused with the term "multiple-inheritance" which signifies the conjoining of two or more distinctly different classes to create an all-purpose class. With single inheritance, each level then takes on the attributes of all of the previous levels, creating a hierarchical structure that is based on abstraction rather than distinction and is hence the preferred method. Inherited classes are also subject to three levels of access security namely *public*, *protected*, and *private*. Our first two examples then will define a simple publicly inherited class as it relates to a set of public and protected accessible member variables and functions (see Examples 6.32 & 6.33). Note: While C++ is still backward compatible with multiply inherited structures, C# is not, thus such techniques will not be discussed.

Example 6.32. Public Inheritance with public members.
```
/* Public Inheritance with public members */
#include "stdafx.h"
#using <mscorlib.dll>
#include <tchar.h>

using namespace System;

__gc public class BaseClass {
public : short Width, Length;

public : BaseClass() {}
public : BaseClass(short w, short l) {Width = w; Length = l;}
public : static void ReadWidth(BaseClass* X)
{Console::WriteLine(X->Width);}
public : static void ReadLength(BaseClass* X)
{Console::WriteLine(X->Length);}};

__gc public class DerivedClass : public BaseClass
{public : DerivedClass(short w, short l) {
Width = w; Length = l;}

public : static void DisplayArea(DerivedClass* Y) {
Console::Write("Area = ");
Console::WriteLine (Y->Width*Y->Length);} };

void _tmain(void) {
DerivedClass* Instance = new DerivedClass(5, 6);
DerivedClass::ReadWidth(Instance);
DerivedClass::ReadLength(Instance);
DerivedClass::DisplayArea(Instance);}
```

Example 6.33. Public Inheritance with protected members.
```
/* Public Inheritance with protected members */
#include "stdafx.h"
#using <mscorlib.dll>
#include <tchar.h>
```

```
using namespace System;

__gc public class BaseClass {
protected:
short Width, Length;

public : BaseClass() {}
public : BaseClass(short w, short l) {
Width = w; Length = l;}
public : static void ReadWidth(BaseClass* X)
{Console::WriteLine(X->Width);}
public : static void ReadLength(BaseClass* X)
{Console::WriteLine(X->Length);}};

__gc public class DerivedClass : public BaseClass {
public : DerivedClass(short w, short l) {
Width = w; Length = l;}
public : static void DisplayArea(DerivedClass* Y)
{Console::Write ("Area = ");
Console::WriteLine (Y->Width*Y->Length);} };

int _tmain(void) {
DerivedClass* Instance = new DerivedClass(5, 6);
DerivedClass::ReadWidth(Instance);
DerivedClass::ReadLength(Instance);
DerivedClass::DisplayArea(Instance);}
```

Inheritance vs. Composition

Inheritance and composition describe to similar, but distinctly different types of references. For one, composition is said to be formed under a "has a" standard. In other words, a shared class "has a" relationship with a linking class. On the other hand, the base component of an inherited class isn't just said to "have a" relationship with its derived class, but instead it is said that the derived class "is an" object of the base class. This relationship then transcends the objects in question and speaks to the very nature of the components. For example, if we were to say that we had a horse and carriage, we'd be implying that the horse was needed to pull that carriage. The carriage then would be said to "have a" relationship connecting its use with that of the horse. Yet, if we were to say that the carriage was made out of wood, it would be understood that the wood "is a" part of the carriage, just as the base class becomes a part of the inherited class.

Inheriting Constructors & Destructors

As was explained in earlier sections, a constructor is a member function often used to initialize our objects as pertaining to the values presented in their declarations or thereby calculated as part of that class. The initialization is done automatically (at the moment of declaration) with reference to one of possibly several overloading constructor references. Once an inherited class is introduced, this initialization is then compounded with the need for both a base class initialization and than an inherited class initialization. Base class constructors, however, are not inherited by derived classes, and thus do not need to be overloaded or overridden. The order of derivation with regards to a constructor of an inherited class is always linked as in from our base class to the derived class, and the reverse order with regards to the destructor as in from the derived class to the base class.

Private vs. Protected Inheritance

Earlier in this chapter *private* and *protected* members seemed to be almost interchangeable. That is, they both protected against unauthorized referencing, granting access to only the properly labeled member functions... They allowed for predicate/ utility member functions and they both seemed to work well with the nested and inherited classes. The uniqueness then of the protected class became evident when we attempted to access a private member variable from inside an inherited class (review examples 5.33 & 5.34). In these differing cases, we found that the protected modifier acted much more like the public modifier than that of its private counterpart, that being to enable public access to our inherited class while still enforcing its rule of privacy on the accompanying program. To the same extent then our protected inherent classes allow for the same sharing of data between our base and derived classes, but private fields and method do not, thus they require methods used to retrieve that data (see Examples 6.34 & 6.35).

Example 6.34. Public inheritance with protected methods and fields.
```
/* Public inheritance with protected methods and fields */
#include "stdafx.h"
#using <mscorlib.dll>
#include <tchar.h>
using namespace System;

__gc public class BaseClass {
protected:
short Width, Length;

protected : BaseClass() {}
protected : BaseClass(short w, short l) {Width = w; Length = l;}
protected : static short ReadWidth(BaseClass* X)
{return (X->Width);}
protected : static short ReadLength(BaseClass* X)
{return(X->Length);}};

__gc public class DerivedClass : public BaseClass {
public : DerivedClass(short w, short l) {
Width = w; Length = l;}
protected : static void DisplayArea(DerivedClass* Y)
{Console::Write ("Area = ");
Console::WriteLine (Y->Width*Y->Length);}

public : static void Application(DerivedClass* Instance) {
Console::WriteLine(ReadWidth(Instance));
Console::WriteLine(ReadLength(Instance));
DisplayArea(Instance); } };

void _tmain(void) {
DerivedClass* Instance = new DerivedClass(5, 6);
DerivedClass::Application(Instance);}
```

Example 5.35. Public inheritance with public methods and private fields.

```
/* Public inheritance with public methods and private fields */
#include "stdafx.h"
#using <mscorlib.dll>
#include <tchar.h>
using namespace System;

__gc public class BaseClass {
private:
short Width;
short Length;

protected : BaseClass() {}
protected : BaseClass(short w, short l) {
Width = w; Length = l;}
public : static short ReadWidth(BaseClass* X) {
return(X->Width);}
public : static void SetWidth(BaseClass* X, short w) {
X->Width = w;}
public : static short ReadLength(BaseClass* X) {
return(X->Length);}
public : static void SetLength(BaseClass* X, short l) {
X->Length = l;}};

__gc public class DerivedClass : public BaseClass {
public : DerivedClass(short w, short l) {
SetWidth(this, w); SetLength(this, l);}
public : static void DisplayArea(DerivedClass* Y) {
Console::Write ("Area = ");
Console::WriteLine (ReadWidth(Y) * ReadLength(Y));}};

void _tmain(void) {
DerivedClass* Instance = new DerivedClass(5, 6);
Console::WriteLine(DerivedClass::ReadWidth(Instance));
Console::WriteLine(DerivedClass::ReadLength(Instance));
DerivedClass::DisplayArea(Instance);  }
```

Using Multiply Linked Single-Inheritance

Once an inherited class is developed it too becomes subject to the renderings of yet another inherited class. The combined attributes then also become part of the third object with the exception of the constructor functions and the assignment statements since neither of these are passed to an inheriting class. Again, the level of access granted to the inheriting class is primarily based on the security established by the specified members. Once a secondary inherited class is established it too becomes subject to other potentially inherited classes and again all security levels are enforced (see Example 6.36).

Example 6.36. Single inheritance.

```
/* Linking Classes */
#include "stdafx.h"
#using <mscorlib.dll>
```

184

```
#include <tchar.h>
using namespace System;

__gc public class BaseClass {
protected : short Width, Length;
protected : BaseClass() {}
protected : BaseClass(short w, short l) {Width = w; Length = l;}
public : static short ReadWidth(BaseClass* X)
{return (X->Width);}
public : static short ReadLength(BaseClass* X)
{return(X->Length);}};

__gc public class DerivedClass : public BaseClass {
protected : DerivedClass() {}
protected : DerivedClass(short w, short l) {
Width = w; Length = l;}
protected : static void DisplayArea(DerivedClass* Y)
{Console::Write("Area = ");
Console::WriteLine (Y->Width*Y->Length);}};

__gc public class DerivedX : public DerivedClass
{public : DerivedX(short w, short l) {Width = w; Length = l;}
public : static void DisplayArea(DerivedX* Z)
{Console::Write ("Area = ");
Console::WriteLine (Z->Width*Z->Length);}
public : static void Triangle(DerivedX* Z)
{Console::Write("The Area of the Triangle is ");
Console::WriteLine(.5*Z->Width*Z->Length);}};

void _tmain(void) {
DerivedX* Instance = new DerivedX(5, 6);
Console::WriteLine(DerivedX::ReadWidth(Instance));
Console::WriteLine(DerivedX::ReadLength(Instance));
DerivedX::DisplayArea(Instance);
DerivedX::Triangle(Instance);}
```

Overriding & Virtual Methods

   In addition to being able to overload a functions (as into changed the signature or parameters of that function), we can also override a function so as to force the compiler to except a secondary version of that function. As its name implies the keyword override is used to override members inherited from a base class. These inherited methods must have matching signatures and be either virtual, abstract, or previously overridden. This technique also allows us to manipulate that programs data so as to give it the illusion of consistency or to save us the trouble of revising our previous class. The secondary version then would become the obvious choice as our instance was declared as part of that inherited class. On a cautionary note, it should also be mentioned that if any of our overriding functions had also referenced their base version (as is commonly done with our privately inherited classes), that function's reference would then be diverted back to the inherited function. Note: we can also return access to the original method via the *base* command.

Following this same line of reasoning, we might mistakenly conclude that privately passed inherited classes are only accessible through internal use as with predicate and/or other unity type functions. This however is not the case, since all the techniques used to access a standard yet privately controlled class are also available to us from within our derived class. Once a need for a privately inherited class is established, the approach then would be to create a set of member functions that relied on indirect access thus creating a relay from our inherited to our base functions, hence the Set methods…

The keyword virtual denotes a modifier that sets a method of a base class so that it can be overridden in a derived class. When a *virtual* function is referenced it searches for an overriding method. Overriding, as was explained earlier, force the compiler to except a secondary version of that function as related to a secondary/ inherited class. Overriding, as was explained earlier, force the compiler to except a secondary version of that function as related to a secondary/ inherited class. The polymorphic affect then is said to be accomplished at run-time (or what is known as through late binding) rather then at compilation (or what is referred to as early binding), as was the case with operator and member style overloading. *Virtual* functions are declared using the standard member's only declaration preceded by the keyword *virtual*, neither constructors nor friend functions can be accessed using this method, but *virtual* destructors are allowed (see example 6.37). Note: In contrast to the definition of an overloading function, a function that is overridden must include an identical list of parameters.

> Note:
> Inherited classes that do not include properly overwritten virtual functions are then subject to the default virtual functions included in their base classes. If a multilevel inherited class cannot find a properly declared virtual function, it may mistakenly revert through each inherited class until an appropriate function is found.

Example 6.37. Single inheritance II.

```
/* Linking Classes II */
#include "stdafx.h"
#using <mscorlib.dll>
#include <tchar.h>
using namespace System;

__gc public class Area {
public :
short Base, Height;
double Radius;
short Base2;

public : Area() {}
public : Area(short w, short h)
{Base = w; Height = h;}
public : Area(double r) {Radius = r;}
public : Area(short a, short b, short h)
{Base = a; Base2 = b; Height = h;}

public : static short ReadBase(Area* X)
{return(X->Base);}
public : static void SetBase(Area* X, short a)
{X->Base = a;}
public : static void SetBase2(Area* X, short b)
```

```
{X->Base2 = b;}
public : static short ReadHeight(Area* X)
{return(X->Height);}
public : static void SetHeight(Area* X, short h)
{X->Height = h;}
public : static double ReadRadius(Area* X)
{return(X->Radius);}
public : static void SetRadius(Area* X, double r)
{X->Radius = r;}
public : static double SumOfBases(Area* X)
{return(X->Base+X->Base2);}
public : virtual void CalculateArea()
{Console::WriteLine("No Shape Found\n");}};

__gc public class Parallelogram: public Area {
public : Parallelogram(short w, short l) {
SetBase(this, w); SetHeight(this, l);}
public : void CalculateArea()
{Console::Write("Area  = ");
Console::WriteLine (ReadBase(this)*ReadHeight(this));}};

__gc public class Triangle : public Area {
public : Triangle(short w, short l)
{SetBase(this, w); SetHeight(this, l);}
public : void CalculateArea()
{Console::Write ("\n Area = ");
Console::WriteLine(ReadBase(this)*ReadHeight(this)/2);}      };

__gc public class Circle : public Area {
public : double PI;
public : Circle(double r)
{PI = 3.14159265358979323846264338327950; SetRadius(this, r);}
public : void CalculateArea()
{Console::Write("\n Area = ");
Console::WriteLine ((PI)*ReadRadius(this)*ReadRadius(this));}};

__gc public class Trapezoid : public Area {
public : Trapezoid(short a, short b, short h) {
SetBase(this, a);
SetBase2(this, b);
SetHeight(this, h);}
public : void CalculateArea()
{Console::Write("\n Area = ");
Console::WriteLine(ReadHeight(this)*(SumOfBases(this))/2);}

public : static void CalculateArea(Area* Relay)
{Relay->CalculateArea();}};

void _tmain(void) {
Area* Shape = new Area();

Parallelogram* Shape1 = new Parallelogram(5, 5);
```

```
Shape1->CalculateArea();

Parallelogram* Shape2 = new Parallelogram(5, 6);
Shape2->CalculateArea();

Triangle* Shape3 = new Triangle(5, 6);
Shape3->CalculateArea();

Circle* Shape4 = new Circle(3);
Shape4->CalculateArea();

Trapezoid* Shape5 = new Trapezoid(4, 5, 6);
Shape5->CalculateArea(); }
```

Inheriting *virtual* functions are also considered *virtual* by default, thus the use of the keyword *virtual* is considered optional and is generally only restated for program clarity. The application then of a *virtual* function should include some type of generalized retrieving notation…

Abstraction Continued:

As was stated and restated throughout this chapter, our primary goal is to develop abstract objected-oriented classes, which will be used as both a foundation and a reusable base that will move us into the higher levels of programming. Our development of classes then must include completely abstracted versions of both our member functions and their variables. Base classes then would be capable of adapting to a host of scenarios that would include creating instances that could calculate either whole of floating-point values, defining Boolean types and reference characters without the need to revise our coding. This should be your continuing goal both while studying C# and once you begin to work in the field.

Exception Handling

Another important feature that helps to perfect our programs is the ability to catch exception errors. Exception errors are errors thrown by our program/Windows during execution and can range from simple input errors to problems such as missing files, division by zero… All questionable coding then is placed inside of what is known as a *try*-block, this is a block of coding that may or may not succeed. If this coding does fail then the program immediately turns to one or an assortment of *catch*-blocks, which can also be either general or specific. Upon completion of either the *try* or the *catch*-block a tertiary block is executed this one is known as the __finally block, the finally-block is always executed with the termination of this set of coding (see Examples 6.40 & 6.41).

Example 6.40. Exception Handling –General.
```
/* General catch */
#include "stdafx.h"
#using <mscorlib.dll>
#include <tchar.h>
using namespace System;

int _tmain(void) {
  int eight = 8, zero = 0;
```

```
try
{Console::WriteLine(eight/zero);}
catch(System::Exception*)
{Console::WriteLine("Error Detected");}
__finally{Console::WriteLine("Program Complete!");}}
```

Example 6.41. Exception Handling –Specific.
```
/* Specific Catch */
#include "stdafx.h"
#using <mscorlib.dll>
#include <tchar.h>
using namespace System;

int _tmain(void) {
int eight = 8, zero = 0;

try
{Console::WriteLine(eight/zero);}
catch(System::ArithmeticException*)
{Console::WriteLine("Error Detected");}
__finally{Console::WriteLine("Program Complete!");}}
```

__except

In addition to the try/catch block, there is also the __try/__except block and the __leave command. Here we'll be using the Microsoft specific version of the try command. While _try and try are basically the same, the new components __except and __leave require its specifications. __except has three orders that can be followed. (-1) EXCEPTION_CONTINUE_EXECUTION: Dismisses the exception and continues the execution at the point where the exception occurred. (0) EXCEPTION_CONTINUE_SEARCH: Recognizes the exception, but then looks for a try-catch sequence or for the handler with the highest precedence. And (1) The exception is recognized and control is transferred to the exception handler with the exception sequence is executed (see Example 6.42).

Example 6.42. Exceptions.
```
/* __except */
#include "stdafx.h"
#using <mscorlib.dll>
#include <tchar.h>
using namespace System;

int _tmain(void) {
 int eight = 8, zero = 0;

__try{Console::WriteLine(zero/zero);}
__except(1){
Console::WriteLine("0/0 = 1");}}
```

__Leave is used like an escape command allowing us to jump out of the try statement (see Example 6.43).

Example 6.43. __leave.
```
/*  __leave */
#include "stdafx.h"
#using <mscorlib.dll>
#include <tchar.h>
using namespace System;

int _tmain(void) {
int eight = 8, zero = 0;

__try
{__leave;
Console::WriteLine(eight/zero);}
__finally{Console::WriteLine("Program Complete!");}}
```

Nested *try*-blocks

In addition to creating simple try-block structures we can also nest those structures to protect against a host of errors and/or deliberately flawed user inputs (see Example 6.44).

> Note:
> The *null* reference refers to an object that has not yet been assigned, it basically serves as a blank or non-value, which can be substituted for later. It is also the default value to any non-assigned reference-types and it can be used to mark a position where no actual reference is needed.

Example 6.44. Nested try-blocks.
```
/* Nested try-blocks */
#include "stdafx.h"
#using <mscorlib.dll>
#include <tchar.h>
using namespace System;

void _tmain(void) {
int X, Y;
Console::WriteLine("Let's divide some numbers...");

while(true)
{Console::Write("Enter your numerator now: ");
X = (Console::ReadLine())->ToInt32(0);
Console::Write("Enter your denominator now: ");
Y = (Console::ReadLine())->ToInt32(0);

try {Console::WriteLine(X/Y);}
catch(System::ArithmeticException*)
{Console::WriteLine("Division by Zero Attempted!\n");
Console::Write("Please enter a new denominator now: ");
Y = Console::ReadLine()->ToInt32(0);
```

```
try {Console::WriteLine(X/Y);}
catch(System::ArithmeticException*) {
  Console::WriteLine("Error!");
      break;}}
catch(System::Exception*)
{Console::WriteLine("Error Detected");}}}
```

The Keyword *throw*

In addition to being able to catch both generalize and specific exceptions, we can also learn to throw a few of our own. This is not usually necessary for the contexts of this book, but the technique can serve to clarify the definitions of some otherwise confusing errors (see Example 6.45).

Example 6.45. Clarifying our exceptions.
```
/* Clarifying our Exceptions */
#include "stdafx.h"
#using <mscorlib.dll>
#include <tchar.h>
using namespace System;

int _tmain(void) {
String* Input;
 int X, Y;
Console::WriteLine("Let's divide some numbers...");

while(true)
{Console::Write("Enter your numerator now: ");
Input = Console::ReadLine();
if(Char::IsNumber(Input, 0))
{X = Input->ToInt32(0);}
else
{throw new System::ArgumentException("\nProgram Error!");}

Console::Write("Enter your denominator now: ");
Input = Console::ReadLine();

if(Char::IsNumber(Input, 0))
{Y = Input->ToInt32(0);}
else
{throw new DivideByZeroException("\nProgram Error!");}

try {Console::WriteLine(X/Y);}
catch(System::ArithmeticException*)
{Console::WriteLine("Division by Zero attempted!\n");
Console::Write("Please enter a new denominator now: ");
Y = (Console::ReadLine())->ToInt32(0);
try{Console::WriteLine(X/Y);}
catch(System::ArithmeticException*) {
```

```
Console::WriteLine("Error!");
break;}}
catch(System::Exception*)
{Console::WriteLine("Error Detected");}}}
```

User-Defined Exception Classes

Occasionally, we'll also want to define our own exception classes, these are special case exceptions that may require additional information and/or input... An exception class is an inherited class that is derived (either directly or indirectly) from form a key base class (namely System.ApplicationException). In all other respects an exception class mimics the rules of a standard inherited class (see Example 5.46).

Example 5.46. User-defined exceptions.
```
/* User-Defined Exceptions */
#include "stdafx.h"
#using <mscorlib.dll>
#include <tchar.h>
using namespace System;

void _tmain(void) {
String* Input;
 int X, Y;

Console::WriteLine("Let's divide some numbers...");

while(true)
{Console::Write("Enter your numerator now: ");
Input = Console::ReadLine();

if(Char::IsNumber(Input, 0))
{X = Input->ToInt32(0);}
else
{throw new IndexOutOfRangeException("\nCharacter Detected where Integer
Value was Excepted!");}

Console::Write("Enter your denominator now: ");
Input = Console::ReadLine();

if(Char::IsNumber(Input, 0))
{Y = Input->ToInt32(0);}
else
{throw new System::IndexOutOfRangeException("\nCharacter Detected where
Integer Value was Excepted!");}

try {Console::WriteLine(X/Y);}
catch(System::ArithmeticException*)
{Console::WriteLine("Division by Zero attempted!\n");
Console::Write("Please enter a new denominator now: ");
Y = (Console::ReadLine())->ToChar(0);
```

```
try{Console::WriteLine(X/Y);}
catch(System::ArithmeticException*) {
Console::WriteLine("Error!");
break;}}
catch(System::Exception*) {
Console::WriteLine("Error Detected");}}}
```

Delegates

Delegates are objects used as references to encapsulate specific methods, which include signatures and formal return types. The __delegate, while similar to the C++ function pointer, is actually type safe and considered OOP (Object-Oriented Programming) compliant. Delegates also allow for both private and public access (the default of private is assumed if no class-visibility-specifier is given). Delegates are most frequently used to pass methods as parameters. Type safety is based on the matching of signatures as part of their declaration—delegates need to be declared before they are called, they are multicast, and are supported through managed extensions. Their returning value can be of any type, but they cannot be overloaded (see Example 6.47).

Example 6.47. A simple delegate.
```
/* A simple delegate */
#include "stdafx.h"
#using <mscorlib.dll>
#include <tchar.h>
using namespace System;
// Prototype
public __delegate void TryDelegate();

static void TryDelegate() {
 Console::WriteLine("Hello World!");
}

void _tmain(void) {
 TryDelegate();
}
```

Events

Events are used to pass information between delegates; they can be applied to method declaration, interface declaration, and data member de4claration. They are null before they're referenced, and their metadata describes their type, raised class, and the methods used to add and remove their handlers. Events are used to specify delegates and are referenced at runtime; they can include multiple methods, and are applicable to other programs (see Example 6.48).

Example 6.48. Events.
```
/* Events */
#include "stdafx.h"
#using <mscorlib.dll>
#include <tchar.h>
```

```
using namespace System;

public __gc class Events {
public : __event void MyEvent();
};

void _tmain(void) {
}
```

Trouble Shooting

If you've gotten the previous programs to run, but you're having trouble with these new ones, then the problem must be in the setup. Trying going back over the steps and repeating those steps for the earlier games. You might also want to try including all the classes as part of the same file, if the combine file runs correctly than there must be something wrong with the way your setting up the secondary files.

Questions

1. Build a simple structure then reference it form the main method, then using public fields rebuild that structure as a class.
2. Form question 2, convert that classes public fields into protected field (build as many secondary methods as you'll need to get the job done).
3. Form question 3, convert those fields into private members, (hint you may need to ad additional methods?
4. Write a class that allows for both overloaded arithmetic and comparison operators.
5. Write a simple public-nested class, and then replace that nested class with an inherited class.

PART THREE

GRAPHIC PROGRAMMING BASICS

Chapter Seven

"The marble not yet carved can hold the form of every thought the greatest artist has."
- Michelangelo

Writing Our First Game

Before we can write a program, game or otherwise, we must first have an idea of what our program is going to be about. Next, we'll have to develop our idea using a list of thoughts usually expanding in phases and always increasing in detail. As we progress, we'll also want to turn those thoughts into a formal document or algorithm. This algorithm could then be enhanced both logically and pictorially through the use of mathematical and graphical designs. For the beginner this usually means peeking into the C# language, but for the moment we won't really begin to write too it. In gaming terms, this also often requires the ability to draw or the enlistment of a graphic artist, but for these examples, we'll rely primarily on simple mouse and hand drawn graphics. In addition, when we do begin to convert to coding, we'll also want to develop our tasks using the simplest coding possible, but with the added criteria that it should be generic in nature. Remember, the higher the level of abstraction the greater the level of reusability.

Brainstorming

Brainstorming is the first creative step. It's nothing more than throwing out ideas, but it's also the foundation for everything that follows. Here's a sample of what we might write if we were planning to create a sports game like paddle tennis, which in fact we're about to do (see example 3.1).

Example 3.1:

Notes:

1. The paddle tennis game should have two players. One placed on the right, the other to the left.
2. There should be a net that divides the screen vertically.
3. The players should move freely as in up, down, left, and right, but they should not be allowed to leave the screen or cross over to the other player's side.
4. There would be a ball that bounces around, which the players can hit back and forth, with the upper and lower limits used to simulate the ground.
5. The ball can increase in size when it's moving closer to the net, thus simulating a 3D environment.
6. When one player misses the ball, the other player should get a point and/or win the serve.
7. The game should start with a simple menu that allows our players to select the type of game as in two players, one player, or demo mode. (Note: Our one player and demo modes will also mean that we'll have to write some simple artificial intelligence coding).
8. The game should also allow our players to quit at any time via the ESC key. Asking the players if they're sure they want too quit before actually ending the program could also be an option.
9. The game should be colorful with a blue background, yellow net and two brightly dressed characters (it would be best if the tennis ball actually looked like a tennis ball).
10. The game should also have sounds when the ball hits the ground (edges of the screen) and/or the players. There should also be a cheer from the unseen viewers when a player scores.
11. You may also want to put in a timer that automatically starts at least the demo mode if

nothing happens for say two minutes.

12. Finally, the game should reset itself, so as to allow for repeated play.

Drawing Characters

Now that we have a general idea of what we'll need pictorially, we'll have to convert those ideas into actual illustrations and then we'll have the fun task of figuring out how those images are going to be manipulated. The actual designs aren't really that important, but the steps used to access and complete those designs are. The first step then would be to formalize ourselves with how the graphic tools work in this new environment. Note: If you're not an artist not to worry, the CD-ROM includes a complete list of pre-drawn images relating to all of the games listed.

To begin, I'll assume you're sitting in front of your computer with your .Net compiler fully loaded and that you have already selected both the "New Project" listing and the "Windows Application" icon (Note: do not confuse this application with the console version used in the pervious chapters). Now change the name of the project to "Chapter3" and press "OK" (see screen shots 3.1 through 3.3).

Screen Shot 3.1   Screen Shot 3.2

Screen Shot 3.3

Note: The first screen you'll see is only the visual portion of our program, to open the text portion, simply double click onto that grid (see example 3.2).

Example 3.2:

```
using System;
using System.Drawing;
using System.Collections;
using System.ComponentModel;
using System.Windows.Forms;
using System.Data;

namespace Chapter3
{public class Form1: System.Windows.Forms.Form
{private System.ComponentModel.Container components = null;

public Form1 ()
{InitializeComponent ();}

#region Windows Form Designer generated code
private void InitializeComponent ()
{this.AutoScaleBaseSize = new System.Drawing.Size (5, 13);
this.ClientSize = new System.Drawing.Size (292, 266);
this.Name = "Form1";
this.Text = "Form1";
this.Load += new System.EventHandler (this.Form1_Load) ;}
#endregion

[STAThread]
static void Main ()
{Application.Run (new Form1 ());}

private void Form1_Load (object sender, System.EventArgs e)
{}}}
```

Next, we'll want to open a new graphics file. To create such a file simply click the "File" menu and select "New" and then the secondary "File" listing. A second window labeled "New File" should appear with a host of options, select the icon titled "Bitmap File" and then press "Open" (see screen shots 3.4 & 3.5).

Screen Shot 3.4

Screen Shot 3.5

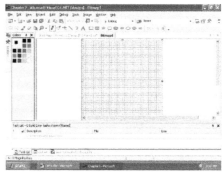

From this point, we'd simply want to use these tools in basically the same manner as any other graphics program, in fact if you'd prefer you could run all your designs through an alternative program just as long as you make those files available to your project(s). The three characters we'll concern ourselves with then are the two players and their tennis ball. To shortcut this further, we'll assume that the two players will just be the reverse of each other (see screen shots 3.6 – 3.8).

Screen Shot 3.6

Screen Shot 3.7

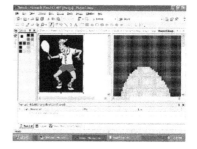

Screen Shot 3.8

Plotting Motions

The next step then will be to plot the motions of our players and their ball. The player's movements are a bit easier to define so we'll discuss those first. The players or at least the characters representing our players should have free and easy two-dimensional movement. Their playing field should be limited to the screen size and they should not be allowed to cross into the other player's area (see example 3.3).

Example 3.3:

One-dimensional movement

Two-dimensional movement

The ball, unlike the players, also requires us to include diagonal movements, which technically are still only two-dimensional movements, but the added visual effect is important when conveying the feel of free motion. This however, will still only total six directions, since we won't allow the ball to travel directly up or directly down (see example 3.4).

Example 3.4:

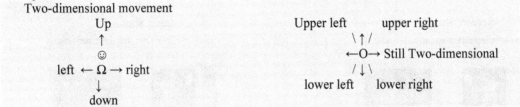

Again, the ball should not be allowed to move outside the viewable screen and it should also bounce off our characters. When the ball is missed, it should automatically reset to the scorers side and from the scoring players position. Finally, the balls initial motion will be decided by a random motion function as in *Random () rnd = new Random ()*. Note: We'll also want to add a random change of motion as the players interact with the ball and potentially we may allow the players to alter the ball's path by striking it form different angles.

Writing Our First Algorithm

After brainstorming, choosing characters, and plotting their motions the next logical step then would be to weave those images into a program document or algorithm. An algorithm, as introduced in chapter one, is an abstract yet detailed list of everything that needs to occur inside our programs. Since this is only a quick look at algorithms and since there are still several programming aspects that haven't been explained, we'll once again, not worry too much about completely defining all the details that make up this program. Eventually however, when our programs actually necessitate an algorithmic breakdown, we'll want to include all such details (see example 3.5).

Example 3.5:
Again, this is an older C++ algorithm and not all the methods will apply directly, yet the steps used to create the program tend to remain the same.
1. *Create a viable Windows handle accessible through the Windows console setting. Declare the handle as both read and write enabled with a call to maximize the screen size. Place this handle in a shared file namely games.cpp. Also, create a program that acts as a menu to our games. This initial program will be used to set the screen size and to access the game subprograms, starting with our first game "paddle tennis."*
2. *Write a function to draw the players' characters: This function has three steps, first it gives the computer our characters' coordinates, and then it moves the cursor to those coordinates. Finally, it displays our character(s) at those coordinates (ultimately, we'll want to use this function with all of our character driven games).*
3. *We'll also need to include a function that paints/clears the screen: Although this technique is a bit cumbersome it also tends to be necessary when dealing with console programs, especially when used to change the color of a background or when erasing a large portion of the screen.*
Referring to games.h;
4. *We'll define most of our variables as class members with the notable exception of the color settings. For example, we'll want to build off of Window's basic BACKGROUND and FOREGROUND RED, BLUE, and GREEN, with the added assignments of YELLOW, ORANGE, and PURPLE...*
Referring to tennis.cpp;

5. *Setting the variables/members: Just as with any other program, we'll have a set of variables that need to be assigned values. A few of these will be assigned at the beginning of the main program, but for practical reasons the rest will be placed at the start of our games do-while loop.*
6. *Setting the ball to a random direction: When converting directions to coding I often use the numeric keypads layout as my foundation (4 equals left, 6 is right, 8 is up, 2 is down and so on). If we apply this technique to a function such as srand () and a random number count form 1 to 9 our game ball will then seem to have random motion.*
7. *Create a while-loop that ends when the game ends: Game loops are real-time loops that <u>are not</u> dependent on the users action, thus there's no grantee that the loop will ever end. However, at the same time when the loop does end it should end in a structured manner and it should give the player the option of playing again or quitting (remember not repeating the loop also mean a return to our main menu).*

Inside the while loop

8. *Call a function that removes all residual images using a combination of calls to blank characters and/or a full-blown clear screen function.*
9. *Set the colors: (since these colors never change this can be done from either the do-while or internal while loop).Later games will require multiple color references.*
10. *Display the players, ball, and the scores (0 to 0 as we start): There are actually five function calls listed here, two for the players, one for the ball, and two for the scores. When called they tell the computer to reprint the erased objects.*
11. *Call a function that reads the players input from the keyboard (located under games2.cpp). Everything inside a real-time loop is made non-input dependent, that means that the loop will continue whether our players play or not. Since standard cin and scanf functions inherently lock-up our programs neither of these can be used. Under our console setting a combination of kbhit() and getch() are used to access player inputs (later we'll learn additional input methods).*
12. *Write a function to propel the ball. As explained in an earlier section the ball will move in one of six directions. This function then modifies the balls location continually in one of those direction based on the selected path. (Note: The function's call should be subject to that balls activation).*
13. *Write a function to limit the area in which the players can traverse. This is our first case of collision detection and as such, we'll make it simple. The characters our placed on the screen based on preset location. When the player inputs a movement, the program processes that movement by adding or subtracting one unit of distance from that player's location. This distance is based on a general understanding that the first space of the first line is coordinate (0, 0). Since the player is now confined to a mathematical grid, we can "lock him down" by not allowing those values to increase or decrease beyond a certain point. The ball works in a similar manner with its deflection being based on a change in path rather than resetting its location.*
14. *We should include sounds when the ball bounces: Sound effects are simple, but important –an enhancement that really makes a big difference in game programming. All the games have there own pre-recorded sounds, but you're welcome to replace them with your own.*
15. *Check to see if the ball and players have collided (collision detection II). The ball will bounce off the player: The actions of the ball on the playing characters would be identical to that of the ball and the wall if not for the additional patterns and added randomness of srand. We've also considered allowing the playing characters to alter the balls course by hitting it form an angle, but we won't discuss how to implement such details until we're in the programming stage.*
16. *If the ball gets to the end of the screen and the player is not there give the other player a point. Now, reset the ball: To add a scoring point we simply increment the players score, but before restarting or redrawing the ball, we'll have to reset/reassign its location to the other player's side. To make things simple we'll just use the scoring player's last position and the spacebar as the shared serving key.*
17. *Repeat the loop until either player scores five points: We'll terminate either the loop on request or when a certain score is reached. Here, we'll also use the two-point rule (explained in coding).*
18. *Ask the player(s) if they want to play again: Remember a good game loop should always allow the player(s) the option of playing again.*
19. *End or repeat game: Ending the gaming loop in our case means ending the game and returning to the menu portion. This then allows the users to either quit the program or continue into another game.*

> <u>Note</u>: When thinking of how we might implement those functions using a C# model, it becomes obvious that the most direct solution would be to convert those tools into methods (methods are functions that are called from the vantage point of a class). Expanding our classes to include multiple tasks also gives them a greater level of control, as well as, a more

practical sense of reusability.

Displaying Graphics –Using Native C++

Once we've completed our drawings and have a basic sense of motion, we'll want to include the appropriate coding as in the visual parameters, setups, and system calls… These commands should seem almost simplistic however, when they're compared to the monstrosity known as the Window's API standard. Of course, the original coding for these games was written in the good old console version of C++, where animation meant reposition our block characters using a COORD command (which stood for coordinates as in the x-y or Cartesian coordinate system) and then setting our window to that position using the "SetConsoleCursorPosition" function. Of course, that also meant that we had too repeatedly remove the previous image and redisplay the new characters to actually see the animation, but that was then and this is now.

Displaying Graphics –Using C#

Despite the advances, we'll still need to understand the basic Cartesian coordinate system, at lest as it pertains to our screen. Here the values start as zeros at the upper left-hand corner and increase both to the right and downward as is shown in example 3.6.

Example 3.6:

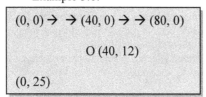

The value of x increases as the ball travels to the right and decreases as it travels back to the left. The value of y behaves in basically the same manner only traveling down as its value increases and up as it moves closer to zero. Thus with a combination of these points our characters can travel anywhere on the screen (see example 3.7).

Example 3.7:

```
/* Animation Test 1 */
using System;
using System.Drawing;
using System.Collections;
using System.ComponentModel;
using System.Windows.Forms;
using System.Data;
using System.IO;
using System.Runtime.InteropServices;

namespace Games
```

```
{public class PaddleTennis : System.Windows.Forms.Form
  {private System.ComponentModel.Container components = null;

Objects Projectiles = new Objects (650, 225, 4, 0, 0, true);
Image DisplayTennisBall;

public PaddleTennis()
{InitializeComponent () ;}

protected override void Dispose( bool disposing )
{if( disposing )
{if (components != null)
{components.Dispose();}}
base.Dispose( disposing );}

#region Windows Form Designer generated code
private void InitializeComponent()
{this.AutoScaleBaseSize = new System.Drawing.Size (5, 13);
this.ClientSize = new System.Drawing.Size (780, 550);
this.Name = "Paddle Tennis";
this.Text = "Paddle Tennis";
this.Load += new System.EventHandler (this.PaddleTennis_Load);
this.BackColor = Color.Blue;

DisplayTennisBall = Image.FromFile
(@"c:\Games.Net\Tennis\TennisBall.Bmp");
this.AutoScrollMinSize = DisplayTennisBall.Size;

Timer Clock = new Timer ();
Clock.Interval = 60;
Clock.Start ();
Clock.Tick += new EventHandler (Ball_Click);}
#endregion

protected override void OnPaint(PaintEventArgs e)
{Graphics Figures = this.CreateGraphics ();
this.Show ();

Graphics dc = e.Graphics;
if (Projectiles.Active == true)
dc.DrawImage (DisplayTennisBall, Projectiles.X.ReadValue (),
Projectiles.Y.ReadValue (), 25, 25);
base.OnPaint (e) ;}

public void Tennis()
{InitializeComponent () ;}

[STAThread]
static void Main()
{Application.Run (new PaddleTennis ()) ;}

public void Ball_Click(object sender, System.EventArgs e)
```

```
{if (Projectiles.Active == true)
{for (int i = 0; i < 3; i++)
{Projectiles.AnimateObject ();
Invalidate () ;}}}

private void PaddleTennis_Load(object sender, System.EventArgs e)
{}}}
```

Note: This program requires class references as explained in the next two sections.

Introducing Object-Oriented Programming

In order to understand the concepts behind the development of object-oriented programming, we must first discuss the principles behind its predecessors as in top-down design, structured programming, and modular programming. Top-down design was a liner approach to programming wherein you basically started at the top and worked your way down, whereas structured programming was more of a systematic approach to problem solving based primarily on the idea of *divido et vinco* (divide and conquer). This process then allowed the programmer to develop larger and more complex programs, but it did not initially allow for reuse without modification. Structured programming complemented top-down design and also lead us to a concept known as generic coding. The combined power of structured programming and generic coding also allowed for the re-stringing of functions to solve additional problems. Modular programming was also developed as an expansion to structured programming allowing for the linkage of files and generically coded subprograms, but this too fell short of meeting the demands placed on today's programmers.

Object-oriented programming is then both a collection of the aforementioned techniques and a progression from object-based programs to object driven programs. Generically written structure and then classes became the emphasis, and objects became the guiding tool used by most programmers. Classes then took on a new approach that included friend and member functions (and now what is referred to as methods) to create a generic framework that can be applied to a multitude of tasks. Inheritance was developed along with a slue of new methodologies and concepts. In this new framework, variables are often replaced by class members and functions by methods. While the coding that defines these objects won't actually be discussed until chapter five, the practical applications that allow for their use will be implemented here. This is possible though the use of the black box method applied to both members and methods (again, see chapter five for details).

Adding Files to Our Projects

Too properly implement the previous program we must first transfer its supplemental files to the appropriate main or subdirectory. This can be done through a simple copy and paste procedure as explained below.

Adding Files to our Projects:
1. Locate the files required by our project (namely this books CD-ROM's source code files referenced in the previous sections). (Note: The necessary files are bundled as part of chapter three's "AnimationTest1").
2. Select and copy the required files as shown in screen shot 3.9 (this will include class1.cs through class5.cs, Player1.bmp, Player2.bmp, TennisBall.bmp...).
3. Open the appropriate directory and paste those files to that directory (this is the directory usually created by the compiler as part of your current project – see screen shot 3.10).

Screen Shot 3.9:   Screen Shot 3.10

Next, we'll need to link these files to our current project. (Note: Included files such as "headers" do not exist in C#). Continuing from 3…

4.   From the C#'s compiler's menu select "<u>F</u>ile" and then the attribute labeled "Add existing item(s)..." Depressing that attribute will bring up the corresponding menu namely "Add existing item – *YourProjectsNameHere*" again make sure to repeat these steps for each item added (see screen shot 3.11).

Screen Shot 3.11:

Programming Our First Character

<u>Real Time Game Programming Basics:</u>
   In the older C++ model we used simple commands like Kbhit() and getch(), which were also the real time equivalents to both cin >> and scanf(), since C# also allows for quick and easy access to both console and windows type applications, we can progress quite easily into "OnKeyDown" and "OnKeyPress" type examples. These Window's commands allow for multitasking or what beginner game programmers might call basic real time programming. "Real time" being the continuation of actions within a particular time frame without regard for the users' response.

Our second step then will be to animate our first character. This is done through a combination of both our "OnPaint" and our "OnKeyDown" commands. We'll once again use the incrementing operator to change our characters position, but this time we'll also need to include the decrementing operator for reversing that motion (remember both of those example are bundle within our first class namely Class1.cs Objects – see chapter 5 for details). We'll use the arrow keys to control our characters as in up, down, left, and right (see examples 3.8 & 3.9).

Example 3.8:

```
protected override void OnKeyDown(KeyEventArgs e)
{string input = e.KeyData.ToString();

switch (input)
{case "Down":
Human.Vector.SetValue (2);
break;

case "Left":
Human.Vector.SetValue (4);
break;

case "Right":
Human.Vector.SetValue (6);
break;

case "Up":
Human.Vector.SetValue (8);
break;}

Human.AnimateObject ();
Human.DeflectPlayers ();

if(Projectiles.Active == false)
Invalidate ();}
```

Example 3.9:

```
/* Animation Test II */
using System;
using System.Drawing;
using System.Collections;
using System.ComponentModel;
using System.Windows.Forms;
using System.Data;
using System.IO;
using System.Runtime.InteropServices;

namespace Games
{public class PaddleTennis : System.Windows.Forms.Form
{private System.ComponentModel.Container components = null;

Objects Human = new Objects (680, 225, 0, 1, 0, true);
Objects Projectile = new Objects (0, 0, 0, 0, 0, false);

Image DisplayHuman;
```

```csharp
public PaddleTennis()
{InitializeComponent () ;}

protected override void Dispose( bool disposing )
{if( disposing )
{if (components != null)
{components.Dispose();}}
base.Dispose( disposing );}

#region Windows Form Designer generated code
private void InitializeComponent()
{this.AutoScaleBaseSize = new System.Drawing.Size (5, 13);
this.ClientSize = new System.Drawing.Size (780, 550);
this.Name = "Paddle Tennis";
this.Text = "Paddle Tennis";
this.Load += new System.EventHandler (this.PaddleTennis_Load);

this.BackColor = Color.Blue;
DisplayHuman = Image.FromFile (@"c:\Games.Net\Tennis\Player2.bmp");
this.AutoScrollMinSize = DisplayHuman.Size ;}
#endregion

protected override void OnPaint(PaintEventArgs e)
{{Graphics Figures = this.CreateGraphics ();
this.Show ();
Graphics dc = e.Graphics;
dc.DrawImage (DisplayHuman, Human.X.ReadValue (),
Human.Y.ReadValue (), 100, 100);
base.OnPaint (e) ;}}
```

Note:
> The player's input is the data gathered by the OnKeyDown Command. This is translated into movements by the computer and it is what allows us to change the direction of the character. The player's x and y components indicate the player's current position. The initial settings would place our first character at about eye level but to the right of the screen (as in the accompanying sketch).

(577, 220) ☺
Ω

```csharp
// Insert Example protected override void OnKeyDown (KeyEventArgs e)

public void Tennis()
{InitializeComponent () ;}

[STAThread]
static void Main()
{Application.Run (new PaddleTennis ()) ;}
```

```
private void PaddleTennis_Load(object sender, System.EventArgs e)
{}}}
```

Erasing Residual Images

Erasing residual images is an important step in the creation of the illusion of animations; each character then must be erased before its temporal counterpart can be displayed. This process is usually handled through the invalidation of a rectangle or defined area. The actual work or process is handled by Windows, but the referencing of that system is done from within our programs. Surprisingly enough, we've already included an invalidating reference, which is almost plugged in without thought. Yet, there should also be a set of cautions that come with this reference, since the overuse of invalidating commands will cause undue flickering and possibly make our games unplayable. For an intermediate reference, we'll also want to localize our rectangles, which will also reduce overall flickering (this will become especially important when we're working with more complex games).

Our third step then, although slightly out of phase with our algorithm, will be to demonstrate these techniques. This task could be accomplished in a number of ways, but to get the best results as in little flickering as possible, we'll have to use our invalidation command sparingly, and thus we'll only call that command when a change in imagery is absolutely necessary. For example if the ball is active we'll have to call it, and if a player moves to a new position we'll have to call it, but if the ball is in motion and the player moves, only the predominating ball movement needs to invalidate the screen, since the entire screen will still be updated (see example 3.10).

Example 3.10:

```
protected override void OnKeyPress(KeyPressEventArgs e)
{switch (char.ToUpper(e.KeyChar))
{case '1':
Human.Vector.SetValue (1);
goto AnimateHuman;

case '2':
Human.Vector.SetValue (2);
goto AnimateHuman;

case '3':
Human.Vector.SetValue (3);
goto AnimateHuman;

case '4':
Human.Vector.SetValue (4);
goto AnimateHuman;

case '6':
Human.Vector.SetValue (6);
goto AnimateHuman;

case '7':
Human.Vector.SetValue (7);
goto AnimateHuman;
```

```
case '8':
Human.Vector.SetValue (8);
goto AnimateHuman;

case '9':
Human.Vector.SetValue (9);
AnimateHuman:
Human.AnimateObject ();
Human.DeflectPlayers ();
break;

case 'Q':
Computer.Vector.SetValue (8);
goto AnimateComputer;

case 'A':
Computer.Vector.SetValue (2);
goto AnimateComputer;

case 'Z':
Computer.Vector.SetValue (4);
goto AnimateComputer;

case 'X':
Computer.Vector.SetValue (6);
AnimateComputer:
Computer.AnimateObject ();
Computer.DeflectPlayers ();
break;

case ' ':
if(Projectiles.Active == false)
{Projectiles.Active.SetValue (true);
SetRandomVectorX ();
PlaySound (@"C:\Games.Net\Tennis\Racket.wav", 0, 0);}
break;}

if(e.KeyChar == Keys.Escape.GetHashCode())
{Cursor.Show ();
if(MessageBox.Show("Are you sure you want to quit?", "Program
Termination!",
            MessageBoxButtons.YesNo) == DialogResult.Yes)
      Application.Exit ();
else
Cursor.Hide () ;}

if(Projectiles.Active == false)
Invalidate ();
base.OnKeyPress (e) ;}
```

Remember, this coding is also listed on the CD-ROM.

Collision Detection –Part I
(The Players Boundaries)

Now that we have a player that can roam around our screen, we'll want to give him some limitation. After all, we cannot have him wondering off now can we? The coding used to stop our character's excess motion is actually quite simple, just a *switch* statement, and some incrementing and decrementing operators. These statements will probably seem a bit more complex and possibly confusing, but that's because we're also using them as part of both our user-defined and class based methods (just remember that the principles are basically the same). If you feel you need a little bit more of an explanation, just have a look at this next example. Here we're looking at a method that is included as part of our first character based class. When we declare an object as in Player1, Player2, or even the ball we'll gain access to that method. Now, when we want to test for those parameters, we'll simply call that method by writing it out as in `OurObject.DeflectPlayers ()`, `OurObject.DeflectBall`... Alternatively, we may want to read a value as in `OurObject.Vector.ReadValue ()` or with the keyword *this* as in `this.OurObject.Vector.ReadValue ()` depending upon the type of reference (see example 3.11).

Example 3.11 (from Class1.cs):

```
public void DeflectPlayers()
{if (this.Y <= 0 ||
this.Y >= 500 ||
this.X > 700 ||
this.X <= 0 ||
this.X == 341)
{this.Vector.SetValue (-this.Vector.ReadValue ());
this.AnimateObject ();
this.Vector.SetValue (-this.Vector.ReadValue ());}
else if(this.Y < 0 || this.Y > 500)
{this.Y.SetValue (225) ;}}
```

Collision Detection –Part II
(The Ball in Motion)

Our next few steps then momentarily abandon the player and put our focus on the ball. The ball, like the player, uses the same character based class and methods, but with a few minor changes. The ball should also be deflected by the walls, but this time we'll want to use those walls to implement changes in that objects direction, this of course should resemble at least a rough physical model (but, not to worry it should all be common sense stuff). The model we'll use is based on the numeric keypad/10-key system with the numbers in their default positions (4 is left, 6 is right, 7 is upper left, 9 is upper right, 1 is lower left, and 3 is lower right –0 and 5 are not used). If the order of our numbers doesn't seem to make sense, try looking at them again from the point of view of the keypad as shown in example 3.12.

Example 3.12:

Upper Left	7 8 9	Upper Right
Left	4 5 6	Right
Lower Left	1 2 3	Lower Right

This is also easily converted to code as in a *switch* statement with the *cases* set to those values (as in; *case* 1:, *case* 2:, *case* 3:...), but we'll save that coding for later. Our next step then will be to redefine or change the paths as our ball collides with the walls. Remember that the ball is guided by an inherent force and when the ball is deflected; its path will not be reversed or made random. Instead we'll use a simple conversion form upper right to lower right and lower left to upper left... Numerically this can be expressed as 9 to 3, 3 to 9, 7 to 1, and 1 to 7 (see example 3.13).

Example 3.13:

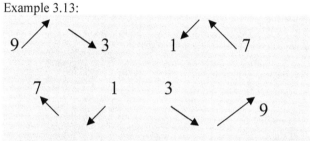

Although technically we <u>did not</u> mathematically map out our ball's path. We did still managed to give the ball a close representation of what would have happened in an actual 2-D elastic collisions (an elastic collision being one that does not alter the shape of the objects impacted).

Still words and pictorials don't teach coding, so here's a stand-alone example of a bouncing ball (see example 3.14). My suggestion is that you study it, alter the balls speed, size, and boundaries, then try to add the player back into the game. If you can't figure out the last part, don't worry about it, I'll definitely do it for you. Next up, we'll go back to our players and give them the ability to deflect the ball.

Example 3.14

```
/* Animation Test III */
using System;
using System.Drawing;
using System.Collections;
using System.ComponentModel;
using System.Windows.Forms;
using System.Data;
using System.IO;
using System.Runtime.InteropServices;

namespace Games
{public class PaddleTennis : System.Windows.Forms.Form
{private System.ComponentModel.Container components = null;

Random rnd = new Random ();
ScreenSize Area = new ScreenSize ();
```

```
GameControls GameSpeed = new GameControls (3);

Objects Human = new Objects (700, 0, 0, 0, 0, false);
Objects Computer = new Objects (0, 0, 0, 0, 0, false);
Objects Projectiles = new Objects (650, 225, 0, 0, 0, false);

Image DisplayTennisBall;

public PaddleTennis()
{InitializeComponent () ;}

protected override void Dispose( bool disposing )
{if( disposing )
{if (components != null)
{components.Dispose();}}
base.Dispose( disposing );}

#region Windows Form Designer generated code
private void InitializeComponent()
{this.AutoScaleBaseSize = new System.Drawing.Size (5, 13);
this.ClientSize = new System.Drawing.Size (780, 550);
this.Name = "Paddle Tennis";
this.Text = "Paddle Tennis";
this.Load += new System.EventHandler (this.PaddleTennis_Load);
this.BackColor = Color.Blue;

DisplayTennisBall = Image.FromFile
(@"c:\Games.Net\Tennis\TennisBall.Bmp");
this.AutoScrollMinSize = DisplayTennisBall.Size;

Timer Clock = new Timer ();
Clock.Interval = 60;
Clock.Start ();
Clock.Tick += new EventHandler (Ball_Click) ;}
#endregion

protected override void OnPaint(PaintEventArgs e)
{Graphics Figures = this.CreateGraphics ();
this.Show ();
Graphics dc = e.Graphics;
if (Projectiles.Active == true)
if (Projectiles.X >= Area.XMax.Value/2-20 && Projectiles.X <=
Area.XMax.Value/2+20)
      dc.DrawImage (DisplayTennisBall, Projectiles.X.ReadValue (),
Projectiles.Y.ReadValue (), 50, 50);
else if(Projectiles.X > Area.XMax.Value/4 && Projectiles.X <
3*Area.XMax.Value/4)
      dc.DrawImage (DisplayTennisBall, Projectiles.X.ReadValue (),
Projectiles.Y.ReadValue (), 35, 35);
else
dc.DrawImage (DisplayTennisBall, Projectiles.X.ReadValue (),
Projectiles.Y.ReadValue (), 25, 25);
```

```
base.OnPaint (e) ;}

protected override void OnKeyPress(KeyPressEventArgs e)
{switch (char.ToUpper(e.KeyChar))
{case ' ':
if (Projectiles.Active == false)
{Projectiles.Active = Projectiles.Active + true;
SetRandomVectorX () ;}
break;}

Invalidate ();
base.OnKeyPress (e) ;}

public void Tennis()
{InitializeComponent ();}

[STAThread]
static void Main()
{Application.Run (new PaddleTennis ());}

public void Ball_Click(object sender, System.EventArgs e)
{if (Projectiles.Active == true)
{for (int i = 0; i < 3; i++)
{DeflectingTheBall ();
Projectiles.AnimateObject ();
Invalidate ();}}}

public void DeflectingTheBall()
{switch (Projectiles.Vector.ReadValue())
{case 1:
if (Projectiles.Y >= Area.YMax.Value)
{Projectiles.Vector.SetValue (7);}
else if(Projectiles.X == Computer.X)
{if (Computer.DeflectingTest(Projectiles))
{SetRandomVectorX ();
if (Projectiles.Vector == 6 ||
Projectiles.Vector == 4)
{Projectiles.Vector.SetValue (6);}
else
Projectiles.Vector.SetValue (3);}
else
{Projectiles.Active.SetValue (false);
Projectiles.Y.SetValue (Human.Y.ReadValue ());
Projectiles.X.SetValue (Human.X.ReadValue ());}}
break;

case 3:
if (Projectiles.Y >= Area.YMax.Value)
{Projectiles.Vector.SetValue (9);}
else if(Projectiles.X >= Human.X)
{if (Human.DeflectingTest(Projectiles))
{SetRandomVectorX ();
```

```
if (Projectiles.Vector == 4 || Projectiles.Vector == 6)
{Projectiles.Vector.SetValue (4);}
else
Projectiles.Vector.SetValue (1);}
else
{Projectiles.Active.SetValue (false);
Projectiles.X.SetValue (Computer.X.ReadValue ());
Projectiles.Y.SetValue (Computer.Y.ReadValue ());}}
break;

case 4:
if (Projectiles.X <= Computer.X)
{if (Computer.DeflectingTest(Projectiles))
{SetRandomVectorX ();
if (Projectiles.Vector >= 7 ||
Computer.Y-3 == Projectiles.Y)
Projectiles.Vector.SetValue (9);
else if (Projectiles.Vector <= 3 ||
Projectiles.Y == Computer.Y+3)
Projectiles.Vector.SetValue (3);
else
{Projectiles.Vector.SetValue (6);}}
else
{Projectiles.Active.SetValue (false);
Projectiles.X.SetValue (Human.X.ReadValue ());
Projectiles.Y.SetValue (Human.Y.ReadValue ());} }
break;

case 6:
if (Projectiles.X >= Human.X)
{if (Human.DeflectingTest(Projectiles))
{SetRandomVectorX ();
if (Projectiles.Vector >= 7 ||
Human.Y-1 == Projectiles.Y)
Projectiles.Vector.SetValue (7);
else if (Projectiles.Vector <= 3 ||
Human.Y+1 == Projectiles.Y)
Projectiles.Vector.SetValue (1);
else
{Projectiles.Vector.SetValue (4);}}
else
{Projectiles.Active.SetValue (false);
Projectiles.X.SetValue (Computer.X.ReadValue ());
Projectiles.Y.SetValue (Computer.Y.ReadValue ());}}
break;

case 7:
if (Projectiles.Y <= Area.YStart.Value)
{Projectiles.Vector.SetValue (1);}
else if (Projectiles.X <= Computer.X)
{if (Computer.DeflectingTest(Projectiles))
{SetRandomVectorX ();
```

```
if (Projectiles.Vector == 6 || Projectiles.Vector == 4)
{Projectiles.Vector.SetValue (6);}
else
{Projectiles.Vector.SetValue (9);}}
else
{Projectiles.Active.SetValue (false);
Projectiles.X.SetValue (Human.X.ReadValue ());
Projectiles.Y.SetValue (Human.Y.ReadValue ()); }}
break;

case 9:
if (Projectiles.Y <= Area.YStart.Value)
{Projectiles.Vector.SetValue (3);}
else if (Projectiles.X >= Human.X)
{if (Human.DeflectingTest(Projectiles))
{SetRandomVectorX ();
if (Projectiles.Vector == 4 ||
Projectiles.Vector == 6)
{Projectiles.Vector.SetValue (4);}
else
{Projectiles.Vector.SetValue (7);}}
else
{Projectiles.Active.SetValue (false);
Projectiles.X.SetValue (Computer.X.ReadValue ());
Projectiles.Y.SetValue (Computer.Y.ReadValue ());}}
break;}}

public void SetRandomVectorX()
{Random rnd = new Random ();
Projectiles.Vector.SetValue ((int) Math.Round (rnd.NextDouble () * 10)
+1);

if(Projectiles.X > Area.XMax.Value/2)
{if(Projectiles.Vector <= 2 ||
Projectiles.Vector == 3)
Projectiles.Vector.SetValue (1);
else if(Projectiles.Vector == 5 ||
Projectiles.Vector == 6)
Projectiles.Vector.SetValue (4);
else if(Projectiles.Vector == 8 ||
Projectiles.Vector >= 9)
Projectiles.Vector.SetValue (7);}
else
{if (Projectiles.Vector <= 1 ||
Projectiles.Vector == 2)
Projectiles.Vector.SetValue (3);
else if(Projectiles.Vector == 4 ||
Projectiles.Vector == 5)
{Projectiles.Vector.SetValue (6) ;}
else if(Projectiles.Vector == 7 ||
Projectiles.Vector >= 8)
Projectiles.Vector.SetValue (9) ;}}
```

```
private void PaddleTennis_Load(object sender, System.EventArgs e)
{}}}
```

Collision Detection –Part III
(Deflecting the Ball)

   The next thing we'll want to do with our players is give them the ability to deflect the ball. This will become ever more useful once we've covered how to combine the two. The first method we'll discussed then changes the ball's direction using the same principles covered in the previous section, but with a different order of deflection. A new order of deflection is necessary to keep the players interest as in a wider variety of patterns to perceive. In addition, as was mentioned, we'll also want to plug-in some random paths, which will allow for other less conditional patterns, but we'll get to those in a moment.

   Our first step then will be to plot our player's patterns of deflection. These, as you should remember, are the patterns that the ball takes after it collides with an object. Once again, we'll use the numeric keypad/ 10-key system as our point of reference (see example 3.15).

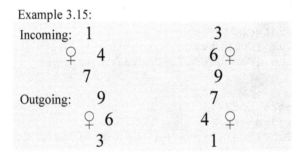

Example 3.15:

   The number scheme for this example splits the numbers up horizontally rather than vertically with 7 to 9, 9 to 7, 1 to 3, and 3 to 1. In addition, two alternate paths are introduced namely path 4 (left) and path 6 (right), these will have to be handled with random functions since they simply do not fall into our basic patterns of change. Reclaiming them as diagonal paths will also be handled by randomization (see example 3.16).

Example 3.16:
```
public void DeflectingTheBall()
{switch (Projectiles.Vector.ReadValue())
{case 1:
if (Projectiles.Y >= Area.YMax.Value)
{Projectiles.Vector.SetValue (7);
PlaySound (@"C:\Games.Net\Tennis\Wall.wav", 0, 0) ;}
else if(Projectiles.X == Computer.X)
{if (Computer.DeflectingTest(Projectiles))
 {SetRandomVectorX ();
if (Projectiles.Vector == 6 ||
Projectiles.Vector == 4)
{Projectiles.Vector.SetValue (6);
GameSpeed--;}
```

```
else
Projectiles.Vector.SetValue (3);

PlaySound (@"C:\Games.Net\Tennis\Racket.wav", 0, 0);}
else
{PlaySound (@"C:\Games.Net\Tennis\Cheer.wav", 0, 0);
GameSpeed++;
Human.Score++;
Projectiles.Active.SetValue (false);
Projectiles.Y.SetValue (Human.Y.ReadValue ());
Projectiles.X.SetValue (Human.X.ReadValue ());}}
break;

case 3:
if (Projectiles.Y >= Area.YMax.Value)
 {Projectiles.Vector.SetValue (9);
PlaySound (@"C:\Games.Net\Tennis\Wall.wav", 0, 0) ;}
else if(Projectiles.X >= Human.X)
 {if (Human.DeflectingTest(Projectiles))
   {SetRandomVectorX ();
   if (Projectiles.Vector == 4 || Projectiles.Vector == 6)
    {Projectiles.Vector.SetValue (4);
     GameSpeed-- ;}
   else
    Projectiles.Vector.SetValue (1);

   PlaySound (@"C:\Games.Net\Tennis\Racket.wav", 0, 0) ;}
  else
   {PlaySound (@"C:\Games.Net\Tennis\Cheer.wav", 0, 0);
    GameSpeed++;
    Computer.Score++;
    Projectiles.Active.SetValue (false);
    Projectiles.X.SetValue (Computer.X.ReadValue ());
    Projectiles.Y.SetValue (Computer.Y.ReadValue ());}}
break;

case 4:
 if (Projectiles.X <= Computer.X)
  {if (Computer.DeflectingTest(Projectiles))
    {SetRandomVectorX ();
    if (Projectiles.Vector >= 7 ||
      Computer.Y-3 == Projectiles.Y)
       Projectiles.Vector.SetValue (9);
      else if (Projectiles.Vector <= 3 ||
            Projectiles.Y == Computer.Y+3)
            Projectiles.Vector.SetValue (3);
      else
      {Projectiles.Vector.SetValue (6);
            GameSpeed--; }
       PlaySound (@"C:\Games.Net\Tennis\Racket.wav", 0, 0) ;}
  else
  {PlaySound (@"C:\Games.Net\Tennis\Cheer.wav", 0, 0);
```

```
 GameSpeed++;
Human.Score++;
Projectiles.Active.SetValue (false);
Projectiles.X.SetValue (Human.X.ReadValue ());
Projectiles.Y.SetValue (Human.Y.ReadValue ()) ;}}
break;

case 6:
if (Projectiles.X >= Human.X)
{if (Human.DeflectingTest(Projectiles))
{SetRandomVectorX ();
if (Projectiles.Vector >= 7 ||
Human.Y-1 == Projectiles.Y)
Projectiles.Vector.SetValue (7);
else if (Projectiles.Vector <= 3 ||
 Human.Y+1 == Projectiles.Y)
Projectiles.Vector.SetValue (1);
else
 {Projectiles.Vector.SetValue (4);
GameSpeed++; }
PlaySound (@"C:\Games.Net\Tennis\Racket.wav", 0, 0);}
 else
 {GameSpeed++;
 Computer.Score++;
PlaySound (@"C:\Games.Net\Tennis\Cheer.wav", 0, 0);
Projectiles.Active.SetValue (false);
Projectiles.X.SetValue (Computer.X.ReadValue ());
Projectiles.Y.SetValue (Computer.Y.ReadValue ());}}
break;

case 7:
if (Projectiles.Y <= Area.YStart.Value)
{Projectiles.Vector.SetValue (1);
PlaySound (@"C:\Games.Net\Tennis\Wall.wav", 0, 0);}
else if (Projectiles.X <= Computer.X)
{if (Computer.DeflectingTest(Projectiles))
{SetRandomVectorX ();
if (Projectiles.Vector == 6 ||
Projectiles.Vector == 4)
{Projectiles.Vector.SetValue (6);
GameSpeed--; }
else
{Projectiles.Vector.SetValue (9);
GameSpeed++; }
PlaySound (@"C:\Games.Net\Tennis\Racket.wav", 0, 0) ;}
else
{PlaySound (@"C:\Games.Net\Tennis\Cheer.wav", 0, 0);
GameSpeed++;
Human.Score++;
Projectiles.Active.SetValue (false);
Projectiles.X.SetValue (Human.X.ReadValue ());
Projectiles.Y.SetValue (Human.Y.ReadValue ()); }}
```

```
break;

case 9:
if (Projectiles.Y <= Area.YStart.Value)
{Projectiles.Vector.SetValue (3);
PlaySound (@"C:\Games.Net\Tennis\Wall.wav", 0, 0);}
else if (Projectiles.X >= Human.X)
{if (Human.DeflectingTest(Projectiles))
{SetRandomVectorX ();
if (Projectiles.Vector == 4 ||
 Projectiles.Vector == 6)
{Projectiles.Vector.SetValue (4);
GameSpeed--; }
else
{Projectiles.Vector.SetValue (7);
GameSpeed++; }
PlaySound (@"C:\Games.Net\Tennis\Racket.wav", 0, 0);}
else
{PlaySound (@"C:\Games.Net\Tennis\Cheer.wav", 0, 0);

GameSpeed++;
Computer.Score++; // += 1;
Projectiles.Active.SetValue (false);
Projectiles.X.SetValue (Computer.X.ReadValue ());
Projectiles.Y.SetValue (Computer.Y.ReadValue ());}}
break;   }

if (GameActive.Test == true &&
(Human.Score == 5 || Computer.Score == 5))
{GameActive.Test = false;
Cursor.Show ();
GameOver ();}}
```

A Few Minor Details
(Scores, Speed Settings, and Additional Graphics)

  Now that we've plotted all the characters motions, including our boundaries and patterns of deflection, and since we've already put together a working example of both the players and their ball. It would seem that there would be little else to do, but to put all these pieces together and call it a game. This, unfortunately, is not the case, since there are still several little issues that need to be addressed. For example, we'll need a way to implement our player's scores and a way to terminate the game when a player reaches a certain score. In addition, we'll also need to discuss adjusting the balls speed, adding in the net, and controlling the serve. Not to worry these are all relatively simple issues and we'll get back to the fun stuff momentarily.

Issue one, keeping score.
  Optimally, in order to maximize the reuse of our program's coding, we'll have to declare most of our variables as members of a class. These members will normally be stored as private members, thus we'll also have to create member function (also known as methods) to access these values. Methods are usually referenced in pairs as in one to store the data and other to retrieve it. At this level however, we won't worry

too much about the details used to create these classes and instead we'll focus on how to use them. The two key references then that control the players scores are SetValue and ReadValue (see example 3.17).

Example 3.17:

```
Human.Score.SetValue (0);
Computer.Score.SetValue (0);
Human.Score.ReadValue ();
Computer.Score.ReadValue ();
```

We also want to create overloaded versions of our incrementing and decrementing operators, which, of course, will be used to alter the player's scores (see example 3.18).

Example 3.18:

```
Human.Score++;
Human.Score--;
Computer.Score++;
Computer.Score--;
```

Displaying our scores is also just a matter of referencing our data in the correct manner, this time in addition to retrieve that data, we'll also need to covert it into a string value before attempting to display it (see example 3.19).

Example 3.19:

```
Brush YellowBrush = new SolidBrush (Color.Yellow);
Graphics MyText = e.Graphics;
Font Normal = new Font ("Times New Roman", 14, FontStyle.Bold);
string HumanScore = (Human.Score.ReadValue()).ToString();
string ComputerScore = (Computer.Score.ReadValue()).ToString();
MyText.DrawString (ComputerScore,
Normal, YellowBrush, new Rectangle (new Point (195, 20), new Size (780,
550)));
MyText.DrawString (HumanScore,
Normal, YellowBrush, new Rectangle (new Point (585, 20), new Size (780,
550)));
```

Note: to learn more about drawing tools, shapes, and colors see appendixes F-H.

Issue two, Game Controls:

Our next step then will be to create a real time loop not unlike a console *while* loop, but this time we'll let Windows handle most the work. Here, we'll rely on our second class GameControls (listed under Class2.cs), which will continually test to see if our value GameActive is true, if not then the playable portion of our game will terminate. We'll also use this class to define our games speed, as in the speed of the ball (see examples 3.20 through 3.23).

Example 3.20:

```
GameControls GameActive = new GameControls (false);
```

Example 3.21:

```
GameActive.SetValue (true);
GameActive.SetValue (false);
```

Example 3.22:

```
if (GameActive.Test == true &&
(Human.Score == 5 || Computer.Score == 5))
{GameActive.Test = false ;}}
```

We can also increase or decrease the playable speed with a simple call to our games speed reference as in GameSpeed.SetValue(X);. Remember increasing the value <u>increases</u> the looping process, which subsequently increases the balls speed. The larger the value the faster the ball will move. Note: This may seem odd to programmers who are use to the older C++ sleep function, since increasing that value had the opposite affect.

Example 3.23:

```
GameControls GameSpeed = new GameControls (3);

GameSpeed.SetValue (5);
GameSpeed.ReadValue ();
```

Issue three, the Net:
  We could draw a net and load it using a few simple commands as in Image `DisplayNet;`
`DisplayNet = Image.FromFile (@"c:\Games.Net\Tennis\Net.bmp");`
`this.AutoScrollMinSize = DisplayNet.Size;`
Followed up with a graphic reference as in dc.DrawImage (DisplayNet, 350, 0, 10, 550); or we could use function from the list presented in the next section (see example 3.24).

Example 3.24:

```
Graphics Figures = this.CreateGraphics ();
this.Show ();
Brush YellowBrush = new SolidBrush (Color.Yellow);
for (int Y = 0; Y <= 550; Y+=15)
{Figures.FillRectangle (YellowBrush, 390, Y, 5, 5) ;}
```

Note: See the next section for details.

Issue four, controlling the serve:
  First, we'll need to develop a random number generator that sets the initial path of our projectile or "ball." Second, we'll need to keep track of our projectile's location and we'll need to setup so scenarios that will allow for the ball to switch sides. For convenience, we'll also want to bundle these procedures into a simple function (see example 3.25).

Example 3.25:

```
public void SetRandomVectorX()
{Random rnd = new Random ();
Projectiles.Vector.SetValue ((int) Math.Round (rnd.NextDouble () * 10)
+1);

if(Projectiles.X > Area.XMax.Value/2)
{Projectiles.X.SetValue (Human.X.ReadValue ());
Projectiles.Y.SetValue (Human.Y.ReadValue ());
if(Projectiles.Vector <= 2 ||
Projectiles.Vector == 3)
```

```
      Projectiles.Vector.SetValue (1);
else if(Projectiles.Vector == 5 ||
Projectiles.Vector == 6)
    Projectiles.Vector.SetValue (4);
else if(Projectiles.Vector == 8 ||
Projectiles.Vector >= 9)
     Projectiles.Vector.SetValue (7);}
else
{Projectiles.X.SetValue (Computer.X.ReadValue ());
Projectiles.Y.SetValue (Computer.Y.ReadValue ());

if (Projectiles.Vector <= 1 ||
Projectiles.Vector == 2)
 Projectiles.Vector.SetValue (3);
else if(Projectiles.Vector == 4 ||
   Projectiles.Vector == 5)
{Projectiles.Vector.SetValue (6) ;}
else if(Projectiles.Vector == 7 ||
Projectiles.Vector >= 8)
Projectiles.Vector.SetValue (9) ;}}
```

Adding Colors

There are two very basic color references as in our background and our foreground, for which we've already referenced the background colors as in `this.BackColor = Color.Blue;`, which, of course, can be changed to a whole slue of references a hundred and forty not including any user-defined references (as shown in screen shot 3.12). The foreground colors are equally obnoxious, I mean beautiful, and again the same plethora of choices are available. We can also set colors using the brush option as in `Brush YellowBrush = Brushes.Yellow;` and/or with another option known as the Pen option as in `Pen YellowPen = new Pen(Color.Yellow, 3);`, wherein the "3" represents the thickness of the pen. Once we have a declared color we might also think about using that color to specify a basic shape as in a square, rectangle, circle and/or ellipse (see example 3.26).

Screen Shot 3.12:

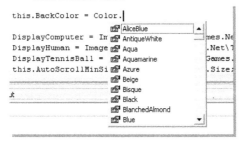

Example 3.26:

```
Graphics Figures = this.CreateGraphics ();
this.Show ();
Brush YellowBrush = Brushes.Yellow;
```

```
Brush YellowBrush = new SolidBrush (Color.Yellow);
Pen YellowPen = new Pen (Color.Yellow, 3);
Figures.DrawEllipse (YellowPen, 390, 200, 25, 25);
Figures.FillRectangle (YellowBrush, 390, Y, 5, 5);
```

Adding Sounds

Another important aspect to game programming is the use of sounds. Sounds can be used to enhance the overall quality of our games, as well as, for other minor tasks such as system notifications, popup ads, and virus alerts. While the recording of our sounds won't be handled through the .Net compiler, the storage for such sounds should be made part of any current project or at least as part of a central media base. Now, there are two key points to reference when declaring sounds as in the Window's reference and then the executing statements (see example 3.27 & 3.28).

Example 3.27:
```
public class PaddleTennis : System.Windows.Forms.Form
{ [DllImport("winmm.dll")]
public static extern long PlaySound(String lpszName,
                  long hModule, long dwFlags);
private System.ComponentModel.Container components = null;}
```

Example 3.28:
```
PlaySound (@"C:\Games.Net\Tennis\Racket.wav", 0, 0);  // as the ball hits the racket
PlaySound (@"C:\Games.Net\Tennis\wall.wav", 0, 0);  // as the ball hits the wall
PlaySound (@"C:\Games.Net\Tennis\cheer.wav", 0, 0); // when the player misses
```

> Note: Sounds may also be copied from the CD-ROM to our local directories. Sounds are listed according to their project reference (see chapter3\project1, project2...).

In addition to inserting such coding, we may also need to modify our compilers settings to include the ability to access these sounds. Here you may need to add an additional library reference or change some other settings with in your project (see your compiler's documentation for details).

> Remember, you can reposition these commands to create sounds anywhere in your programs, but be careful not to over use them. Multiple sound references can disrupt the game flow and cause other minor errors.

Adding in the Mouse

Another increasing feature we'll want to add to our games, is the little object sitting to the side of our keyboards (yes, I mean the mouse). The mouse was invented in the 60's, by a man named Douglas C. Engelbart of Stanford Research Institute (SRI) and later put to use at the Xerox Palo Alto Research Center (known as PARC) as part of the first graphical users interface (or GUI). The mouse was also made popular by a man named Steven Jobs with the release of a primitive type of computer known historically as the Macintosh.... The mouse is a fine tool especially when we're working with games that would otherwise require a trackball or paddle type joystick. The basic controls we'll want to work with include the OnMouseUp, OnMouseDown, OnMouseMove, and the OnMouseWheel (Note: the OnMouseWheel also requires an IntelliMouse; a specially designed three button mouse, which is manufactured by Microsoft). The two key functions we'll work with here then are OnMouseMove and OnMouseDown events, but the other two can be applied in basically the same manner.

Here we'll also want to use the X, Y properties to mark the mouse's position as pertaining to our preset area (see example 3.29).

Example 3.29:

```
protected override void OnMouseMove (MouseEventArgs e)
{if (GameActive.Test == true)
{Human.X.SetValue (e.X.GetHashCode ());
Human.Y.SetValue (e.Y.GetHashCode ());

if (Human.X < 341)
  Human.X.SetValue (341);

if (Projectiles.Active == false)
  Invalidate (); }}
```

Next, we'll want to add some button controls as in our players ability to serve the ball, this again can be done with either an OnMouseDown or an OnMouseUp command (see example 3.30).

Example 3.30:

```
protected override void OnMouseDown (MouseEventArgs e)
{if (GameActive.Test == true)
if (Projectiles.Active == false)
{Projectiles.Active.SetValue (true);
SetRandomVectorX ();
PlaySound (@"C:\Games.Net\Tennis\Racket.wav", 0, 0) ;}}
```

In addition, we'll want to reference our cursors with the show and/or hide functions. It is important to keep a balance between these two features as in calling only one hide and then one show per cycle. If a programmer fails to keep track of these procedures, the hides and/or the shows will end up overlapping and the cursor will may be lost indefinitely (see example 3.31).

Example 3.31:

```
Cursor.Hide ();
Cursor.Show ();
```

Finally, you may wish to alter the icon used to represent your mouse as in the arrow, hand… This can be done through a simple reassignment as in `Cursor.Current = Cursors.Hand;` (see table 3.1).

Table 3.1:

```
Cursor.Current = Cursors.AppStarting;
```

Appstart.ani

```
Cursor.Current = Cursors.Arrow;
```

Arrow_m.cur

```
Cursor.Current = Cursors.Cross;
```
Cross.cur

```
Cursor.Current = Cursors.Default;
```
Current
System
Default.

```
Cursor.Current = Cursors.Hand;
```
Harrow.cur

```
Cursor.Current = Cursors.Help;
```
Help_l.cur

```
Cursor.Current = Cursors.HSplit;
```
Hsplit.cur

```
Cursor.Current = Cursors.IBeam;
```
Beam_l.cur

```
Cursor.Current = Cursors.No;
```
No_i.cur

```
Cursor.Current = Cursors.NoMove2D;
```
Im_panhv.cur

```
Cursor.Current = Cursors.NoMoveHoriz;
```
Im_panh.cur

```
Cursor.Current = Cursors.NoMoveVert;
```
Im_orgv.cur

```
Cursor.Current = Cursors.PanEast;
```
Im_pane.cur

```
Cursor.Current = Cursors.PanNE;
```
Im_panne.cur

```
Cursor.Current = Cursors.PanNorth;
```
Im_pann.cur

```
Cursor.Current = Cursors.PanNW;
```
Im_pannw.cur

```
Cursor.Current = Cursors.PanSE;
```
Im_panse.cur

```
Cursor.Current = Cursors.PanSouth;
```
Im_pans.cur

```
Cursor.Current = Cursors.PanSW;
```
Im_pansw.cur

```
Cursor.Current = Cursors.PanWest;
```
Im_panw.cur

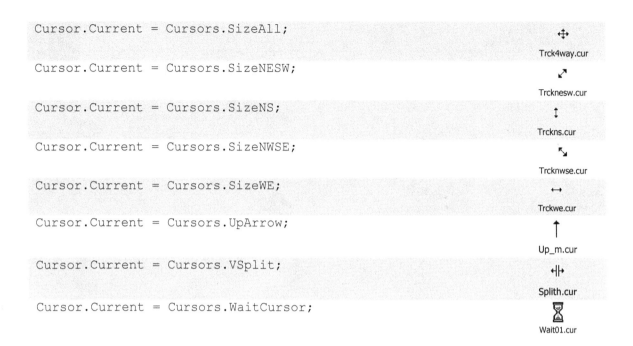

Code	Cursor	File
`Cursor.Current = Cursors.SizeAll;`	✛	Trck4way.cur
`Cursor.Current = Cursors.SizeNESW;`	↙	Trcknesw.cur
`Cursor.Current = Cursors.SizeNS;`	↕	Trckns.cur
`Cursor.Current = Cursors.SizeNWSE;`	↘	Trcknwse.cur
`Cursor.Current = Cursors.SizeWE;`	↔	Trckwe.cur
`Cursor.Current = Cursors.UpArrow;`	↑	Up_m.cur
`Cursor.Current = Cursors.VSplit;`	⊣⊢	Splith.cur
`Cursor.Current = Cursors.WaitCursor;`	⌛	Wait01.cur

Introducing Menus

Another interesting feature that is available to us as Visual C# programmers is the ability to create a host of menus both visually and through basic text references. The visually method, while fairly straightforward, is not always as complete as the text based method, hence the need to understand both techniques. Our first look then will be at how to create a basic visual menu. (Note: this technique would also apply to labels, buttons, boxes, and pictures...). First, we'll need to reference our design window (as in Forms.cs [Design]), next we'll need to reference the toolbox menu (located to the left side of our screen). Note: we can also open the toolbox using the view/toolbox submenu or by hitting the Ctrl-Alt and X keys in sequence. Next, we'll want to choose the appropriate interface (in this case the Main Menu), from there we'll simply drag and drop that selection onto our grid... (See screen shots 3.13 & 3.14).

Screen Shot 3.13:

Screen Shot 3.14:

Now to add they appropriate menu items, simply double click onto that menu (or submenu) and type in the appropriate heading(s) (see screen shot 3.15). For reference, I've labeled those items with the numbers one, two, and three. You should also notice the secondary listing, becoming available to the right, clicking onto this option allows us to create additional submenus (see screen shot 3.16).

Screen Shot 3.15:

Screen Shot 3.16:

Now, simply switch back to the text portion of our project (as in our original file "Forms.cs") and note the changes. Here we'll find everything from the basic references to the names we inserted as our menu items (see example 3.32). Of course, if we wanted to create these files by hand, then it would just be a question of inputting those references manually. Here it's important to remember to list each item, as well as their accompanying index points.

Example 3.32:

```
using System;
using System.Drawing;
using System.Collections;
using System.ComponentModel;
using System.Windows.Forms;
using System.Data;

namespace Menu
{public class Form1 : System.Windows.Forms.Form
{private System.Windows.Forms.MainMenu mainMenu1;
private System.Windows.Forms.MenuItem menuItem1;
private System.Windows.Forms.MenuItem menuItem2;
private System.Windows.Forms.MenuItem menuItem3;
private System.Windows.Forms.MenuItem menuItem4;
private System.ComponentModel.Container components = null;

public Form1()
{InitializeComponent ();}

protected override void Dispose( bool disposing )
{if( disposing )
{if (components != null)
{components.Dispose();}}
base.Dispose( disposing );}
```

```
#region Windows Form Designer generated code
private void InitializeComponent()
{this.mainMenu1 = new System.Windows.Forms.MainMenu ();
this.menuItem1 = new System.Windows.Forms.MenuItem ();
this.menuItem2 = new System.Windows.Forms.MenuItem ();
this.menuItem3 = new System.Windows.Forms.MenuItem ();
this.menuItem4 = new System.Windows.Forms.MenuItem ();
this.mainMenu1.MenuItems.AddRange (new System.Windows.Forms.MenuItem []
{                                 this.menuItem1});
this.menuItem1.Index = 0;
this.menuItem1.MenuItems.AddRange (new System.Windows.Forms.MenuItem []
{this.menuItem2,
this.menuItem3,
this.menuItem4});
this.menuItem1.Text = "Menu";
this.menuItem2.Index = 0;
this.menuItem2.Text = "One";
this.menuItem3.Index = 1;
this.menuItem3.Text = "Two";
this.menuItem4.Index = 2;
this.menuItem4.Text = "Three";
this.AutoScaleBaseSize = new System.Drawing.Size (5, 13);
this.ClientSize = new System.Drawing.Size (292, 266);
this.Menu = this.mainMenu1;
this.Name = "Form1";
this.Text = "Form1";
this.Load += new System.EventHandler (this.Form1_Load);}
#endregion

[STAThread]
static void Main()
{Application.Run (new Form1 ()) ;}

private void Form1_Load(object sender, System.EventArgs e)
{}}}
```

From here, we'll want to link those items to a specific function and or a set of functions, depending upon what we're using those items to reference. In our key example the Paddle Tennis game, we'll uses these points to reference our games starting points as in our "Two-Player," "Single-Player," and "Demo Version want" options (see examples 3.33 – 3.36).

Example 3.33:

```
private void TwoPlayer_Click(object sender, System.EventArgs e)
{SinglePlayer = false;
Demo = false;
Setup () ;}
```

Example 3.34:

```
private void SinglePlayer_Click(object sender, System.EventArgs e)
{SinglePlayer = true;
```

```
Demo = false;
Setup () ;}
```

Example 3.35:
```
private void DemoVersion_Click(object sender, System.EventArgs e)
{SinglePlayer = true;
Demo = true;
Setup () ;}
```

Example 3.36:
```
public void Setup()
{GameActive.Test = true;
Cursor.Hide ();
GameSpeed.SetValue (3);
Human.X.SetValue (680);
Human.Y.SetValue (225);
Human.Score.SetValue (0);
Computer.X.SetValue (5);
Computer.Y.SetValue (225);
Computer.Score.SetValue (0);
Projectiles.Active.SetValue (false);
Projectiles.X.SetValue (Human.X.ReadValue ());
Projectiles.Y.SetValue (Human.Y.ReadValue ());
Invalidate () ;}
```

Artificial Intelligence –Part I

Artificial Intelligence, in its simplest form, is essentially the modeling or simulation of human responses that pertain to a certain situation or set of conditions. These responses might be based on patterns or mathematically equation such as tracking or evasion, but the initial reactions are usually random base movements. Artificially driven programs must include both a realistic representation of human limitation as in the ability to make errors and/or the occasional lucky shot, but it must also represent an impersonal-consistent opponent as in its ability to repeat the same level of skill over and over at least until we tire and shut it off. Of course, the AI we'll discuss here is only a minor introduction to that subject, but don't let the simplicity of these references fool you, programming for artificial intelligence can be surprisingly thought provoking, tactically tricky, and well worth the time it will take to master. To begin, we'll focus on the key points needed to complete this game as in a model on tracking and random motion (see the segments below).

Concept one – Tracking:
Tracking, as its name implies, is the ability to keep track of or follow a moving character as it travels across a predefined area. This is accomplished by an independent portion of programming as in a subroutine that can either implement position changes or send that information to a secondary subroutine. The coding used to track an object then resembles the coding used to implement our character's movements. The only difference then being that it's implemented by the computer's judgment as in when a comparison tells it that the tracked object is higher or lower allowing it to adjust its position. Unfortunately, this technique does have one fault, that being, that the computer cannot make mistakes, which breaks the primary rule of humanistic realism. Luckily, we can over come this need for perfection by adding in random events, hence the necessity of applying these techniques in unison.

Concept two – Random Motion:

In the last two chapters, we've used random numbers several times to create new information and too dynamically change the results of otherwise predictable behaviors. This process is also very useful when attempting to break the monogamy of projected movements and is the primary source of new input used by our artificial characters. The one key twisted then that will make this procedure a bit different is that we'll use that random input to reduce the artificial players' ability to seek the projectile. The idea behind this maneuver will be to increase the level of error and hence the playability of the game (see examples 3.37 & 3.38).

Example 3.37:

```
public void TennisAI()
{if (Projectiles.Active == true)
{switch (Projectiles.Vector.ReadValue())
{case 1:
 if (Projectiles.Y > Computer.Y)
{Computer.Vector.SetValue (2);}
else
Computer.Vector.SetValue (8);
break;

case 4:
if (Projectiles.Y < Computer.Y)
{Computer.Vector.SetValue (8);}
else if(Projectiles.Y > Computer.Y)
{Computer.Vector.SetValue (2);}
break;

case 7:
if (Projectiles.Y < Computer.Y)
 {Computer.Vector.SetValue (8);}
else
Computer.Vector.SetValue (2);
break;}

Computer.AnimateObject ();
Computer.DeflectPlayers ();}
else
 Computer.Y.SetValue (225);}
```

Example 3.38:

```
public void TennisAI2()
{GameSpeed.SetValue (4);

if (Projectiles.Active == false)
{Projectiles.Active.SetValue (true);
SetRandomVectorX ();
PlaySound (@"C:\Games.Net\Tennis\Racket.wav", 0, 0);
Human.Y.SetValue (225);}

switch (Projectiles.Vector.ReadValue())
```

```
{case 3:
if (Projectiles.Y > Human.Y)
{if (Projectiles.Y < Area.XMax.Value/2)
 Human.Vector.SetValue (1);
else
 Human.Vector.SetValue (2);}
else
Human.Vector.SetValue (6);
break;

case 4:
case 6:
if (Projectiles.Y < Human.Y)
{if (Human.X < Area.XMax.Value/2)
 Human.Vector.SetValue (7);
else
Human.Vector.SetValue (8);}
else if(Projectiles.Y > Human.Y)
 {if (Human.X < Area.XMax.Value)
 Human.Vector.SetValue (1);
   else
Human.Vector.SetValue (2);}
else
Human.Vector.SetValue (6);
break;

case 9:
if (Projectiles.Y < Human.Y)
{if (Human.X < Area.XMax.Value/2)
 Human.Vector.SetValue (7);
 else
 Human.Vector.SetValue (8);}
else
 Human.Vector.SetValue (6);
break;}

Human.AnimateObject ();
Human.DeflectPlayers ()  ;}
```

Putting It All Together
(Paddle Tennis)

Finally, as a last course of business, we'll need to develop what is commonly referred to as the main or master program. This lead program is used to reference our components, as well as the attached classes... This program will include all of the components listed earlier as well as the based class library developed in chapter five (see example 3.39).

Example 3.39 (Note: Remember to add the proper links):

```
/* Paddle Tennis v2.0 - by Salvatore A. Buono */
using System;
```

```
using System.Drawing;
using System.Collections;
using System.ComponentModel;
using System.Windows.Forms;
using System.Data;
using System.IO;
using System.Runtime.InteropServices;

namespace Games
{public class PaddleTennis : System.Windows.Forms.Form
{[DllImport ("winmm.dll")]
public static extern long PlaySound(String lpszName, long hModule, long
dwFlags);
private System.Windows.Forms.MainMenu mainMenu1;
private System.Windows.Forms.MenuItem menuItem1;
private System.Windows.Forms.MenuItem menuItem2;
private System.Windows.Forms.MenuItem menuItem3;
private System.Windows.Forms.MenuItem menuItem4;
private System.ComponentModel.Container components = null;

Random rnd = new Random ();
ScreenSize Area = new ScreenSize ();
GameControls GameSpeed = new GameControls (3);
GameControls GameActive = new GameControls (false);

Objects Computer = new Objects (5, 225, 0, 0, 0, true);
Objects Human = new Objects (680, 225, 0, 1, 0, true);
Objects Projectiles = new Objects (0, 0, 0, 0, 0, false);

Image DisplayComputer, DisplayHuman, DisplayTennisBall;
bool Demo = false, SinglePlayer = false;
Point Mouse = new Point (680, 225);

public PaddleTennis()
{InitializeComponent () ;}

protected override void Dispose( bool disposing )
{if( disposing )
{if (components != null)
{components.Dispose();}}
base.Dispose( disposing );}

#region Windows Form Designer generated code
private void InitializeComponent()
{this.mainMenu1 = new System.Windows.Forms.MainMenu ();
this.menuItem1 = new System.Windows.Forms.MenuItem ();
this.menuItem2 = new System.Windows.Forms.MenuItem ();
this.menuItem3 = new System.Windows.Forms.MenuItem ();
this.menuItem4 = new System.Windows.Forms.MenuItem ();

this.mainMenu1.MenuItems.AddRange (new System.Windows.Forms.MenuItem []
{this.menuItem1});
```

```csharp
this.menuItem1.Index = 0;
this.menuItem1.MenuItems.AddRange (new System.Windows.Forms.MenuItem []
{this.menuItem2,
this.menuItem3,
this.menuItem4});
this.menuItem1.Text = "Paddle Tennis";

this.menuItem2.Index = 0;
this.menuItem2.Text = "Two-Player";
this.menuItem2.Click += new System.EventHandler (this.TwoPlayer_Click);

this.menuItem3.Index = 1;
this.menuItem3.Text = "Single-Player";
this.menuItem3.Click += new System.EventHandler
(this.SinglePlayer_Click);

this.menuItem4.Index = 2;
this.menuItem4.Text = "Demo Version";
this.menuItem4.Click += new System.EventHandler
(this.DemoVersion_Click);

this.AutoScaleBaseSize = new System.Drawing.Size (5, 13);
this.ClientSize = new System.Drawing.Size (780, 550);
this.Name = "Paddle Tennis";
this.Text = "Paddle Tennis";

this.Menu = this.mainMenu1;
this.Load += new System.EventHandler (this.PaddleTennis_Load);

this.BackColor = Color.Blue;

DisplayComputer = Image.FromFile (@"c:\Games.Net\Tennis\Player1.bmp");
DisplayHuman = Image.FromFile (@"c:\Games.Net\Tennis\Player2.bmp");
DisplayTennisBall = Image.FromFile
(@"c:\Games.Net\Tennis\TennisBall.Bmp");
this.AutoScrollMinSize = DisplayComputer.Size;
this.AutoScrollMinSize = DisplayHuman.Size;
this.AutoScrollMinSize = DisplayTennisBall.Size;

Timer Clock = new Timer ();
Clock.Interval = 60;
Clock.Start ();
Clock.Tick += new EventHandler (Ball_Click);}
#endregion

protected override void OnPaint(PaintEventArgs e)
{if (GameActive.Test == false)
{Graphics Intro = e.Graphics;
Brush YellowBrush = Brushes.Yellow;
Font LargeAlgerianFont = new Font ("Algerian", 72);
Font MidAlgerianFont = new Font ("Algerian", 36);
```

```csharp
Intro.DrawString ("Paddle Tennis", MidAlgerianFont,
YellowBrush, 60, 25);
Intro.DrawString ("By Salvatore A. Buono", MidAlgerianFont, YellowBrush,
60, 450) ;}
else
{Graphics Figures = this.CreateGraphics ();
this.Show ();
Brush YellowBrush = new SolidBrush (Color.Yellow);
for (int Y = 0; Y <= 550; Y+=15)
{Figures.FillRectangle (YellowBrush, 390, Y, 5, 5);}
Graphics MyText = e.Graphics;
Font Normal = new Font ("Times New Roman", 14, FontStyle.Bold);
string HumanScore = (Human.Score.ReadValue()).ToString();
string ComputerScore = (Computer.Score.ReadValue()).ToString();
MyText.DrawString (ComputerScore,
Normal, YellowBrush, new Rectangle (new Point (195, 20), new Size (780,
550)));
MyText.DrawString (HumanScore,
Normal, YellowBrush, new Rectangle (new Point (585, 20), new Size (780,
550)));
Graphics dc = e.Graphics;
dc.DrawImage (DisplayComputer, Computer.X.ReadValue (),
Computer.Y.ReadValue (), 100, 100);
dc.DrawImage (DisplayHuman, Human.X.ReadValue (), Human.Y.ReadValue (),
100, 100);
if (Projectiles.Active == true)
if (Projectiles.X >= Area.XMax.Value/2-20 && Projectiles.X <=
Area.XMax.Value/2+20)
dc.DrawImage (DisplayTennisBall, Projectiles.X.ReadValue (),
Projectiles.Y.ReadValue (), 50, 50);
else if(Projectiles.X > Area.XMax.Value/4 && Projectiles.X <
3*Area.XMax.Value/4)
dc.DrawImage (DisplayTennisBall, Projectiles.X.ReadValue (),
Projectiles.Y.ReadValue (), 35, 35);
else
dc.DrawImage (DisplayTennisBall, Projectiles.X.ReadValue (),
Projectiles.Y.ReadValue (), 25, 25);
base.OnPaint (e);}}

// Insert all the previous gaming examples

public void Tennis()
{InitializeComponent () ;}

public void GameOver()
{GameActive.Test = false;
SinglePlayer = false;
Demo = false;
Projectiles.Active.SetValue (false) ;}

[STAThread]
static void Main()
```

```
{Application.Run (new PaddleTennis ()) ;}

public void Ball_Click(object sender, System.EventArgs e)
{if (Projectiles.Active == true)
{for (int i = 0; i < GameSpeed.ReadValue(); i++)
  {DeflectingTheBall ();
   Projectiles.AnimateObject ();
if (SinglePlayer)
{TennisAI () ;}
if (Demo)
{TennisAI2 () ;}
Invalidate () ;}}}

private void PaddleTennis_Load(object sender, System.EventArgs e)
{}}}
```

Bonus Games
(Spaces Fighters & Asteroid Minor)

Okay, before jumping back into the thick of C#, I thought you might enjoy crunching out a few more games. This will also give us an opportunity to introduce a few more topics and some time to improve upon our initial techniques. For this second game, I'll then assume that you've already mastered the techniques presented earlier and that you'd prefer a shorter review. I will however, still take the time to mimic the creation of the game and to give a realistic view of how one might go about developing it, keeping everything in real time of course... Our second game "Space Fighters," although simple, does include several techniques that you should find useful. We'll begin then by jotting down a quick list of thoughts AKA brainstorming and we'll take a few moments to develop our characters...

Space Fighters
(Brainstorming)

Brainstorming List:
1. The game should have two players just as our last game did, but this time they'll appear as spaceships.
2. Again, one will be placed on the right and the other on the left. Letting the game start the moment it's loaded.
3. The players' movements should be two-dimensional in respect to the screen, but it should also include diagonal movements.
4. These ships should have a thrust, but not a brake or reverse. Allowing momentum to carry them forward.
5. The two ships will have weapons or at least one weapon, namely a missile that can be fired at its opponent, but to keep things simple, the missiles won't be able to injure its own ship.
6. Again, we'll set up a menu option for one or two and again we'll add in some AI for a one-player option.
7. We'll use a black background with stars randomly placed across it. The stars will be smaller versions of our sun.
8. The ships should have contrasting colors with those colors reflecting their weapons color.
9. The ships should make sounds including a thrust, weapon's fire, and an explosion when hit.
10. The ships should not be able to fire when there dead nor should they be able to get hit.
11. Set the game to end once a player gets say five kills, also if a player is killed by crashing into the sun... have him loose a point.
12. They'll have to restart after they die and we'll also give them the power to hyperspace.
13. We'll also place a sun in the middle of the screen and we'll use a set number of cycles to simulate the force of gravity pulling the ships into that sun. Gravity will also make a sound as it pulls in the ships.

Selecting Characters & Plotting Motions

Our second step then will be to draw out some basic images as in our spaceships, their exhaust trails, and a large sun that will be conspicuously placed in the center of our screen. The ships will be basically identical, but with contrasting colors, and the exhaust trail will be superimposed onto those ships when the engines are active (see screen shots 3.17 – 3.19).

The movements for these characters will be simple enough with one key set aside as a thrust and two others set to turn the crafts to alternate sides (see example 3.40). We'll continue to use both the arrow keys and the numeric keypad for such movements with left and right being used to adjust the direction of the vessel and the upward arrow/8-key being used as the thrust. We'll also use the downward arrow/2-key to reviving the characters and to send our ships into hyperspace. The zero key will be used to fire our weapons. The second player will use the keys <Q> (to turn left), <A> (to turn right), <X> (to thrust), <S> (for hyperspace), and the spacebar (to fire weapons).

We'll also need two characters to represent their missiles and another image to represent explosions (see screen shot 3.21).

Finally, we'll want to give our crafts some momentum (momentum being the force that keeps our ships gliding in one direction even after we've turned it to another). Our momentum will fade within a few program cycles, but the affects will combine when the thrust key is applied at more frequent intervals (see example 3.41).

Writing the Algorithm

The comments listed here are supplemental to our first algorithm. Here, we'll want to expand those descriptions to include the details of these secondary subprograms. Again, these instructions are in reference to the older version of this program, but there are still many similarities between the two languages (see the list below).

Algorithm:
1. *Link our program to the previous game, using menu.cpp, games.cpp...*
2. *Reference our main function screen size and access the proper subprograms.*
3. *Write a function to handle the unique turning motions required by this game (see example 3.37).*
4. *We'll also need to include a function that paints the stars and the screen black*
5. *Again, we'll want to access our variables as class members listed in an additional subprogram.*
6. *Setting the variables/members including paths...*

Inside the while loop
7. *Write a function that removes all residual images using a combination of calls to blank characters and the paint star function. .*
8. *Set the colors remembering to change the color for each vessel. Each change in color will require its own declaration:*
9. *Display all characters...*
10. *We'll still need to animate our weapon – this time we'll use all eight directions.*
11. *Our limits will no longer stop the characters; instead we'll want to wrap their movements around the screen. Projecting our characters to the opposite side, this also means that we won't have to alter their paths.*
12. *There are four sounds associated with this game namely Hit.wav (used when a player dies), Fire.wav (used to represent weapons fire), Gravity.wav (used to emphasis the pull of gravity), and thrust.wav (used to represent the ship's engine).*

13. *Collision detection (usually ends up in the destruction of a ship). Activate the collision detection routine whenever a weapon is active.*
14. *Set the weapons movement: Make it equal to the path each ship is facing at the moment the weapons are fired. If the missiles reach the end of the screen, they'll also be rerouted (traveling a total of 100 cycles before termination).*
15. *Add a force of momentum that keeps the ship moving in one direction even if the ship turns.*
16. *Only Display the characters when they're active, if they're not then display the exploding ship in their place.*
17. *Repeat the loop until either player scores five kills: either we'll terminate the loop on request or when that goal is reached.*
18. *Ask player(s) if they want to play again: Remember a good game loop should always allow the player(s) the option of playing again.*
19. *End or repeat game: Ending the gaming loop in our case means ending the game and returning to the menu portion. This then allows the users to either quit the program or continue into another game.*

Starting Our Second Game

Our fourth step then will be to get our compilers up and running; this includes repeating the steps used to link our class base and all of its counterparts. If you'd prefer to use chapter3's\project2 you can just load it up, but if you're building from scratch you'll have to remember to add each file to the project and in some cases you'll have to remember to load the Window's multimedia library. Again, we'll need to build several user-defined functions with a final main function that controls this game… (Refer to the pervious sections as needed).

Animating Our Characters –Part I
(Animating Our Spaceships)

While most of our characters will share the same generic methods, the spaceships also require two secondary display specifiers. These secondary functions also allow the programmer to indicate which of the many choices should be used and displayed. An "*if*" or preferable a "*switch*" statement can be used to direct the program to the correct data. Since, we'll want this subroutine to apply to both characters we'll use the variable id to indicate a changing identity (see examples 3.43 through 3.45). (Note: adding a second ship includes only the matter of calling that function using a second identity).

Note: As with the ships images, displaying the exhaust trail is simply a matter of reading in the ship's coordinates and displaying the appropriate image.

Animating Our Characters –Part II
(Projectiles & Explosions)

As with their character counterparts our projectiles must rely on a combination of functions and events including activation, animation, collision detection, and deactivation. While, most of these attributes are integrated within other functions we can still define our projectile's behavior based on a few lines of coding (see examples 3.46 & 3.47). Example 3.46 also denotes are secondary keyboard configuration.

Of course, we can also use a smaller version of the sun, to represent our ships as they burst into flames. (Note: A ship that has been destroyed should are not affected by additional weapons fire nor should it be effected by our sun's gravity). Again, a combination of both if and switch statements are used to reduce clutter.

OnPaint

Here we'll want to display our characters, as well as a few minor images as in our stars and eventually our asteroids (see examples 3.48 & 3.49). Notice how I've setup multiple possibilities, which ultimately allows for an area of possible appearances.

Boundaries & Projectile Limits

The next two key components then will be to add our ship's boundaries and also to limit our ships projectiles. Since this game wasn't based on a set field as in our traditional screen limits, our previous limitations should not apply. Instead, here we'll use those boundaries to indicate a chance to loop or reposition using x, y- zero to x, y- max as our coordinates. Our player's paths will not change nor will our ship's vectors (see example 3.50).

Additionally, our WeaponLimits function will also be used to access that rerouting subroutine. The secondary purpose of this function however, will be to terminate our weapon's fire if it fails to make contact with an object after a set limit of one hundred cycles. This combination will aid in creating the illusion of a truly open environment (see examples 3.51 – 3.58).

Artificial Intelligence –Part II
(Evasion)

Previously we explained the basic concepts of tracking and random motions, but we left out the third key concept, most commonly known as, evasion. Evasion in coding terms is simply the reverse of tracking. Here rather than moving closer to an object our opponent's characters are total to avoid it, thus creating the illusion of intelligently driven tactics. We'll also need to include a four function that allows of weapon's fire these functions are listed as examples 3.59 – 3.62.

Including Obstacles –Part I
(The Sun)

Another sure fire way of increasing a games enjoyment is in the insertion of field obstacles. The first obstacle we'll create then places a small sun in the middle of our screen. This sun is used like a little gravity well, slowly pulling in its prey until Bang! The ships make contact with its center. We'll setup the force of gravity to pull once every twenty cycles displacing our ships with increasing increments (see examples 3.63 & 3.64).

Gaining Momentum

Also, unlike our tennis game, we'll also want to think about how our ships might experience motion. For example, how far should the thrusters push our characters, and what happens if we change course after we apply those thrusts. This question can be answered quite simply through a solid function dedicated to the concept of momentum. Here, we won't really have to stress over any of the physical details and instead only focus on the appearance of the movement. This can be accomplished through the use of some simple timer and animation calls as shown in examples 3.65.

Including Obstacles –Part II
(Asteroids as Extra Credit)

Once again, we'll want to develop a secondary set of characters that can be used to increase the difficulty of our second game. This time however, we'll also want to give those characters a list of attributes that allow for independent interaction. These attributes should include character positioning, object animation, and partial to full destruction with multiple strikes. The asteroids bodies then should be developed using the ASCII code characters 219 (as our block) and 32 (as our blank). A combination of these characters including varying sizes is give as example 3.66.

As with the pervious characters, we'll also want to give our asteroids some unique patterns of movement. Here, the asteroids will both travel across the screen and change direction as their struck by our player's fire. The asteroids will also need to be rerouted to the opposite side of the screen whenever those screen limits are reached. Since we'll be writing for four asteroids, we'll conveniently use the four basic directions as in upper right (9), lower right (3), upper left (70), and lower left (1) (see examples 3.67).

Here, we'll want to include a few functions to handle our asteroids collision detection this should include both weapons fire and ships collision. We will not however, allow our asteroids to collide with each other or the sun character developed earlier

Menus

Again, we'll want to add in the appropriate menu options, but this time we won't include any additional mouse controls (see examples 3.68 – 3.71).

Putting it all together II

Again, a managing subprogram is necessary to weave these components into what we'd refer too as our Space Fighter game. These subprograms will also require the linkage of the menu.cpp, games.cpp... (See example 3.72).

Asteroid Miner

We can also introduce a third game that relies mostly on what we've already developed. The third game then would include the goal of destroying the asteroids rather than an enemy's vessel. Here, we'll also want too completely rewrite our space fighters managing program (see example 3.73).

Note: This program requires all of the pervious files and links (for details see chapter three's project3).

Trouble Shooting

Common Errors, Problems, and Pits:

1. If the games are compiling, but your getting a runtime error and/or your only detecting the default sound. This would indicate that your references are not to the appropriate director. For example, if you've copied the games to your D drive then the C:\ listings would all be in error. Make sure all the bitmaps, wav files and classes are not only included as part of your project, but also referenced at the appropriate locations.
2. check to make sure your files are listed with the appropriate director. For example, the games listed in the text are clearly marked as coming from the C drive under the subfolder Games.Net, while the CD-ROM versions are marked as SourceCode\...
3. Are you using Microsoft Visual C# version 7?
- If your answer was yes, go to Question 2.
- If your answer was no, try looking up any errors or warnings in your compiles help menu.
4. Can you get any of the animation test programs to work?
- If your answer was yes, go to question 3.
- If your answer was no, chances are there's a human error. Try beginning with a simple program. Make sure it runs and then add sets of coding in slowly.
5. Are you having problems with the linker or the compiler?
6. If you answered linker, your problem lies with either your settings or your subprograms.
7. If you said compiler your more than likely dealing with one of the three basic errors explained in the first two chapters.
8. Did you forget to add a subprogram?
9. Did you open two files and attempt to compile – solution, close everything and start a new workspace with the proper *.CS file.
10. If all the programs give you the same error the problem may lie in your setup.
11. If you got the Paddle Tennis program to work (project1), but are having trouble with either Space Fighter (project2) or Asteroid Belt (project3), then just try starting again and rebuilding slowly. The only real differences between the two programs are perceptual and will not affect the compiler or computer.
12. If you cannot get the game programs to run on your system, try continuing with the chapters and attempt to recompile these files after you've gained greater experience.

Things to Remember

1. Game programming starts with an idea, first you brainstorm, and then you refine. Use diagrams and algorithm as necessary.
2. Always list algorithms in English not coding –you won't always know what language you'll need to write the program in.

3. Use top-down design to simplify your tasks and write your code in modules so that they can be reused.
4. <u>Do not</u> color your characters using the same colors as their backgrounds.
5. Make backups of any and all of the games you create. You won't want to lose your hard work.
6. Write everything to be reusable… trying to limit the number of variables used in the main function.

Questions

1. Using what we've discussed in the last three games, rewrite our first game "paddle tennis" to include three characters on each side. These players should move in unison with all three characters playing as one. Give this altered game the new file name and title (soccer would be a good choice). You could also limit the scoring area as in a goal post, redesign the ball...
2. Using the second game, add a second computer controlled spaceship. Have it come on only when the users choose the deluxe version.

Direct X

What is DirectX?

DirectX is an alternative set of Window's functions, also developed by Microsoft, which were written to handle the higher demands of games. They allow for near direct access to video, sound, joysticks, and keyboards... bypassing layer upon layer of coding used by the API and .Net frameworks. Bypassing such layers however, also means forfeiting a certain level of protection, easy in programming..., but if you want the speed, well then, you'll have to pay the price.

Note: DirectX 9.0 is the first .Net version, the programs listed in this text being tested for both DirectX 9.0a and the .Net 1.1 platform. If you're using a newer version that should also be fine; one of DirectX's key features is backward compatibility.

There are several components that makeup DirectX including Direct3DIM, Direct3DRM, DirectDraw, DirectInput, DirectMusic, DirectPlay, DirectSetup (Auto Play), DirectShow, DirectSound, and DirectSound3D. Here, I've cover all of these in brevity (see the listed definitions).

Direct3D: Direct3D is used to render three-dimensional graphics, wherein Direct3DIM represents the lower-level Immediate Mode and Direct3DRM represents the higher-level Retained Mode.

DirectDraw: DirectDraw is used to render two-dimensional graphics and to display bitmaps. Unlike GDI+, DirectDraw can only access files saved under the bitmap format.

DirectInput: DirectInput is used to access input devices including the keyboard and mouse... DirectInput also allows for special features like joysticks.

DirectMusic: DirectMusic is use in association with MIDI technology and DLS (Downloadable Sounds). It allows for digital instruments and includes features like low-latency sink and clock time loops.

DirectPlay: DirectPlay is a networking tool that allows for internet and network communications. Through DirectPlay we can send and receive data packets, which can include virtually any type of information, supporting both sessions and lobbies.

DirectSetup: DirectSetup also known as AutoPlay is a automated program that can be used to install CD-ROM contain including DirectX and game programs.

DirectShow: DirectShow, originally dubbed ActiveMovie, is a media platform used to manipulate multimedia streams such as MPEG, AVI, MP3, and Wav files.

DirectSound: DirectSound is used to play digital sound waves as in Wav files. It is limited to non-compressed date, which must be set to a fixed rate.

DirectSound3D: DirectSound3D attempts to create the illusion of distance and three-dimensional placement by manipulating its speaker set. Too properly test DirectSound you'll also need to have speakers that support 3D effects.

Inside DirectX

Again, while DirectX does bypass several layers of API/.Net coding, there are two underline layers that do intercede on DirectX's behalf. The first is known as the HAL (Hardware Abstract Layer). This is usually code, written by the manufacture, and included on our systems as device drivers. These device drivers then communicate directly with the hardware and allow for the fastest level of acceleration.

Second, there is what is known as the HEL (Hardware Emulation Layer), this sec
ondary layer takes over when our device drivers cannot handle a certain feature or request. This secondary layer works through a set of algorithms, thus it is not as fast as the HAL layer, but overall, this is still a very fast set.

Installing DirectX

Before we can use DirectX, we'll first have to install it. Installing DirectX should be as simple as downloading the software (http://www.microsoft.com/windows/ directx/default.aspx.) and clicking the eventual "Install.exe" icon. You'll be given two choices Debug and Release; both can handle the contents of this chapter.

Note: If you've already installed DirectX 9.0 for your C++ and/or Visual Basic compilers, you'll have to remove that install and re-run the installation program after installing C# or any new compiler. Attempting to re-run the install program without first removing the previous or same version of DirectX will result in an installation error.

Referencing DirectX

Now that we have DirectX installed, it is important to remember that this does not mean that DirectX will be automatically included with our projects, no in fact, it's quite the opposite. Thus, we'll have to remember to include DirectX and its components throughout this chapter. To include these links just follow the steps listed below.

Step 1: From the Window's fold-down menu: first, select "Project," and then "Add Reference" (see screen shot 6.1).

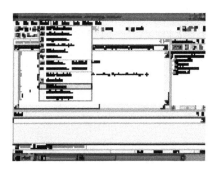

Step 2: As the "Add Reference" popup window appears, simply scroll down, noting the listings "Microsoft.DirectX," "Microsoft.DirectX.DirectDraw," "Microsoft.DirectX.DreictInput," and "Microsoft.DirectX.DirectSound." Double click on all four of these entries and then press "OK" (see screen shot 6.2).

FIGURE 1._

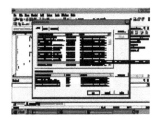

Step 3: Now, in order to use these links you'll have to include a set of using statements as in "using Microsoft.DirectX," "using Microsoft.DirectX.DirectDraw," "using Microsoft.DirectX.DirectSound," "using Buffer = Microsoft.DirectX.DirectSound.SecondaryBuffer," and "using Microsoft.DirectX.DirectInput." To see how these statements are placed in a program see example 6.1.

Example 6.1

```
using System;
using System.Drawing;
using System.Windows.Forms;

using Microsoft.DirectX;

using Microsoft.DirectX.DirectDraw;

using Microsoft.DirectX.DirectSound;
using Buffer =
Microsoft.DirectX.DirectSound.SecondaryBuffer;

using Microsoft.DirectX.DirectInput;

namespace Chapter6
{public class LearningDirectX : System.Windows.Forms.Form
{public LearningDirectX()
{InitializeComponent();}

#region Windows Form Designer generated code
private void InitializeComponent()
{
this.AutoScaleBaseSize = new
System.Drawing.Size(5, 13);
this.ClientSize = new System.Drawing.Size(292, 266);

this.Name = "LearningDirectX";
this.Text = "LearningDirectX";
this.Load += new System.EventHandler(this.Form1_Load);}
#endregion

[STAThread]
```

```
static void Main()
{Application.Run(new LearningDirectX());}

private void Form1_Load(object sender,
System.EventArgs e) {}}}
```

Beginning DirectDraw

The first thing that our games are going to need is a way of handling the video content, the solution to this is to use DirectDraw. DirectDraw as its name implies allows for direct or near direct access to our video hardware. As was explained in the previous sections, DirectDraw would need to be installed, referenced, and then declared as part of our programs before we could begin to code, but I'll assume that you've completed these steps (see Installing and Referencing DirectX for details).

The first thing we'll want to add to our programs is the declaration "private Microsoft.DirectX.DirectDraw.Device draw = null;" Here, the word "draw" could be replaced with any word that is clear to you as a programmer; examples include "Draw," "ScreenDisplay," "Pizza,"... Still, what this statement does is it creates a DirectDraw variable. The variable begins with a null value, but it must be assigned before any content is executed.

Next, we'll need to declare the primary and secondary surfaces; the primary surface is the screen area used by our game, the secondary surface would be a character's surface. The variable name primary is commonly used as in "private Surface primary = null;" The secondary surface is commonly dubbed "offscreen," but in cases were there are more than one secondary surface descriptive names may be more useful as in "private Surface BallDraw = null;"

Another essential part to creating our primary and secondary surfaces is the concept of clipping. Clipping can be a rather large and somewhat confusing subject, but for the most part, it simply means too NOT display bitmaps beyond the defined area. For example, without clipping our little tennis player might be inclined to sneak off the screen and find his way into Atari's Pong, -bad, bad tennis player. Using the variable name "clip" is very common as in "private Clipper clip = null;"

Finally, we'll want to define our area as in a simple rectangle, again the name "destination" is common among DirectX programmers as in "private Rectangle destination = new Rectangle();" The initial setting then would appear as so (see example 6.2).

Example 6.2:

```
using System;
using System.Drawing;
```

```
using System.Windows.Forms;

using Microsoft.DirectX;
using Microsoft.DirectX.DirectDraw;

namespace Chapter6
{public class LearningDirectDraw : System.Windows.Forms.Form
{private System.ComponentModel.Container
components = null;


private Microsoft.DirectX.DirectDraw.Device
draw = null;

private Surface primary = null;

private Surface BallDraw = null;

private Clipper clip = null;

private Rectangle destination = new Rectangle();
public LearningDirectDraw()
{InitializeComponent();}
...
```

Creating Surfaces

Now that we have our preliminaries in order, we'll want to build a CreateSurface function. This function will be the assignment area for our DirectX variables as in primary, clipper... as well as a crux for our bitmap references. Note: before calling CreateSurface, we will need to assign draw as in "draw = new Microsoft.DirectX.DirectDraw.Device();" (see example 6.3).

Example 6.3:

```
using System;
using System.Drawing;
using System.Windows.Forms;
using Microsoft.DirectX;
using Microsoft.DirectX.DirectDraw;
```

1

```
namespace Chapter6
{public class LearningDirectDraw : System.Windows.Forms.Form
{

as in draw, primary, clip, and destination
only the non-generic DrawBall will change */
private Microsoft.DirectX.DirectDraw.Device
draw = null;
private Surface primary = null;

which will be included in the next example */
private Surface DrawBall = null;
private Clipper clip = null;
private Rectangle destination = new Rectangle();
public LearningDirectDraw()
{InitializeComponent();

draw = new Microsoft.DirectX.DirectDraw.Device();

        draw.SetCooperativeLevel(this,Microsoft.DirectX.DirectD
raw.CooperativeLevelFlags.Normal);

CreateSurfaces();}



private void CreateSurfaces()
{SurfaceDescription description = new
SurfaceDescription();



description.SurfaceCaps.PrimarySurface = true;
primary = new Surface(description, draw);


clip = new Clipper(draw);
clip.Window = this;
primary.Clipper = clip;
description.Clear();
```

2

```
DrawBall = new Surface("..\\..\\TennisBall.bmp",
description, draw);}
```
. . .

Exception Handling with DirectDraw

Once all the other components are in place, it becomes a simple matter of setting the coordinates and referencing the bitmap. These are done with a call for a new rectangle and the primary.Draw command (see example 6.4).

Example 6.4:

```
destination = new Rectangle(PointToScreen(new
Point(X, Y)), new Size(width, height));

primary.Draw(destination, BallDraw, DrawFlags.Wait);
```

Nevertheless, nothing in life is really that simple. In this instance, nearly anything could go wrong and well, oops, the entire program could be rendered useless. The solution, we should always include a basic exception handler when dealing with a primary surface (see example 6.5).

Example 6.5:

```
try{destination = new Rectangle(PointToScreen(new
Point(X, Y)), new Size(width, height)); primary.Draw(destination, BallDraw, DrawFlags.Wait);}

catch(SurfaceLostException)
{CreateSurfaces();}
```

Here the caught exception allows us to recreate the surface, allowing the program to continue, minus one image. In most cases, this would only mean a minor disruption, one missing frame or at worst, a character that does not appear through out the game, but keep in mind that these errors should have been tested out and all errors fixed before adding-in these safeties.

Finally, we'll want to place this collection of functions into a single working example (see example 6.6).

Example 6.6:
```
using System;
```

```csharp
using System.Drawing;
using System.Windows.Forms;
using Microsoft.DirectX;
using Microsoft.DirectX.DirectDraw;

namespace Chapter6
{public class LearningDirectDraw : System.Windows.Forms.Form
{private Microsoft.DirectX.DirectDraw.Device
draw = null;
private Surface primary = null;
private Surface BallDraw = null;
private Clipper clip = null;
private Rectangle destination = new Rectangle();

public LearningDirectDraw()
{InitializeComponent();

draw = new Microsoft.DirectX.DirectDraw.Device();

draw.SetCooperativeLevel(this,Microsoft.DirectX.DirectD raw.CooperativeLevelFlags.Normal);
CreateSurfaces();}


private void CreateSurfaces()
{SurfaceDescription description = new
SurfaceDescription();
description.SurfaceCaps.PrimarySurface = true;
primary = new Surface(description, draw);
clip = new Clipper(draw);
clip.Window = this;
primary.Clipper = clip;
description.Clear();
BallDraw = new Surface("..\\..\\TennisBall.bmp", description, draw);}


#region Windows Form Designer generated code
private void InitializeComponent()
{this.Paint += new System.Windows.Forms.PaintEventHandler
(this.ShowMeTheBall);
this.AutoScaleBaseSize = new
System.Drawing.Size(5, 13);
this.ClientSize = new System.Drawing.Size(292, 266);
```

2

```
this.Name = "LearningDirectDraw";
this.Text = "LearningDirectDraw";
this.BackColor = Color.Blue;
this.Load += new System.EventHandler(this.Form1_Load);}
#endregion

private void ShowMeTheBall(object sender,
System.Windows.Forms.PaintEventArgs e)
{
destination = new Rectangle(PointToScreen(new
Point(10, 50)), new Size(25, 25));

try{primary.Draw(destination,
BallDraw, DrawFlags.Wait);}

catch(SurfaceLostException)
{CreateSurfaces();}}

[STAThread]
static void Main()
{Application.Run(new LearningDirectDraw());}
private void Form1_Load(object sender,
System.EventArgs e) {}}}
```

Introducing DirectInput

There are actually several aspects to DirectInput, but again, this is just an introduction, so we'll try to focus on the minimal coding required to get our games up and running. The two key issues then will be the keyboard and the joystick. The GDI+ keyboard for example, becomes overrun when you hold down too many buttons, and as for the GDI+ joystick controls, well, they don't exist.

Note: The nice thing about DirectInput is that it doesn't require as much background referencing, the downside to this is that the applications require a bit more coding.

The first step then will be to declare our DirectInput variables, yes variables as in one for the keyboard and one for the joystick. It is possible to create a working program that will run off a single variable, but ultimately this will lead to unpredictable errors. Note: I would also caution you against using the variable name "input" unless you were to add a more descriptive phrase such as KeyboardInput or inputJoystick (see example 6.7).

Example 6.7:
```
private Microsoft.DirectX.DirectInput.Device
```

```
keyboard = null;
private Microsoft.DirectX.DirectInput.Device
joystick = null;
```

Here we'll also need to include a JoystickState declaration and our Window's Timer references (see example 6.8)

Example 6.8:
```
public JoystickState State = new JoystickState();
private System.Windows.Forms.Timer JoyStick;
private System.Windows.Forms.Timer Keyboard;
```

Note: We'll include a KeyboardState state = keyboard.GetCurrentKeyboardState(); as part of our OnKey functions Keyboard_Tick.

Keyboard_Tick

Now that the DirectInput preliminaries have been completed, we'll want to jump into our keyboard applications. Here we'll be replacing the GDI+ OnKeyDown and OnKeyPress methods with a single Keyboard_Tick method. Keyboard_Tick as the name implies is based on the timer reference explained in the last section. From within the Keyboard_Tick method, we'll need too:

1. Assign our variable; keyboard = new Microsoft.DirectX.DirectInput.Device(SystemGuid.Keyboard);

2. Set a buffer (this is a portion of memory used to store the data retrieved from the keyboard); keyboard.Properties.BufferSize = 8;

3. Acquire that data; keyboard.Acquire();

4. Reassign that data to the variable state; KeyboardState state = keyboard.GetCurrentKeyboardState();

From here, we'd simply need to test for a Key value as in Key.Escape through Key.MediaSelect (see example 6.9).

Example 6.9:
```
keyboard = new
Microsoft.DirectX.DirectInput.Device(
SystemGuid.Keyboard);
keyboard.Properties.BufferSize = 8;
keyboard.Acquire();
KeyboardState state =
```

```
keyboard.GetCurrentKeyboardState();
for (Key k = Key.Escape; k <= Key.MediaSelect; k++)
{if (state[k] && k == Key.DownArrow)
...
```

Note: In order for this new method to run correctly, you'll also have to include a "this.components = new System.ComponentModel.Container();" statement, to be called from the InitializeComponent().

JoyStick_Tick

Next, we'll want to add-in our joystick references. There generally are a repeat of the statements used to explain the keyboard, but again, it is important to include a distinct referencing variable.

Important: in order too properly run the joystick sequence you'll actually have to have a joystick physically plugged into and installed on your system. If you do not have a joystick, you can still insert the coding, but you must include the safety "if (joystick == null) {return;}" statement or your applications will fail. The safety then is used to abort the coding before execution, thus the data will be untested.

Further, there are many different types of joysticks, and there is a chance that the coding listed here might not work with your particular controller, if you do have a problem try calibrating and retesting your joystick using one of the pre-assembled games. If that doesn't work, try using a third party game, if your joystick works under calibration and through some third party software, the problem probably lies in the State.X and State.Y comparisons, the possibility being that the input range is set too high or too low. The DirectX sample browser included with the SDK (Software Development Kit) also includes a joystick test program, which can give you, your joysticks range, the SDK can be downloaded as www.microsoft.com/windows/directx.

Now, assuming that you do have a joystick...

Building our joystick method:

First, we'll want to test for each joystick linked to your system this can be down with a "foreach (DeviceInstance instance in Manager.GetDevices(DeviceClass.GameControl, EnumDevicesFlags.AttachedOnly))" statement. If a joystick is found, it will then be assigned using a "joystick = new Microsoft.DirectX.DirectInput.Device(instance.InstanceGuid);" If it is not found the assignment will bring back a null value. This is were we should include our safety "if(joystick == null) {return;}"

We will now be able to read streams of data. Here we'll set our format as in joystick.SetDataFormat(DeviceDataFormat.Joystick); Testing for each instance with foreach (DeviceObjectInstance d in joystick.Objects) {if ((0!= (d.ObjectId & (int)DeviceObjectTypeFlags.Axis))).

Defining our input range may also be a problem input is read as X, Y coordinates, if the numbers that I've set don't seem to work, try changing them. The definition is written as {joystick.Properties.SetRange(ParameterHow.ById, d.ObjectId, new InputRange(-1000, 1000));}} joystick.Acquire(); does as it name indicates, but it should be noted that Acquire is a structure that does not return a value, as in public struct void, after acquire, we poll as in joystick; joystick.Poll(); for another again without assignment.

Finally, will read in our joysticks key state, as in State = joystick.CurrentJoystickState; As I said, this number can differ between joysticks, the joystick I'm using reads at around negative 450 X-axis without being pressed, thus I've been using a negative 400 to negative 500 setting throughout the games. The coding is "if (-400 < State.X) and (-500 > State.X)" Your Y-axis will also need to be tested, my numbers come back in the negative 550's, to I've set my why states to -600 and -500, if(-600 > State.Y) and (-500 < State.Y). Again, if you are having problems, chances are these numbers are the cause, if nothing else try changing them to see what happens, if you can get even one direction to work, well then, you'll know that this is the problem and you'll be able to fine tune the other values.

Of course, no joystick function would be complete without at least, one reference to its buttons as in "byte[] buttons = State.GetButtons();" The buttons, then use there own set of comparisons, as in a foreach statement and a hexadecimal reference, here we simply test through the b array, and it b is not zero, then this indicates a press. Nearly any reaction can be set in response to either a pad or button press, but generally pad movements control characters, buttons weapons, of course for fun you might try reversing those choices. The JoyStick_Tick method is given as example 6.10.

Example 6.10:
```
private void JoyStick_Tick(object sender, System.EventArgs e)
{
foreach (DeviceInstance instance in
Manager.GetDevices(DeviceClass.GameControl,
EnumDevicesFlags.AttachedOnly))
{joystick = new Microsoft.DirectX.DirectInput.Device
(instance.InstanceGuid);
break;}

if(joystick == null) {return;}

joystick.SetDataFormat(DeviceDataFormat.Joystick);
foreach (DeviceObjectInstance d in joystick.Objects)
{if ((0 != (d.ObjectId & (int)DeviceObjectTypeFlags.Axis)))
{joystick.Properties.SetRange(ParameterHow.ById, d.ObjectId, new
InputRange(-1000, 1000));}}
```

```
joystick.Acquire();
joystick.Poll();

State = joystick.CurrentJoystickState;
if(-400 < State.X)
{this.X--;
Invalidate();}
else if(-500 > State.X)
{this.X++;
Invalidate();}
if(-600 > State.Y)
{this.Y++;
Invalidate();}
else if(-500 < State.Y)
{this.Y--;
Invalidate();}

byte[] buttons = State.GetButtons();
foreach (byte b in buttons)
{if (0 != (b & 0x80))
{          }}}
```

Introducing DirectSound

Sound is probably the simplest of the DirectX standards. Here we'll merely have to insert a few background variables as in private "Microsoft.DirectX.DirectSound.Device sound = null;" and "private SecondaryBuffer SoundBuffer = null;" Include a assignment and a cooperation level "sound = new Microsoft.DirectX.DirectSound.Device();" "sound.SetCooperativeLevel(this, CooperativeLevel.Priority);" Load the buffer with a standard sound file as in "SoundBuffer = new SecondaryBuffer("..\\..\\Racket.wav", sound);" And play the sound with a call to "SoundBuffer.Play(0, BufferPlayFlags.Default);"

Of course, there are a few faults with this simplicity. One, if the file is not in the designated location, the game crash. Two, DirectSound is loaded on the fly and there is no grantee that the sound wave will load correctly, this will also cause the entire game to crash. In contrasts, the higher level GDI+ merely skips the sound, no crashes, no fuss although they also cause the games to slowdown -even freeze. Luckily, however, the solution is relatively simple, all we'll need to do is add a try- catch block as in try{SoundBuffer = new SecondaryBuffer("..\\..\\Racket.wav", sound); SoundBuffer.Play(0, BufferPlayFlags.Default);} catch {}. Where catch is really, a do nothing place meant.

In addition, in the games, I also allow the catch to substitute the higher level GDI+ reference when the sound file cannot be played. This may subsequently slowdown some of the game-play, but ultimately the sound are better off heard. The alternate catch statement can be written as catch{PlaySound("..\\..\\Racket.wav", 0, 0);}, but this would also require that we include the older "[DllImport ("winmm.dll")]" and "public static extern long PlaySound(String lpszName, long hModule, long dwFlags);" references. Another alternative could be to call a second DirectX sound, which should include its own try-catch block, or to flag the potential error with a default sound. In any case, all sounds should be tested and confirmed before a secondary catch is added. Note: the sounds loaded as part of the Tennis Arcade version were intentionally flawed and always invokes the GDI+ catch statements "PlaySound("Pong.wav", 0, 0);" and "PlaySound("Miss.wav", 0, 0); -a nice fix, if I say so myself (see examples 6.11 and 6.12).

Example 11:

```
SecondaryBuffer("..\\..\\Racket.wav", sound);

SoundBuffer.Play(0, BufferPlayFlags.Default);}
```

Example 12:

```
try {
SoundBuffer = new SecondaryBuffer
("..\\..\\Racket.wav", sound);

SoundBuffer.Play(0, BufferPlayFlags.Default);}

catch{PlaySound("..\\..\\Racket.wav", 0, 0);}
```

Finally, we'll want to see how the three DirectX standards combine to creating a simple, but complete model -this model also includes all of the references needed to create the DirectX versions of our first seven games (see example 6.13)

Example 6.13:

```
using System;
using System.Drawing;
using System.Windows.Forms;
using Microsoft.DirectX;
using Microsoft.DirectX.DirectDraw;
using Microsoft.DirectX.DirectInput;
using Microsoft.DirectX.DirectSound;
```

```
using Buffer = Microsoft.DirectX.DirectSound.SecondaryBuffer;

namespace Chapter6
{public class DirectXModel : System.Windows.Forms.Form
{private System.ComponentModel.Container
components = null;
private Microsoft.DirectX.DirectDraw.Device
draw = null;
private Microsoft.DirectX.DirectInput.Device
keyboard = null;
private Microsoft.DirectX.DirectInput.Device
joystick = null;
private Microsoft.DirectX.DirectSound.Device
sound = null;
private SecondaryBuffer SoundBuffer = null;
public JoystickState State = new JoystickState();
private Surface primary = null;
private Surface BallDraw = null;
private Clipper clip = null;
private Rectangle destination = new Rectangle();
private System.Windows.Forms.Timer Keyboard;
private System.Windows.Forms.Timer JoyStick;
private int X, Y;

public DirectXModel()
{InitializeComponent();
draw = new Microsoft.DirectX.DirectDraw.Device();
draw.SetCooperativeLevel(this,Microsoft.DirectX.DirectD
raw.CooperativeLevelFlags.Normal);
CreateSurfaces();

sound = new Microsoft.DirectX.DirectSound.Device();
sound.SetCooperativeLevel(this, CooperativeLevel.Priority);}

private void CreateSurfaces()
{SurfaceDescription description = new
SurfaceDescription();
description.SurfaceCaps.PrimarySurface = true;
primary = new Surface(description, draw);
clip = new Clipper(draw);
clip.Window = this;
primary.Clipper = clip;
```

```csharp
description.Clear();
BallDraw = new
Surface("..\\..\\TennisBall.bmp", description, draw);}

#region Windows Form Designer generated code private
void InitializeComponent()
{this.components = new
System.ComponentModel.Container();
this.Paint += new
System.Windows.Forms.PaintEventHandler
(this.ShowMeTheBall);
this.AutoScaleBaseSize = new
System.Drawing.Size(5, 13);
this.ClientSize = new
System.Drawing.Size(292, 266);
this.Name = "DirectX";
this.Text = "DirectX";
this.BackColor = Color.Blue;
this.Load += new System.EventHandler
(this.Form1_Load);

this.Keyboard = new
System.Windows.Forms.Timer(this.components);
this.Keyboard.Tick += new
System.EventHandler(this.Keyboard_Tick);

this.JoyStick = new
System.Windows.Forms.Timer(this.components);
this.JoyStick.Tick += new
System.EventHandler(this.JoyStick_Tick);}
#endregion

private void ShowMeTheBall(object sender,
System.Windows.Forms.PaintEventArgs e)
{try{destination = new Rectangle(PointToScreen(new
Point(X, Y)), new Size(25, 25));
primary.Draw(destination, BallDraw,
DrawFlags.Wait);}
catch(SurfaceLostException)
{CreateSurfaces();}}

private void Keyboard_Tick(object sender,
```

```
System.EventArgs e)
{keyboard = new
Microsoft.DirectX.DirectInput.Device
(SystemGuid.Keyboard);
keyboard.Properties.BufferSize = 8;
keyboard.Acquire();
KeyboardState state =
keyboard.GetCurrentKeyboardState();
for (Key k = Key.Escape; k <= Key.MediaSelect; k++)
{if (state[k] && k == Key.Space)
{this.X++;
Invalidate();
try
{SoundBuffer = new
SecondaryBuffer("..\..\Racket.wav", sound);
SoundBuffer.Play(0, BufferPlayFlags.Default);}
catch{      }
break;}}}

private void JoyStick_Tick(object sender, System.EventArgs e)
{
foreach (DeviceInstance instance in Manager.GetDevices(DeviceClass.GameControl,
EnumDevicesFlags.AttachedOnly))
{joystick = new Microsoft.DirectX.DirectInput.Device
(instance.InstanceGuid);
break;}

if(joystick == null) {return;}

joystick.SetDataFormat(DeviceDataFormat.Joystick);
foreach (DeviceObjectInstance d in joystick.Objects)
{if ((0 != (d.ObjectId & (int)DeviceObjectTypeFlags.Axis)))
{joystick.Properties.SetRange(ParameterHow.ById, d.ObjectId, new InputRange(-1000, 1000));}}

joystick.Acquire();
joystick.Poll();

State = joystick.CurrentJoystickState;

if(-400 < State.X)
{this.X--;
Invalidate();}
```

```
else if(-500 > State.X)
{this.X++;
Invalidate();}

if(-600 > State.Y)
{this.Y++;
Invalidate();}
else if(-500 < State.Y)
{this.Y--;
Invalidate();}
byte[] buttons = State.GetButtons();
foreach (byte b in buttons)
{if (0 != (b & 0x80))
{try{SoundBuffer = new SecondaryBuffer("..\\..\\Racket.wav", sound);
SoundBuffer.Play(0, BufferPlayFlags.Default);}
catch{            }}}}

[STAThread] static void Main()
{Application.Run(new DirectXModel());}

private void Form1_Load(object sender,
System.EventArgs e)
{Keyboard.Start();
JoyStick.Start();}}}
```

Vector Graphics (GDI+)

As I stated at the top of this chapter, there are also Arcade versions to our games. These again, build off the same object-oriented models, but there is a twist. Their visible components are reflected using shapes rather than bitmaps. The drawings are rendered using simple rectangles, ellipses, pies, arcs, and the more complex polygons. Brushes and pens are used to color these images, although DirectX and GDI+ differ in the way that those shapes are colored. Again, while I don't really want to get into the specifics of game play, I do want to give you an overview of how these shapes were created. The next few sections then cover the shape class for the GDI+ versions. The DirectX versions are explained as a follow-up, since several of the GDI+ tools do not have DirectX equivalence.

Paddle Tennis

Paddle Tennis uses two basic shapes, namely the FillRectangle and the FillEl
lipse. The rectangle is used to create both the players and their net. The net is merely a decoration, which does not affect game play. The players are constructed using a simple format, FillRectangle(System.Drawing.Brush brush, int x, int y, int width, int height), with the x, y-values denoted the player's coordinates. All colors need to be declared before being reference as in "Brush WhiteBrush = new (Color.White);" The player's positions are read from the AnimatingImage class as in imagePosX, imagePosY. The word "SCALE" refers is a constant that is used to control the size; in this case, the value is 25, so the width is 12, the height 25, giving the paddle a rectangular shape (see figure 6.1 and example 6.14).

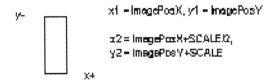

Example 6.14:
```
g.FillRectangle(WhiteBrush, playerL.imagePosX,
playerL.imagePosY, SCALE/2, SSCALE);
g.FillRectangle(WhiteBrush, playerR.imagePosX,
playerR.imagePosY, SCALE/2, SSCALE);
```

The ellipse, which is used to represent the ball, is also defined by the (System.Drawing.Brush brush, int x, int y, int width, int height) format. This also give the ellipse much more of a rectangular appearance (see figure 6.2 and example 6.15). Note: for a true circle one might look to the DrawArc reference (defined later in this chapter).

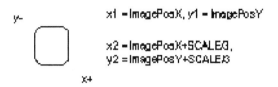

Example 6.15:
```
g.FillEllipse(WhiteBrush,
theBall.imagePosX, theBall.imagePosY,
SCALE/3, SCALE/3);
```

Space Fighter & Asteroid Miner

Both Space Fighter and Asteroid Miner use several new brushes and pens, these colors are explicated by their names as in RedPen, OrangeBrush... both also use the DrawPie function as in FillPie(System.Drawing.Pen pen, int x, int y, int width, int height, int startAngle, int sweepAngle). The angles listed are given to create the illusion of a ship pointing in different directions; a secondary FillEllipse is also used to create the illusion of exhaust (see figure 6.3 and example 6.16).

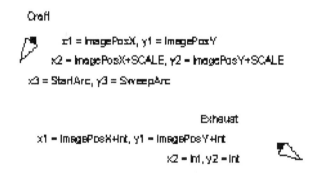

Example 6.16:

```
DrawPie(BluePen, X, Y, S, S, 290, 50);
FillEllipse(OrangeBrush, X+21, Y-1, SC/5, S/5);
```

2

```
DrawPie(BluePen, X, Y, S, S, 250, 50);
FillEllipse(OrangeBrush, X+10, Y-4, S/5, S/5);

DrawPie(BluePen, X, Y, S, S, 200, 50);
FillEllipse(OrangeBrush, X, Y, S/5, S/5);

DrawPie(BluePen, X, Y, S, S, -25, 50);
FillEllipse(OrangeBrush, X+25, Y+10, S/5, S/5);

DrawPie(BluePen, X, Y, S, S, 155, 50);
FillEllipse(OrangeBrush, X-5, Y+10, S/5, S/5);

DrawPie(BluePen, X, Y, S, S, 25, 50);
FillEllipse(OrangeBrush, X+20, Y+22, S/5, S/5);

DrawPie(BluePen, X, Y, S, S, 65, 50);
FillEllipse(OrangeBrush, X+10, Y+25, S/5, S/5);

DrawPie(BluePen, X, Y, S, S, 105, 50);
FillEllipse(OrangeBrush, X, Y+22, S/5, S/5);
```

   Of course, the most interesting of all the shapes is the polygon, written as DrawPolygon and FillPolygon. The polygon is a limitless line graphing option that can be used to create virtually any shape. Here, we'll use FillPolygon to define our interstellar vortex (used with Space Fighter) and the asteroids that we'll need for both games. Since the asteroids are identical, we'll also want to build them into a reusable method, note: this method will be part of a inheriting class titled "Shapes," but for now let's just focus on the coding at hand (see figures 6.4 and 6.5, with examples 6.17 and 6.18).

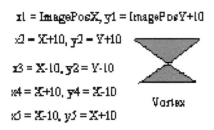

Example 6.17:
```
Point[] Vx = {new Point(Vx.imagePosX, Vx.imagePosY+10),
new Point(Vx.imagePosX+10, Vx.imagePosY+10),
new Point(Vx.imagePosX-10, Vx.imagePosY-10),
```

```
new Point(Vx.imagePosX+10, Vx.imagePosY-10),
new Point(Vx.imagePosX-10, Vx.imagePosY+10)};

g.FillPolygon(YellowBrush, Vx);


if(Asteroid1.Active == true)

{Asteroid1.Asteroid(Figures, BlueBrush);}
...
```

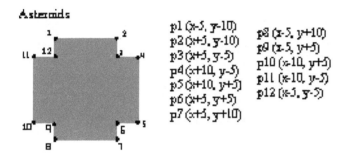

Example 6.17:

```
public void Asteroid(Graphics g,  Brush bAsteroidColor)
{
Point[] PolyRoid =
{
new Point(this.X.ReadValue()-this.ImageX/5, this.Y.ReadValue()-2*this.ImageY/5),
new Point(this.X.ReadValue()+this.ImageX/5, this.Y.ReadValue()-2*this.ImageY/5),
new Point(this.X.ReadValue()+this.ImageX/5, this.Y.ReadValue()-this.ImageY/5),
new Point(this.X.ReadValue()+2*this.ImageX/5, this.Y.ReadValue()-this.ImageY/5),
new Point(this.X.ReadValue()+2*this.ImageX/5, this.Y.ReadValue()+this.ImageY/5),
new Point(this.X.ReadValue()+this.ImageX/5, this.Y.ReadValue()+this.ImageY/5),
new Point(this.X.ReadValue()+this.ImageX/5, this.Y.ReadValue()+2*this.ImageY/5),
new Point(this.X.ReadValue()-this.ImageX/5, this.Y.ReadValue()+2*this.ImageY/5),
new Point(this.X.ReadValue()-this.ImageX/5, this.Y.ReadValue()+this.ImageY/5),
new Point(this.X.ReadValue()-2*this.ImageX/5, this.Y.ReadValue()+this.ImageY/5),
new Point(this.X.ReadValue()-2*this.ImageX/5, this.Y.ReadValue()-this.ImageY/5),
new Point(this.X.ReadValue()-this.ImageX/5, this.Y.ReadValue()-this.ImageY/5),};
```

g.FillPolygon(bAsteroidColor, PolyRoid);}

Battle Wave

Here, our main concern will be the construction of our polygons (note: for coding references see the section titled "Ground Assault" listed in this chapter). The next set of polygons then are used to represent Battle Wave's invading Aliens. As with the previous drawings, these again, will be set to a 20x20 Scale with the position (x = imagePosX, y = imagePosY), being the center of the model (see Figure 6.6 through 6.9). Note: these polygons we'll also be incorporated into an inheriting class, which will be defined in the next section.

Alien1

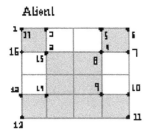

p1 (x-10, y-10)
p2 (x-5, y-10)
p3 (x-5, y-5)
p4 (x+5, y-5)
p5 (x+5, y-10)
p6 (x+10, y-10)
p7 (x+10, y-5)
p8 (x+5, y-5)
p9 (x+5, y+5)
p10 (x+10, y+5)

p11 (x+10, y+10)
p12 (x-10, y+10)
p13 (x-10, y+5)
p14 (x-5, y+5)
p15 (x-5, y-5)
p16 (x-10, y-5)
p17 (x-10, y-10)

Alien2

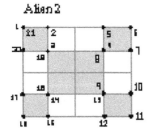

p1 (x-10, y-10)
p2 (x-5, y-10)
p3 (x-5, y-5)
p4 (x+5, y-5)
p5 (x+5, y-10)
p6 (x+10, y-10)
p7 (x+10, y-5)
p8 (x+5, y-5)
p9 (x+5, y+5)
p10 (x+10, y+5)
p11 (x+10, y+10)

p12 (x+5, y+10)
p13 (x+5, y+5)
p14 (x-5, y+5)
p15 (x-5, y+10)
p16 (x-10, y+10)
p17 (x-10, y+5)
p18 (x-5, y+5)
p19 (x-5, y-5)
p20 (x-10, y-5)
p21 (x-10, y-10)

Alien3

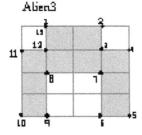

p1 (x-5, y-10)
p2 (x+5, y-10)
p3 (x+5, y-5);
p4 (x+10, y-5)
p5 (x+10, y+10)
p6 (x+5, y+10)
p7 (x+5, y)
p8 (x-5, y)

p9 (x-5, y+10)
p10 (x-10, y-5)
p11 (x-10, y-5)
p12 (x-5, y-5)
p13 (x-5, y-10)

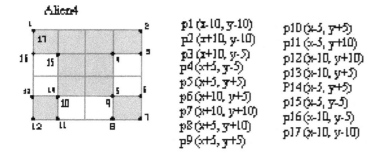

p1 (x-10, y-10) p10 (x-5, y+5)
p2 (x+10, y-10) p11 (x-5, y+10)
p3 (x+10, y-5) p12 (x-10, y+10)
p4 (x+5, y-5) p13 (x-10, y+5)
p5 (x+5, y+5) P14 (x-5, y+5)
p6 (x+10, y+5) p15 (x-5, y-5)
p7 (x+10, y+10) p16 (x-10, y-5)
p8 (x+5, y+10) p17 (x-10, y-10)
p9 (x+5, y+5)

Battle Tennis

With Battle Tennis, the polygons start to become a bit more complex, but if we change the method behind our drawings. Converting them to a component-based configuration, the workload is not only reduced, but we have the advantage of multiple colors, reusable forms, and program independence. The idea then would be to create an inheriting class, which I've titled "Shapes." This class would inherit from the character's "Animating Image" class, thus allowing for simple integration into our gaming model. To begin, we'll want to create two basic methods, namely a trapezoid and a sharpTriangle (see examples 6.18 and 6.19).

Example 6.18:
```
public Point[] Trapezoid()
{Point[] Trapezoid = {

new Point(this.imagePosX-5, this.imagePosY-10),
new Point(this.imagePosX+5, this.imagePosY-10),

new Point(this.imagePosX+10, this.imagePosY),
new Point(this.imagePosX-10, this.imagePosY)};

return(Trapezoid);}
```

Example 6.19:
```
public Point[] sharpTriangle()
{Point[] sharpTriangle = {

new Point(this.imagePosX, this.imagePosY-5),
```

2

```
new Point(this.imagePosX+3, this.imagePosY+10),
```
new Point(this.imagePosX-3, this.imagePosY+10)};
```
return(sharpTriangle);}
```

With the first two methods in place, we now want to implement a third method, this method would be titled "Lamp," since that is the object that we hope to create. The Lamp method then will take the parameters (Graphics g, Brush bLampColor, Brush bLampshadeColor), the graphic information, thus is passed to allow our method to display the data, the first brush is used to set the lamp's color, the second to color its shade (see Figure 6.10).

The Lamp

Note: while both shapes are called in unison, the sharp triangle should always be drawn first, since this will allow the trapezoids color dominance (see example 6.20).

Example 6.20:
```
public void Lamp(Graphics g, Brush LampColor, Brush
LampshadeColor)
```
{Point[] DrawLamp = this.sharpTriangle();
 Point[] DrawLampshade = this.Trapezoid();
```
 g.FillPolygon(LampColor, DrawLamp);

 g.FillPolygon(LampshadeColor, DrawLampshade);}
```

The next image we'll define then is the television, this will require several references to both the FillEllipse and the FillRectangle. This time however, we'll include all of the images are part of a single method (see figure 11 and example 6.21).

TV

2

Example 6.21:
```
public void TV(Graphics g, Brush bTVColor, Pen pTVColor)
{Brush GrayBrush = new SolidBrush(Color.Gray);
g.FillRectangle(GrayBrush, this.ImagePosX,
this.ImagePosY, 25, 15);
g.FillEllipse(bTVColor, this.ImagePosX+1,
this.ImagePosY+1, 15, 13);
g.FillEllipse(bTVColor, this.ImagePosX+18,
this.ImagePosY+2, 5, 5);
g.FillEllipse(bTVColor, this.ImagePosX+18,
this.ImagePosY+7, 5, 5);
g.DrawLine(pTVColor, this.ImagePosX+12,
this.ImagePosY, this.ImagePosX+5,
this.ImagePosY-5);
g.DrawLine(pTVColor, this.ImagePosX+14, this.ImagePosY,
this.ImagePosX+19, this.ImagePosY-5);}
```

Now, we'll want to design our flower, this of course, could be done in several ways, but here I want to introduce the DrawArc method. There are actually four ways to define DrawArc, but they are all essentially the same reference, two handle integers, two handle floats. Two use the Rectangle, two use four points that make a Rectangular shape. The most delineated integer version then would be the DrawArc(System.Drawing.Pen pen, int x, int y, int width, int height, int startAngle, int sweepAngle). Here, we already worked with the first five units, thus it's really only the last two that need to be defined.

startAngle and sweepAngle: Start and sweep do just as their names imply. Start denotes the point where the arc begins, sweep tells the graph how far to take it. For example, a 360 degree sweep starting at 0, would create a circle. a 360 degree sweep starting and 180, would also create a circle, a 180 degree sweep, thus starting anywhere would create a half circle (see Figure 6.12).

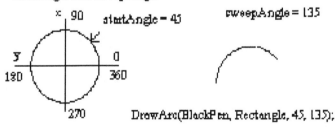

Of course, to create something that resembles a flower we'll have to rake havoc with the curves, we'll also want to reenlist our sharp triangle, this will serve as our stem and vase (see figure 6.13 and example 6.22)

The Flower

Example 6.22:
```
public void Flower(Graphics g,
Brush bFlowerColor, Pen pFlowerColor)
{g.DrawArc(pFlowerColor, this.imagePosX,
this.imagePosY-8, 5, 15, 0, 180);
g.DrawArc(pFlowerColor, this.imagePosX-10,
this.imagePosY-8, 15, 5, 90, 180);
g.DrawArc(pFlowerColor, this.imagePosX,
this.imagePosY-17, 5, 15, 180, 180);
g.DrawArc(pFlowerColor, this.imagePosX+1,
this.imagePosY-8, 15, 5, 270, 180);
g.FillEllipse(bFlowerColor, this.imagePosX-2,
this.imagePosY-10, 10, 10);
Point[] Vase = this.sharpTriangle();
g.FillPolygon(bFlowerColor, Vase);}
```

The most simplest of our design then would have to be the window. Here we are only repeating four rectangles, but the layering is significant. The frame then is drawn first, followed by the glass, then the beam, and finally the window lock (see figure 14 and example 6.23).

The Window

Example 6.23:

```
public void Window(Graphics g, Brush bWindowColor)
{Brush GrayBrush = new SolidBrush(Color.Gray);
g.FillRectangle(GrayBrush, this.imagePosX,
this.imagePosY, 24, 24);
g.FillRectangle(bWindowColor, this.imagePosX+2,
this.imagePosY+2, 20, 20);
g.FillRectangle(GrayBrush, this.imagePosX+11,
this.imagePosY, 3, 24);
g.FillRectangle(GrayBrush, this.imagePosX+11,
this.imagePosY+11, 5, 3);}
```

Ground Assault

Ground Assault is actually a continuation of Battle Wave, just as Battle Wave was a continuation of Battle Bit (chapter two). The idea here is that the aliens finally landed and are now attempting an occupation. In any case, this really wouldn't explain how the aliens are able to fly through space without spaceships, but that's a different issue. The designs to Ground Assault we're are given as coding here,
whereas their images were given as figures 6.6 through 6.9 for coding details see example 6.25.

Example 6.25:

```
public void Alien0(Graphics g, Brush bAlienColor)
{Point[] Alien =
{new Point(imagePosX-10, this.imagePosY-10),
new Point(this.imagePosX-5, this.imagePosY-10),
new Point(this.imagePosX-5, this.imagePosY-5),
new Point(this.imagePosX+5, this.imagePosY-5),
new Point(this.imagePosX+5, this.imagePosY-10),
new Point(this.imagePosX+10, this.imagePosY-10),
new Point(this.imagePosX+10, this.imagePosY-5),
new Point(this.imagePosX+5, this.imagePosY-5),
new Point(this.imagePosX+5, this.imagePosY+5),
new Point(this.imagePosX+10, this.imagePosY+5),
new Point(this.imagePosX+10, this.imagePosY+10),
new Point(this.imagePosX-10, this.imagePosY+10),
new Point(this.imagePosX-10, this.imagePosY+5),
new Point(this.imagePosX-5, this.imagePosY+5),
new Point(this.imagePosX-5, this.imagePosY-5),
new Point(this.imagePosX-10, this.imagePosY-5),
new Point(this.imagePosX-10, this.imagePosY-10)};
```

```
g.FillPolygon(bAlienColor, Alien);}

public void Alien1(Graphics g, Brush bAlienColor)
{Point[] Alien =
{new Point(this.imagePosX-10, this.imagePosY-10),
new Point(this.imagePosX-5, this.imagePosY-10),
new Point(this.imagePosX-5, this.imagePosY-5),
new Point(this.imagePosX+5, this.imagePosY-5),
new Point(this.imagePosX+5, this.imagePosY-10),
new Point(this.imagePosX+10, this.imagePosY-10),
new Point(this.imagePosX+10, this.imagePosY-5),
new Point(this.imagePosX+5, this.imagePosY-5),
new Point(this.imagePosX+5, this.imagePosY+5),
new Point(this.imagePosX+10, this.imagePosY+5),
new Point(this.imagePosX+10, this.imagePosY+10),
new Point(this.imagePosX+5, this.imagePosY+10),
new Point(this.imagePosX+5, this.imagePosY+5),
new Point(this.imagePosX-5, this.imagePosY+5),
new Point(this.imagePosX-5, this.imagePosY+10),
new Point(this.imagePosX-10, this.imagePosY+10),
new Point(this.imagePosX-10, this.imagePosY+5),
new Point(this.imagePosX-5, this.imagePosY+5),
new Point(this.imagePosX-5, this.imagePosY-5),
new Point(this.imagePosX-10, this.imagePosY-5),
new Point(this.imagePosX-10, this.imagePosY-10)};

g.FillPolygon(bAlienColor, Alien);}

public void Alien2(Graphics g, Brush bAlienColor)
{Point[] Alien =
{new Point(this.imagePosX-5, this.imagePosY-10),
new Point(this.imagePosX+5, this.imagePosY-10),
new Point(this.imagePosX+5, this.imagePosY-5),
new Point(this.imagePosX+10, this.imagePosY-5),
new Point(this.imagePosX+10, this.imagePosY+10),
new Point(this.imagePosX+5, this.imagePosY+10),
new Point(this.imagePosX+5, this.imagePosY),
new Point(this.imagePosX-5, this.imagePosY),
new Point(this.imagePosX-5, this.imagePosY+10),
new Point(this.imagePosX-10, this.imagePosY+10),
new Point(this.imagePosX-10, this.imagePosY-5),
new Point(this.imagePosX-5, this.imagePosY-5),
```

new Point(this.imagePosX-5, this.imagePosY-10)};

g.FillPolygon(bAlienColor, Alien);}

public void Alien3(Graphics g, Brush bAlienColor)
{Point[] Alien =
{new Point(this.imagePosX-10, this.imagePosY-10),
new Point(this.imagePosX+10, this.imagePosY-10),
new Point(this.imagePosX+10, this.imagePosY-5),
new Point(this.imagePosX+5, this.imagePosY-5),
new Point(this.imagePosX+5, this.imagePosY+5),
new Point(this.imagePosX+10, this.imagePosY+5),
new Point(this.imagePosX+10, this.imagePosY+10),
new Point(this.imagePosX+5, this.imagePosY+10),
new Point(this.imagePosX+5, this.imagePosY+5),
new Point(this.imagePosX-5, this.imagePosY+5),
new Point(this.imagePosX-5, this.imagePosY+10),
new Point(this.imagePosX-10, this.imagePosY+10),
new Point(this.imagePosX-10, this.imagePosY+5),
new Point(this.imagePosX-5, this.imagePosY+5),
new Point(this.imagePosX-5, this.imagePosY-5),
new Point(this.imagePosX-10, this.imagePosY-5),
new Point(this.imagePosX-10, this.imagePosY-10)};

g.FillPolygon(bAlienColor, Alien);}

We'll also need to include one addition configuration, namely the player's tank, the tank is also equipped with a massive cannon, which is created through the use of a recalculating FillPie (see figure 6.15 and Example 6.26).

The Tank

Example 6.24:
```
public void Tank(Graphics g, Brush bTankColor,
Brush bCannonColor)
```

```
{Point[] tank =
{new Point(this.imagePosX-10, this.imagePosY-10),
new Point(this.imagePosX+10, this.imagePosY-10),
new Point(this.imagePosX+10, this.imagePosY-5),
new Point(this.imagePosX+5, this.imagePosY-5),
new Point(this.imagePosX+5, this.imagePosY+5),
new Point(this.imagePosX+10, this.imagePosY+5),
new Point(this.imagePosX+10, this.imagePosY+10),
new Point(this.imagePosX-10, this.imagePosY+10),
new Point(this.imagePosX-10, this.imagePosY+5),
new Point(this.imagePosX-5, this.imagePosY+5),
new Point(this.imagePosX-5, this.imagePosY-5),
new Point(this.imagePosX-10, this.imagePosY-5),
new Point(this.imagePosX-10, this.imagePosY-10)};

g.FillPolygon(bTankColor, tank);
g.FillPie(bCannonColor, this.imagePosX-12,
this.imagePosY-12, this.imageWidth, this.imageLength,
this.imagePosX, this.imageLength);}
```

Rat Racer

Rat Racer, technically, does not use any new shapes, all we've done here is substitute the walls with FillRectangles and the cheese with FillPies.The most unique feature than, would have to be the way the maze was constructed, a for-loop, used to reference an array of instances, the x, y values referencing it position, the width, height referencing its dimensions (see figure 6.16 and example 6.25).

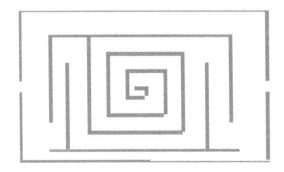

Example 6.25:
```
for(int i = 0; i < 24; i++)
{dc.FillRectangle(BlueBrush, Walls[i].imagePosX, Walls[i].imagePosy,
```

```
Walls[i].imageWidth, Walls[i].imageLength);}
```

Vector Graphics (using DirectDraw)

Another exciting feature included with the DirectDraw package is the ability to create vector graphics. Vector graphics are graphics created through drawing tools, such as DrawBox, DrawCircle, DrawEllipse, DrawLine, and DrawRoundedBox. These DirectDraw versions then can be used to replace at least, some of our GDI+ tools, making for a few more interesting combinations. Let's begin with DrawBox.

DrawBox: DrawBox is written as public void DrawBox(int left, int top, int right, int bottom) it is used in combination with ColorFill, written as public void ColorFill(Rectangle destRectangle, Color fillValue). DrawBox with ColorFill then can be used to recreate anything that FIllRectangle can manage (see examples 6.26).

Example 6.26:
```
for (int Y=50; Y <= this.ClientSize.Height; Y+=15)
{primary.ColorFill(new Rectangle(400, Y,
10, 10), Color.White);
primary.DrawBox(400, Y, 410, Y+10);}
```

DrawCircle: DrawCircle written public void DrawCircle(int x, int y, int radius) is is also used in combination with ColorFill, DrawCircle can actually produce a much better quility circle then the standard FillEllipse (see example 6.27).

Example 6.27:
```
if(theBall.isActive == true)
{primary.ColorFill(new Rectangle(theBall.imagePosX,
theBall.imagePosY, 5, 5), Color.White);
primary.DrawCircle(theBall.imagePosX, theBall.imagePosY, 5);}
```

DrawEllipse: DrawEllipse written public void DrawEllipse(int x1, int y1, int x2, int y2), is combined with ColorFill, DrawEllipse simular to FillEllipse (see example 6.28).

Example 6.28:
```
primary.ColorFill(new Rectangle(theBall.imagePosX,
theBall.imagePosY, 5, 5), Color.White);

primary.DrawEllipse(theBall.imagePosX, theBall.imagePosY, 5, 5);
```

DrawLine: Drawline is written public void DrawLine(int x1, int y1, int x2, int y2), it is also used with ColorFill, DrawLine is simular to Drawline GDI+ (see example 6.29).

Example 6.29:
```
for(int i = 0; i < 24; i++)
{primary.ColorFill(new Rectangle(Walls[i].X.ReadValue(), Walls[i].Y.ReadValue(), Walls[i].ImageX,
Walls[i].ImageY), Color.Blue);
primary.DrawLine(Walls[i].X.ReadValue(), Walls[i].Y.ReadValue(),
Walls[i].ImageX, Walls[i].ImageY);}
```

DrawRoundedBox: DrawRoundedBox written public void DrawRoundedBox(int left, int top, int right, int bottom, int rw, int rh), combined with ColorFill, DrawRoundedBox is simular to FillRectangle (see example 6.30).

Example 6.30
```
primary.ColorFill(new Rectangle(100, 100,
125, 125), Color.Red);
primary.DrawRoundedBox(100, 100, 125, 125, 25, 25);
```

Trouble Shooting

Here we are again; back in troubleshoot, this time however, we're more like seasoned veterans, working through the details of games that seemed foreign to us just a few weeks ago. We've build the standard games, we modified them once, twice, a third time maybe, and now we're just trying to figure out the end pieces. Sure, there's obviously something wrong, but try looking at it other way, look how far we've come. And if it takes a few more days to reach that next level, we'll then, that's what it takes.

Note: If however, you happen to be a skimmer, someone who is not already a C# guru, well then, I recommend that you stop, go back, and do the work that it takes to get here. There's really no point in struggling through the problems of DirectX, if you haven't already master the safer, yet equally rich coding presented under GDI+. Remember, much of the gaming structures are identical, so you might as well learn them under a simpler format.

In any case, the problems and solutions found in this section are exclusively for DirectX 9.x, listed under the categories of Installing, DirectDraw, DirectInput, and DirectSound. If you have any other compiling or trouble-shooting questions, please see the trouble shooting sections listed on the last five chapters.

Installing DirectX: First, you'll need to install you're compiler -let's assume that you've done that. Second, you'll need to download you're DirectX 9.0 SDK, located at www.microsoft.com/windows/directx. Again, let's assume that you've not only downloaded that, but that you've installed it too. So, what is the problem? Well, one error that can occur, happens when DirectX 9 was previously installed on your system without your C# compiler. Possible scenarios; One, you installed it with the C# beta version. Two, you installed it with your C++ compiler, three you installed it with your Visual Basic compiler, four, you eagerly installed it first and then installed C#, gees. The solution, remove all DirectX components and install/ reinstall DirectX 9.0

We'll what if this is the future and there is a problem with DirectX 10, 11, or 12? They had it working with 9.0 and then they got discombobulated. Well then, obviously, that's what my E-mail address is for. Remember the E-mail address posted at the beginning of the text, it's plague@iwon.com. When you write, be very clear, explain your problem in detail, all the steps that you've taken, anything new that you did before the error occurred...

DirectDraw: DirectX seems to have this nasty way of crashing even when the error is relatively small. DirectDraw for example, produces this ominous red X, just to tell you that a single file is missing. Why can't it just look for the file ahead of time and tell us, "Hey! There's a file missing." The answer, it can, but only if we program it to do so. The coding could of course, be done in a number of ways, but probably the simplest example would be a try-block with a MessageBox that alerts us of the error before the game begins (see example 6.31)

Example 6.31:
```
try
{PlayerLDraw = new Surface("..\..\PlayerL.bmp", description, draw);}
catch (FileNotFoundException ex)
{MessageBox.Show("Hey!
ex.Message + "\n\nThere's a file missing.",
"File Not Found!");
Application.Exit();}
```

This makes a nice compliment to the continuing try-block "try{destination = new Rectangle(PointToScreen(new Point(X, Y)), new Size(width, height)); primary.Draw(destination, BallDraw, DrawFlags.Wait);}catch(SurfaceLostException) {CreateSurfaces();}," which prevents errors that occur on the fly. Remember that with this second catch in place a missing or damaged file cannot cause the dreaded red X error, so if you're still having problems, remember that any other visual errors would appear as missing files or blank spots on the screen.

Again, if you've coded for both of these exceptions, then the only other drawing error that you are likely to encounter is an absences of an image. For this I'd try replacing the image with a proven bitmap, if that doesn't resolve the error, try testing the coordinates of the image and the width and height displayed, maybe the image is there, but it's off to the side, too small, or perhaps the coding is not even being accessed.

Files executed from the debug and/or release folders, also, may not be able to find the image and/or sound files listed in the working folders. A simple solution to this would be to transport the files to the appropriate folder; other approaches could include hard coding to a certain file or partial hard coding to a general file with defined sub-folders.

Note: DirectDraw is only compatible with bitmaps other formats such as jpegs, giffs... will compile, but the programs will not run, sparking instead an argument
exception error.

DirectInput: The most detrimental error caused in DirectInput is a crash when the computer cannot find your joystick. If you've included the "if(joystick == null) {return;} statement then this error should also have been averted. Therefore, if you're still having trouble, the problem is probably more along the lines of not being able to get our input devices to work. Let's begin with the joystick.

The Joystick: Remember I cautioned you about the State setting as in State.X and State.Y, the range here could be off, you should also try manipulating the input range itself, perhaps setting it to 0, 1 here you'd be looking for a response in either direction, again, if you get one response, you'll be able to find the others.

Another possibility is that you've improperly setup your bitmap; does it move with the keyboard, if not can you set it to move on a for-loop? Check for a changing variable, an invalidating statement. Does the joystick's input include an invalidating statement? Do the pre-assembled programs work with the joystick, how about a third party game? If you're using a special type of joystick like a steering wheel or multiple joysticks, try replacing them with a simple two button pad (for additional possibilities read through this sections portion on the keyboard).

The Keyboard: Here you're far more likely to have forgotten something. A missing command, did you forget to include a Keyboard.Start()? Did you include the timer coding. Remember the key states they began with the lowest setting and worked their way through to the top, did you start the search at a different point? Also, check the obvious, forget to include an invalidating reference? (For additional possibilities read through this sections portion on the joystick).

DirectSound: Now with DirectSound at least, the program doesn't stop. After an error is detected you can hit continue and actually watch to see where the error occurs. This can also give you a reasonable idea as to which sound is malfunctioning, where that code might be located. The first error you might check for then would be the missing file, but chances are you wouldn't have forgotten to include those files. Next, you'll add your try-catch block, but that merely hides the error, and you end up with a soundless game. You might, as I sometimes do, revert back to the older PlaySound function, so as to hear the sound you want to hear. Noting that winmm.dll allows for most formats, where as DirectX does not. That's right; you've just found the most common error, using a format that doesn't compile with DirectX, and the most common of these formats is the compressed wave. Compressed waves don't work with DirectSound; compressed waves don't work with DirectSound, okay now you have it. The simplest solution, use a different sound, another possibility would be to change the format, or remake the sound, or again, you could use the safety.

Note: If you simply forgot to add sound, you would hear silence is that position. You should check for that as well.

In addition, there are several optimizing techniques that we can use to enhance our future games.

1. Use public reference as in public methods and public fields. Avoid passing unnecessary values, as in entire instances when only a single point is required.

2. Don't use classes where structures would serve. Structures are faster, so if you do not need the properties of the class, don't waste the resource.

3. Breakdown instructions into single statements, write code so that calculations are not wrapped together, the results will be both faster and easier to debug.

4. Binary shifts can be used in place of multiplication and division, the results are the same, but several cycles can be saved with every reference.

5. Don't over complicate your coding. Yes, some coding tricks do look cool, but always be aware of their speed costs. Complex can often become messy.

Finally thoughts:

1. I would also recommend backing up your work. While writing this text I made daily backups. Later, as I reached the end of the project, I found that I could skim and reincorporate ideas that were completely forgotten.

2. Use comments, even the brightest programmers forget things, after I wrote the code for the TV and flower patterns, I couldn't remember which line was which, I ended up having to go back and retest each line.

Appendix A: Keywords/Reserved Identifiers

__abstract	__alignof	__asm	__assume
__based	__box	__cdecl	__declspec
__delegate	__event	__except	__fastcall
__finally	__forceinline	__gc	__hook
__identifier	__if_exists	__if_not_exists	__inline
__int8	__int16	__int32	__int64
__interface	__leave	__m64	__m128
__m128d	__m128i	__multiple_inheritance	__nogc
__noop	__pin	__property	__raise
__sealed	__single_inheritance	__stdcall	__super
__try_cast	__try/__except, __try/__finally	__unhook	__uuidof
__value	__virtual_inheritance	__w64	bool
break	case	catch	char
class	const	const_cast	continue
default	delete	deprecated	dllexport
dllimport	do	double	dynamic_cast
else	enum	explicit	extern
false	float	for	friend
goto	if	inline	int
long	mutable	naked	namespace
new	noinline	noreturn	nothrow
novtable	operator	private	property
protected	public	register	reinterpret_cast
return	selectany	short	signed
sizeof	static	static_cast	struct
switch	template	this	thread
throw	true	try	typedef
typeid	typename	union	unsigned
using declaration, using directive	uuid	virtual	void
volatile	__wchar_t, wchar_t	while	

3

Appendix B: Reserved Identifiers Defined

__alignof

__asm

The keyword __asm (a synonym to _asm), is useful when we want to include assembly language coding as part of our programs. Assembly coding can be included as part of a block or as part of a single line (see Example B.1).

Example B.1:
__asm {
// insert assembly coding here
}
__asm assembly instructions...;

__assume

abstract

  Another useful feature when dealing with inheritance is the abstract modifier. This is a modifier used to declare a class that is intended only to be used as a base class. Abstract classes cannot be instantiated nor can they be modify with a sealed modifier. Only abstract classes may use abstract methods and assessors, but all non-abstract classes derived from those classes must include implementations of those references. Abstract methods are also implicitly virtual, their properties can be overridden, and they cannot be intermixed with static properties (see example B.1).

Example B.1:
```
public abstract class Area {}
class Appendix_B
{static void Main(){}}
```

as

  As is a binary operator that allows for a conversion from an expression to a data type. This is also a useful tool when attempting to avoid exceptions, since as will return a null if the conversion fails (see example B.2).

Example B.2:
```
public class Appendix_B
{public static void Main()
{object MyString = new object();
string s = MyString as string;}}
```

base

Base is the keyword used to access members of a base class. In principle it works the same way as the *this* command, but from within a derived class. A base class can be accessed as a constructor, an instances of a method, or as an instances of a property accessor. These methods can be overridden, but they cannot be used with static methods (see example B.3).

Example B.3:

```
namespace Appendix_B
{public class BaseClass {
public BaseClass() {}
public virtual void DisplayArea() {}}
public class DerivedClass : BaseClass
{DerivedClass() {}
public override void DisplayArea()
{base.DisplayArea();}
static void Main(){}}}
```

bool

Boolean expressions are mathematical representations for the concepts of both true and false. That is, while their actual evaluations are based on mathematical data, their outcomes are in fact determined by a conceptual understanding. This type of determination is represented in the C# languages as the data type bool, with its variables assigned to the Boolean constants *true* or *false* (see example B.4)

Example B.4:

```
class Appendix_B
{static void Main ()
{bool Variable1 = true;}}
```

break

Break as its name implies, terminates any enclosed loop or conditional statement (see example B.5).

Example B.5:

```
class Appendix_B
{static void Main()
{while(true)
{break;}}}
```

byte

Byte is an unsigned 8-bit integral date type that stores whole numbers with a range listed from 0 to 255 (see example B.6).

Example B.6:

```
class Appendix_B
{static void Main ()
{byte Number = 100;}}
```

case

The keyword "*case*" is written and used multiple times from within the *switch* statement, each *case* statement holds a numeric or character value for comparison. If the value held by a *case* statement matches the value read by the *switch* statement then everything following that case statement would be executed (see example B.7).

Example B.7:

```
class Appendix_B
{static void Main ()
{char test = 'A';
switch (test)
{case 'A':
break;}}}
```

catch

The catch statement is part of the try-block, it is used to literally catch and then to possibly repair a program when an exception is thrown. Its clauses can include system exceptions, user defined material, and/or a blank or generalized catch. Note: A try-block normally includes multiple catch statement with the most specific statements listed first and the blank or general statement placed in the furthest position. Failure to list your catches in that order may result in a less specific catch being executed. It is also possible to re-throw an exception from within the catch statement (see example B.8).

Example B.8:

```
public class Appendix_B
{static void Main()
{try {}
catch {}}}
```

char

The character references char, is used to declare 16-bit Unicode characters which have ranges from U+0000 to U+ffff. Unicode characters are 16-bit characters used to represent nearly all of the known languages as well as most if not all of the traditional mathematical and literary symbols. Chars are also used to two represent combined values such as hexadecimal codes and escape sequences (see example B.9).

Example B.9:

```
class Appendix_B
{static void Main()
{char Symbol = 'A';}}
```

checked

Checked is used to monitor both operators and statements for numeric overflow errors as they occur in integral-type arithmetic operations and conversions (see example B.10).

Example B.10:
```
class Appendix_B
{static void Main ()
{byte Max255 = 254;
checked{Max255++;}}}
```

class

Classes are an advanced data type, a few levels beyond a simple byte, but not too dissimilar. They are similar to arrays, yet they're capable of holding tasks and multiple data types (more formally known as tags, fields, methods…). They are called as instances which also can be thought of as variables that hold multiple bits of information. They are limited and/or enhanced by modifiers, classes can also be inherited (see example B.11).

Example B.11:
```
class Appendix_B
{static void Main ()
{}}
```

const

The keyword constant (*const*) notifies the compiler of its unchanging nature and allows it to optimize that appropriate values (see example B.12).

Example B.12:
```
class Appendix_B
{static void Main()
{const int OurVariable = 1;}}
```

continue

Continue, like break, shortcuts its iterations, but rather than ending the loop, it merrily brings the loop back to the top. The loop continues form with a new iteration and everything else continues accordingly (see example B.13).

Example B.13:
```
class Appendix_B
{static void Main ( )
```

```
{while (true)
{continue;}}}
```

decimal

Decimal is a 128-bit date type that stores rational and irrational numbers with a range listed from 1.0×10^{-28} to 7.9×10^{28} its precision level is between 28-29 significant digits, which makes it suitable for nearly all monetary calculations (see example B.14).

Example B.14:
```
class Appendix_B
{static void Main()
{decimal Number1, Number2;
Number1 = 1.0M;
Number2 = 1.1m;}}
```

default

Default is usually placed at the end of a *switch* statement, thus allowing us to execute selected statements based on the fact that they do not match any of the pervious values (see example B.15).

Example B.15:
```
using System;
class Appendix_B
{static void Main()
{int byNumber = Console.Read ();
switch (byNumber)
{default:
break;}}}
```

delegate

Delegates are references used to encapsulate specific methods. A delegate instance encapsulates a static or an instance method. The delegate, while similar to the C++ function pointer, is actually type safe and considered OOP sound. Delegates also allow for six key modifiers namely *new, public, protected, internal, private,* and *unsafe* (*unsafe* need only be used when dealing with parameters that are also pointers). Delegates are most frequently used to pass methods as parameters, the type safety of delegates is based on the matching of signatures as part of their declaration. Delegates are also declared before they are called, like C++ prototypes (see example B.16).

Example B.16:
```
public delegate void TryDelegate();
public class Appendix_B
{static void Main()
{TryDelegate();}
public static void TryDelegate()
```

{}}

do

Do as part of the do-while combination allows for the execution of a set of statements or block. This block will execute indefinably terminating only when a false expression is found. Do-while loops begin by executing their blocks, then they test and repeat, guaranteeing at least one execution before the process is terminated (see example B.17).

Example B.17:

```
class Appendix_B
{static void Main ()
{do
{} while (true);}}
```

double

Double is a 64-bit data type used to store floating-point values ranging from $\pm 5.0 \times 10^{-324}$ to $\pm 1.7 \times 10^{308}$ its precision level is between 15-16 digits (see example B.18).

Example B.18:

```
class Appendix_B
{static void Main()
{double Number1, Number2;
Number1 = 1.0;
Number2 = 1.1;}}
```

else

Else is the first logical extension to the questioning *if-statement*. It adds an additional line of reasoning and an additional path for our programs to follow. *Else* cannot be used independently, yet it links easily to the tail end of the "*if*" structure (see example B.19).

Example B.19:

```
using System;
class Appendix_B
{static void Main()
{double Answer = double.Parse(Console.ReadLine());
if (Answer == 5)
 Console.WriteLine ("\n That is correct!\n");
else
 Console.WriteLine("\n Wrong!!!\n");}}
```

enum

The enumerator is a basic aggregated type that promotes simple reference manipulations. It also allows for some unique references as in user-defined data structures and lists of assignments to those declarations. Initial structures are declared using the keyword *enum* with instances of those values declared and assigned as if they were class references. If no values are assigned to these references than the initial, point would be zero and each new component would automatically increment by one. However, we can also short step this process by beginning at some arbitrary point or we could individually declare each value (see example B.20).

Example B.20:

```
class Appendix_B
{public enum Months {Jan = 1, Feb, Mar, Apr,
       May, Jun, Jul, Aug, Sep, Oct, Nov, Dec}
public enum Day {AprilFools = 1, Birthday = 16,
       XMas = 25, Feb29 = 29, NYeve = 31}
public enum Year {Year2 = 2002, Year3, LeapYear}
static void Main ()
{}}
```

event

We can also specifically state our delegates and then reference them using another keyword namely the event. These events are also then dependent on the program including a delegate to reference. Events are also used with accessor functions namely add and remove, which need to be declared collectively. Note: Events can also be shared through the Common Language Runtime, which also requires that we know which delegates to reference (see example B.21).

Example B.21:

```
using System.Collections;
namespace Appendix_B
{public delegate void TryDelegate(int i);
public class EventSetup
{private Hashtable Test = new Hashtable();
public event TryDelegate Event
{add{Test["Event"] = (TryDelegate)Test["Event"] + value;}
remove{Test["Event"] = (TryDelegate)Test["Event"] - value;}}}
public class Events
{public static void Main()
{}}}
```

explicit

An explicit declaration is a declaration used to express a conversion from a larger to smaller value. Express permission is required because of the potential for lost data. The programmer in so using this declaration must also safeguard against errors manually (see example B.22).

Example B.22:

```
namespace Appendix_B
{class IsByte
```

```
{byte value;
public IsByte(int value)
{this.value = (byte)value;}
public static explicit operator IsByte(byte Byte)
{return new IsByte(Byte);}
public static void Main()
{}}}
```

extern

The extern modifier as it's name implies, indicates that the method will implemented externally, such as the such as with the DllImport attribute.. The external method will contain all appropriate declarations, but it does not require a function body (note: it does require a terminating semicolon). C++ users will find this version of extern a bit more constrictive (see example B.23).

Example B.23:
```
using System;
using System.Windows.Forms;
using System.Runtime.InteropServices;
namespace Appendix_B
{public class Form1 : System.Windows.Forms.Form
{[DllImport("winmm.dll")]
public static extern long PlaySound(String lpszName,
long hModule, long dwFlags);
public Form1()
{PlaySound(@"C:\SourceCode\Mouse.wav", 0, 0);}
static void Main()
{Application.Run(new Form1());}}}
```

false

A user-defined Boolean type operator that returns and the value false (see example B.24).

Example B.24:
```
class Appendix_B
{static void Main ()
{bool Variable1 = false;}}
```

finally

The finally-block is the last block listed in a try-catch-finally set, it statements are always executed with the completion of that set (see example B.25).

Example B.25:
```
public class Appendix_B
{static void Main()
```

```
{try
{}
finally
{}}}
```

fixed

The keyword fixed, used only in unsafe mode, is a modifier that sets unmanaged-pointers to managed variable locations. These positions are then fixed, to prevent there automatic deletion, as is normally done with C# garbage collection (see example B.26).

Example B.26:
```
namespace Appendix_B
{class ClassFixed
{public int variable;}
class Class1
{static unsafe void Main ()
{ClassFixed TestFixed = new ClassFixed();
TestFixed.variable = 7;
fixed (int* pointer = &TestFixed.variable)
{}}}}
```

float

Float is a 32-bit data type used to store floating-point values ranging from $\pm 1.5 \times 10^{-45}$ to $\pm 3.4 \times 10^{38}$ with a precision level is 7 digits. Note: since doubles are the default, it is also important to include a suffix when attempting to assign irrational numeric, failure to do so will result in a compilation error (see example B.27).

Example B.27:
```
namespace Appendix_B
{class Class1
{static void Main( )
{float Number1, Number2;
Number1 = 1.0f;
Number2 = 1.1f;}}}
```

for

The *for*-loop, also known as the *for*-statement, is a repetitive process that is setup under certain conditions to run a particular number of times. This terminating factor will also help us to separate it from the other two looping processes, because it's not dependent on an unknown variable. The *for*-loop thus predefines its variable as part of its initial statement. The comparison operators are still used to determine whether to continue or terminate, but this will always happen at a predetermined point in the loop, as when our variable equals 10, 100, or X number of cycles. The *for*-statement is constructed much like the *while*-loop, but with its initializing variable and its incrementing operator both becoming one with its declaration (see example B.28).

Example B.28:

```
class Appendix_B
{static void Main ()
{for(int i = 0; i < 5; i++)
{/* */}}}
```

foreach

The foreach-loop is a specialized process that is used to skim or scan through an array elements without the common drudgery usually associated with listing that array's components. It is generally written to include both the keywords *"foreach"* and *"in"* and it, for the most part, physically resembles the notation used when describing the for-loop process. One key difference however, is that the indexing or searching value is not allowed to be altered; this would include even subtle manipulation such as the incrementing or decrementing operators (see example B.29).

Example B.29:

```
class Appendix_B
{static void Main()
{char[] integer = {'a', 'g', 'n', 'u'};
foreach (char find in integer)
{/* */ }}}
```

goto

The *goto* statement is probably the most picked on of all the keywords. Its use is consider poor programming habit. Yet, somehow it manages to endure. Its fault lies in its ability to transgress order, the C# help files even mark it as useful way of getting out of nested statements, but, of course, that would be breaking the rules. Still, there is at least one practical reason for using the goto statement in C#, that is to allow for artificial drops when dealing with switch statements. Remember C# no longer allows us to drop between switch statements that contain executable statements, so goto makes a good fix. C#'s goto also has some limitations including not being able to jump into localized block, between classes, nor can or should it be used to alter our try-catch blocks (see example B.30).

Example B.30:

```
class Appendix_B
{static void Main ()
{char Character = '1';
switch (Character)
{case '1':
goto case2;
break;
case '2':
case2:
goto case3;
break;
case '3':
case3:
```

```
break;}}}
```

if

The if statement is a conditional statement that tests an expression or set of expressions and executes a statement or block of statements when that expression is found to be true (see example B.31).

Example B.31:
```
class Appendix_4
{static void Main ( )
{int Number = 7;
if (Number == 7)
Number++;}}
```

implicit

The keyword implicit is used when attempting to declare a user-defined conversion operator. Implicit conversions can improve source code readability, safety, and generally occur without the programmer's awareness. (Note: Implicit operators should not throw exceptions - see example B.32).

Example B.32:
```
namespace Appendix_B
{class IsByte
{byte value;
public IsByte(byte value)
{this.value = value;}
public static implicit operator byte(IsByte Byte)
{return Byte.value;}
public static void Main() {}}}
```

in

The keyword in is used with the foreach statement when reading the contains of an array (see example B.33).

Example B.33:
```
using System;
class Appendix_B
{static void Main ()
{char[] integer = {'a', 'g', 'n', 'u'};
foreach(char find in integer){/* */}}}
```

int

Int, as in integer is a 32-bit integral data type used to store values ranging from -2,147,483,648 to 2,147,483,647 (see example B.34).

Example B.34:

```
class Appendix_1
{static void Main()
{int OurVariable = 1;}}
```

interface

To create a *interface* is to declare a reference type that is noted for having only abstract members. Once created it can exist as either a independent body or as part of a class reference. Interfaces are also capable of inheriting from other interfaces including multiple inheritance (not allowed with C# classes). Note: when creating a inherited class with a combined interface, remember to include the base class first (see example B.35).

Example B.35:

```
using System;
namespace Appendix_B
{interface BaseInterface
{short Width {get; set;}
short Length {get; set;}}
public class BaseClass : BaseInterface
{private short BIWidth;
private short BILength;
protected BaseClass() {}
protected BaseClass(short Width, short y)
{BIWidth = Width; BILength = y;}
public short Width {get{return(BIWidth);} set{BIWidth = value;}}
public short Length {get{return(BILength);} set{BILength = value;}}
public static void Main()
{}}}
```

internal

An internal access modifier is a type member used to access class components. The advantage of the internal modifier is that it allows for limited access from within a single assembly. A key disadvantage then would be that it is only accessible from within that assembly. In addition to the basic internal modifier we can also use the keyword internal in combination with protected to create a internal protected modifier (see example B.36).

Example B.36:

```
namespace Appendix_B
{internal class BankAccount
{internal protected string first_name;
internal void ViewFiles(BankAccount acc)
{}}
class Class1
```

```
{static void Main ()
{}}}
```

is

The is operator is used as part of a Boolean expression to test the compatibility of a specific object type. An is expression will evaluate to true if one, the expression is not null and two, the expression can be cast without throwing an exception (see example B.37).

Example B.37:

```
using System;
namespace Appendix_B
{class TestClass
{}
public class Class1
{public static void Test (object ob)
{TestClass test;
if (ob is TestClass)
{test = (TestClass)ob;}}
public static void Main() {}}}
```

lock

A *lock* is a temporary mutual-exclusion used to insure that multiple threads do not inadvertently access the same section of coding. Locks are used with both the *this*-statement and the *typeof*-command and are written as *lock* (expression) executable block. Note: *lock* statements also require that their expressions be reference types (see example B.38).

Example B.38:

```
namespace Appendix_B
{class MyName
{private string name;
protected MyName(string fn) {this.name = fn;}
protected string TestName(string fn)
{lock (this)
{if (fn != null)
{return (this.name);}}
return(null);}
public static void Main()
{}}}
```

long

Long is a 64-bit data type used to store values ranging from –9,223,372,036,854,775,808 to 9,223,372,036,854,775,807 (see example B.39).

Example B.39:

```
class Appendix_B
{static void Main()
{long Number;}}
```

namespace

When we encompass our coding inside a namespace, we are actually declaring a scope or globally unique partition. The types contained in that namespace are then accessible through both direct access (from within that body) and through the using-namespace-directive, which allows us to use its values without qualification (B.40)

Example B.40:

```
namespace Appendix_B
{class Class1
{static void Main()
{}}}
```

new

The keyword new is used as both an operator and a modifier. As an operator, it is used to declare instances and to create objects. As a modifier it is used to hide members inherited from a base class. Note: the new operator cannot be overloaded nor can it be used with the override statement (see example B.41).

Example B.41:

```
namespace Appendix_B
{public class BaseClass
{public short x;
protected BaseClass() {}
public short X {set{x = value;}}}

public class DerivedClass : BaseClass
{protected DerivedClass() {}
public new short X {get{return(x);}}}

static void Main()
{}}}
```

null

The *null* reference refers to an object that has not yet been assigned, it basically serves as a blank or non-value, which can be substituted for later. It is also the default value to any non-assigned reference-types and it can be used to mark a position where no actual reference is needed (see example B.42).

Example B.42:

```
namespace Appendix_B
```

```
{public class TestAS
{public static void Main()
{object MyString = new object();
MyString = 123;
string s = MyString as string;
if (s != null)
MyString = "X";}}}
```

object

The keyword object is used to assign values to objects. We can apply these techniques to include both value to reference and reference to value conversions. This process is most commonly referred to as "boxing" with the term "unboxing" denoting the returning of those values to their original state. The process follows the same steps used with basic type casting, but with an added note of caution, when attempting to return or unbox our values. Since they can return to new variables, but those variables must be of the originally boxed data type. The conversions are done using the keyword object as is shown below.

Example B.43:
```
public class Appendix_B
{public static void Main()
{object MyString = new object();}}
```

operator

Operator overloading is the reapplication of our operators to include class manipulations. The standard class operator overloads include object-to-object and object-to-numeric values (including variables). The most important point when dealing with operator overloading is the understanding that all abbreviated forms should be made implicit.

Example B.44:
```
namespace Appendix_B
{public class Objects
{int Number;
public Objects(int Value){this.Number = Value;}
public static Objects operator +(Objects Ob, int Value)
{Ob.Number += Value; return(Ob);}
static void Main()
{}}}
```

out

The keyword *out* is basically a special exception marker, which notifies the compiler so that the variable under scrutiny, does not need to be assigned before it can be passed as a referenced variable. This is usually the case when dealing with values that wouldn't otherwise have a meaningful value before the appropriate functions can be executed. Since an *out* value is also a referenced value, this keyword then negates the need for the second reference (*ref*) (see example B.45).

Example B.45:

```
using System;
class Appendix_B
{static void Main()
{int iNumber1;
TheRace (out iNumber1);}

static void TheRace (out int Num)
{Num = 1;}}
```

override

In addition to being able to overload a functions (as into changed the signature or parameters of that function), we can also override a function so as to force the compiler to except a secondary version of that function. As its name implies the keyword override is used to override members inherited from a base class. These inherited methods must have matching signatures and be either virtual, abstract, or previously overridden. This technique also allows us to manipulate that programs data so as to give it the illusion of consistency or to save us the trouble of revising our previous class. The secondary version then would become the obvious choice as our instance was declared as part of that inherited class (see example B.46). On a cautionary note, it should also be mentioned that if any of our overriding functions had also referenced their base version (as is commonly done with our privately inherited classes), that function's reference would then be diverted back to the inherited function. Note: we can also return access to the original method via the *base* command.

Example B.46:

```
namespace Appendix_B
{public class Area {
public Area() {}
public virtual void CalculateArea()
{}}
public class Parallelogram: Area {
override public void CalculateArea()
{}
static void Main(){}}}
```

params

The keyword params is used to pass an array of any object type without explicitly declaring that data as an array. Only one object may be passed as a params per declaration and any other declaration must proceed that statement (see example B.47).

Example B.47:

```
public class Appendix_B
{public static void Params(params string[] list)
{}
public static void Main()
{}}
```

private

These are class or structure members that allow for restricted or limited access based on user-defined methods that were written specifically for those values. These user-defined methods are declared as part of that class's internal structure with the option of either being declared as *public*, *protected*, or *private* members functions (see example B.48).

Example B.48:

```
namespace Appendix_B
{class BankAccount
{private string first_name;
private void ReadFiles (ref BankAccount acc)
{}
static void Main ()
{}}}
```

Note: While *private* is the default setting, many programmers choose too explicitly restate that command thus removing any ambiguity.

protected

These are class or structure members that allow for restricted or limited access based on user-defined methods that were written specifically for those values. These user-defined methods are declared as part of that class's internal structure with the option of either being declared as *public*, *protected*, or *private* members functions (see example B.49).

Example B.49:

```
namespace Appendix_B
{class BankAccount
{protected string first_name;
protected void ReadFiles (ref BankAccount acc)
{}
static void Main (){}}}
```

public

These are class or structure members that allow for restricted or limited access based on user-defined methods that were written specifically for those values. These user-defined methods are declared as part of that class's internal structure with the option of either being declared as *public*, *protected*, or *private* members functions (see example B.50).

Example B.50:

```
namespace Appendix_B
{class BankAccount
{public string first_name;
public void ReadFiles (ref BankAccount acc)
```

```
{}
static void Main ()
{}}}
```

readonly

Readonly is a constant data type used as part of a class reference declared as a field. That is assignable at only one point in the program and then acts as a constant (see example B.51).

Example B.51

```
class Appendix_B
{public readonly double variable2 = 3.14159;
static void Main()
{}}
```

ref

The keyword ref is used to reflect a variables control back to the original parameters, there by allowing the methods or functions alterations to be known by the main or calling body (see example B.52).

Example B.52:

```
class Appendix_B
{static void Main ( )
{int iNumber1 = 0;
TheRace (ref iNumber1);}

static void TheRace (ref int Num)
{}}
```

return

The keyword return is used to pass back a single value to that of the calling function. The value in question must be of the qualified type and in cases where the returning type is void it can be omitted. Return statements are required with all non-void user-defined functions and methods (see example B.53).

Example B.53:

```
using System;
class Appendix_B
{static void Main ( )
{RandomNumber();}

static int RandomNumber ()
{return (0);}}
```

sbtye

The keyword sbtye is a 8-bit integer used to store values ranging from -128 to 127 (see example B.54).

Example B.54:
```
class Appendix_B
{static void Main()
{sbyte Number1 = 1;}}
```

sealed

Occasionally, we'll want to prevent other programmers from overriding our mission critical methods. This can be done through the use of our sealed modifier. Once a class is sealed it can no longer be inherited, hence it cannot be overridden or altered in any other way. By this same reasoning we cannot use sealed with the abstract modifier. Note: The structures we learned about at the start of this chapter were also implicitly sealed, thus they cannot use inherited (see example B.55).

Example B.55:
```
sealed class Appendix_B
{static void Main (){}}
```

short

The keyword short is a 16-bit integer data type used to store values ranging from -32,768 to 32,767 (see example B.56).

Example B.56:
```
class Appendix_B
{static void Main()
{short Number1 = 1;}}
```

sizeof

The *sizeof* keyword is used to gather information pertaining to the size of our data types. Unfortunately, this also requires the use of a secondary command namely unsafe, which is used to mark the unsafe nature of that code (see example B.57).

Example B.57:
```
using System;
class Appendix_B
{static unsafe void Main()
{Console.WriteLine ("Byte = " + sizeof (byte));}}
```

stackalloc

The keyword stackalloc, as in stack allocating, is used to allocate blocks of memory referenced from a stack (this should also not be confused with the heap as explained previously). The addresses of these blocks are stored as pointers and they are protected from garbage collection, thus they do not have to be fixed/pinned (see example B.58). Note: all blocks are lost when their methods are terminated.

Example B.58:

```
class Appendix_B
{public static unsafe void Main()
{int* pointer1 = stackalloc int[3];
pointer1[0] = 1;}}
```

static

The keyword static is used to modify constructors, fields, methods, operators, and properties. Static constructors for example are called automatically and are used to initialize the rest of the class before any members are referenced. Static fields then are not part of a specific instance and instead are referenced as a single memory address.

Example B.59:

```
class Appendix_B
{static void Main ()
{}}
```

string

A string is a reference data type that encompasses the more recently developed Unicode characters. These characters can be transferred to string references using simple quotation marks, these expressions can also be made literal by first delineating them with the @ symbol (see example B.60).

Example B.60:

```
class Appendix_B
{static void Main()
{string MyDog = "Brownie";}}
```

struct

Structures are user-defined data types that allow for groupings of similar or related data that do not have a single base data type. These groups can include all the basic value data-types as well as a list of methods used to manipulate those values. The data types declared inside a structure are referred to as the structure's members (or fields), while their declarations are referred to as its instances. The correlations between these internal values and our structures are usually guided by some common theme or purpose. A structure is made up of the keyword "*struct*," the structure's tag (or name), a list of the fields (written as declared members), and a list of possible methods used to manipulate that data. Structures are generally contained within a single block placed inside our referencing namespace, but as is shown below they can also be used to invoke our main method (see example B.61). Note: While the use of a C++-style terminating semicolon is allowed, it is not required when working with the C# language.

Example B.61:

```
struct Appendix_B
{static void Main (){}}
```

switch

The *switch* statement, like the "*if*" and "*else-if*" statements, is used to execute a statement or set of statements that equal the variables value. However, unlike the "*if*" and "*else-if*" statements the *switch* statement doesn't use comparison operators instead it simply reads the value of the variable and attempts to direct the program to the proper channel. A second keyword "*case*" is also used in this process. The keyword "*case*" is written and used multiple times from within the *switch* statement, each *case* statement holds a numeric or character value for comparison. If the value held by a *case* statement matches the value read by the *switch* statement then everything following that case statement would be executed.

Example B.62:

```
class Appendix_B
{static void Main ()
{int Grades = 1;
switch (Grades)
{case 1:
break;
default:
break;}}}
```

this

The keyword "*this*" is a specialized reference signature used to indicate the referencing object of a passing class, "*this*" is then a longhand version for the otherwise abbreviated member. While the "*this*" reference is implied, its definitions can become ambiguous and should be included to prevent this error (see example B.63).

Example B.63:

```
class Appendix_B
{protected short pin_number;
private void ReadFiles ()
{this.pin_number = 1;}
static void Main (){}}
```

throw

In addition to being able to catch both generalize and specific exceptions, we can also learn to throw a few of our own. This is not usually necessary for the contexts of this book, but the technique can serve to clarify the definitions of some otherwise confusing errors (see example B.64).

Example B.64:

```
using System;
public class Appendix_B
{static void Main()
{int Y = 0;
if(Y == 0)
{throw new DivideByZeroException("\nProgram Error!");}}}
```

true

A user-defined Boolean type operator that returns and the value false (see example B.65).

Example B.65:
```
class Appendix_B
{static void Main ()
{bool Variable1 = true;}}
```

try

Another important feature that helps to perfect our programs is the ability to catch exception errors. Exception errors are errors thrown by our program/Windows during execution and can range from simple input errors to problems such as missing files, division by zero... All questionable coding then is placed inside of what is known as a *try*-block, this is a block of coding that may or may not succeed. If this coding does fail then the program immediately turns to one or an assortment of *catch*-blocks, which can also be either general or specific. Upon completion of either the *try* or the *catch*-block a tertiary block is executed this one is known as the final or *finally*-block, the finally-block is always executed with the termination of this set of coding (see example B.66).

Example B.66:
```
public class Appendix_B
{static void Main()
{try
{}
catch
{}
finally
{}}}
```

typeof

The typeof operator is used to determine an objects type, fields, methods, properties (see example B.67)

Example B.67:
```
using System;
namespace Appendix_B
{public class Class1
{public static void Main()
```

```
{Type Ob = typeof(Class1);
Console.WriteLine(Ob.GetFields());
Console.WriteLine(Ob.GetMethods());}}}
```

uint

The keyword *uint* is a unsigned 32-bit integral type used to store values ranging from 0 to 4,294,967,295 (see example B.68).

Example B.68:
```
class Appendix_B
{static void Main()
{uint Number1 = 1;}}
```

ulong

The keyword ulong denotes a unsigned 64-bit integral type used to store values ranging from 0 to 18,446,744,073,709,551,615 (see example B.69).

Example B.69:
```
class Appendix_B
{static void Main()
{ulong Number1 = 1;}}
```

unchecked

The keyword unchecked is used to block the Solution Explorer\ Configuration Properties\ Build \ Check for arithmetic overflow/underflow - true statement. Note: this statement is false by default, but if we were to change this default and then attempt to break the barriers of our designated type then we could block the error with the unchecked statement (see example B.70).

Example B.70:
```
class Appendix_B
{static void Main ()
{byte Max255 = 255;
unchecked {Max255 += 1 ;}}}
```

unsafe

The keyword unsafe denotes a change in settings to that of the unsafe mode. The unsafe feature was developed to aid in bridging the gap between C++ and C# programming allowing us to use time tested techniques that are not officially permitted under C#'s safe mode (see example B.72). Note: in addition to including the keyword unsafe to our coding we must also change the compilers settings in Configuration manager (Chapter ones - sizeof and unsafe coding for details).

Example B.71:

```
class Class1
{static unsafe void Main(){}}
```

ushort

The keyword ushort denotes a 16-bit integral data type used to store values ranging from 0 to 65,535 (see example B.72).

Example B.72

```
class Appendix_B
{static void Main()
{ushort Number1 = 1;}}
```

using

The using directive allows us to include a host of System and user-defined namespaces. Note: including a namespace is not equivalent to including a file as was done in C++. Here, we'll only be notifying the compiler of where to find the references we'll be writing in shorthand. User-defined namespaces are accessed in exactly the same manner as the System type (see example B.73).

Example B.73:

```
using System;
class Appendix_B
{static void Main()
{}}
```

virtual

The keyword virtual denotes a modifier that sets a method of a base class so that it can be overridden in a derived class. When a *virtual* function is referenced it searches for an overriding method.

Example B.74:

```
namespace Appendix_B
{public class Area
{public Area() {}
public virtual void CalculateArea()
{}}
public class Parallelogram: Area {
public Parallelogram(){}
override public void CalculateArea() {}
static void Main()
{}}}
```

void

Void is a data type that holds no data. It thus severs the purpose of telling the compiler that no data will be required by this variable or returning function. This is logical since the ending of the main function is also the ending of the program and there would be no program to send information too. *Void* is also most commonly associated with user-defined functions that use reference-variables (explained in chapter two) and generalized pointers-variables (explained in chapter four). Unlike the other data types *void* does not take a position in memory. Therefore, we won't need to measure its size in bytes

Example B.75:

```
class Appendix_B
{static void Main()
{}}
```

volatile

The keyword volatile is used to denote a variable that cannot be optimized, this is usually do to some unpredictable change or reference made to it usually from an outside source such as the operating system or hardware device (see example B.76).

Example B.76:

```
class Appendix_B
{public volatile char variable3 = 'A';
static void Main()
{}}
```

while

The *while-loop* can be setup to repeat and/or terminate in several different ways. The most common include using a predetermined count (as in to repeat an iteration five times then end), using the users input (end by request), and a termination command (a command that short-steps or breaks the loop – see example B.77).

Example B.77

```
class Appendix_B
{static void Main()
{while(true)
{}}}
```

Appendix C: Accessors

get & set

The *get* and *set* accessors aren't officially keywords, actually they are parameterless methods named to match certain fields and used in classes and interfaces that hold a body of executable data pertaining to the storage and retrieval of those fields. Their executable statements may include calculations, conversions, and a large host of other tasks, but their underline purpose must include reading or recording to those properties. The body of a accessor is considered equivalent to a method although they do not include identify signatures. The get accessor returns a value and may be set to throw a value when needed, the set accessor by contrast is always set to void. The key word value is also used as an implicit parameter with setting our fields. Value, thus takes on the value of any passed variables. Note: The get and the set accessors always share the same user-defined name, thus they cannot exist in the same base class. It is then considered natural to place the set accessor in the base class with the get accessor listed in the nest derived class. It is also important to remember that the value retrieved by the get property is for reference only, while the value recorded in the set property is write only (see example C.1).

Example C.1:

```
namespace Appendix_C
{public class BaseClass
{public short width;
protected BaseClass() {}
public short Width {set{width = value;}} }
public class DerivedClass : BaseClass
{protected DerivedClass() {}
public new short Width {get{return(width);}}
static void Main()
{}}}
```

value

Value types are implicit fields declared as part of a methods signature and are referenced as if they were actual fields. They have the same limitations and abilities associated with a field of their declared type and should be treated as such (see example C.2).

Example C.2:

```
namespace Appendix_C
{public class Objects
{int Number;
public Objects(int value)
{this.Number = value;}
static void Main()
{}}}
```

Appendix D: Order of Precedence

Precedence of Operators; (Note: the operators are listed by level of precedence).

Symbol(s)	Description
.	Dot operator
[ ]	Array indexing
( )	Function call
++	Postfix increment operator (placed after the variable)
--	Postfix decrement operator (placed after the variable)
new, typeof	
checked, unchecked	
++	Prefix increment operator (placed before the variable)
--	Prefix decrement operator (placed before the variable)
!	Not
-	Unary minus
+	Unary Plus
~	Unary
(T)x	
*	Multiply
/	Divide
%	Remainder
+	Addition
-	Subtraction
<<	Shift
>>	Shift
<	Less than
>	Greater than
<=	Less than or equal to
>=	Greater than or equal to
as, is	
==	Equal to
!=	Not equal to
&	Logical AND
^	Logical XOR
|	Logical OR
&&	And
||	Or
?:	IF
= += -= *=	Assignment, add, subtract, multiply, divide, remainder...
/= %= <<= >>=	
|= &= ^=	

Appendix E: Displaying Message Boxes

Message boxes are predefined dialog boxes that are used to send and receive simple data streams between the user and the program. These Messages may include titles, comments, and buttons which allow for a short list of responses as in yes, no, ok, and cancel (see examples E.1 – E.17).

Example E.1:

```
/* The Message Box */
using System;
using System.Drawing;
using System.Collections;
using System.ComponentModel;
using System.Windows.Forms;
using System.Data;
using System.IO;
using System.Runtime.InteropServices;

namespace Appendix_E
{public class Form1 : System.Windows.Forms.Form
{[DllImport("winmm.dll")]
public static extern long PlaySound(String lpszName,
                    long hModule, long dwFlags);

public Form1()
{MessageBox.Show("Place message here");}

[STAThread]
static void Main()
{Application.Run(new Form1());}

private void Form1_Load(object sender, System.EventArgs e)
{}}}
```

Note: We can also this message boxes with the example shown below.

Example E.2:
```
MessageBox.Show("Place message Here", "Place caption here");
```

Example E.3:
```
MessageBox.Show("Place message Here", "Place caption here",
            MessageBoxButtons.OK);
```

Example E.4:
```
MessageBox.Show("Place message here", "Place caption here",
            MessageBoxButtons.AbortRetryIgnore);
```

Example E.5:
```
MessageBox.Show("Place message here", "Place caption here",
            MessageBoxButtons.OKCancel);
```

Example E.6:
```
MessageBox.Show("Place message here", "Place caption here",
```

```
                MessageBoxButtons.RetryCancel);
```

Example E.7:
```
MessageBox.Show("Place message here", "Place caption here",
                MessageBoxButtons.YesNo);
```

Example E.8:
```
MessageBox.Show("Place message here", "Place Caption here",
                MessageBoxButtons.YesNoCancel);
```

Example E.9:
```
MessageBox.Show("Place message here", "Place caption here",
        MessageBoxButtons.OK, MessageBoxIcon.Asterisk);
```

Example E.10:
```
MessageBox.Show("Place message here", "Place caption here",
        MessageBoxButtons.OK, MessageBoxIcon.Error);
```

Example E.11:
```
MessageBox.Show("Place message here", "Place caption here",
        MessageBoxButtons.OK, MessageBoxIcon.Exclamation);
```

Example E.12:
```
MessageBox.Show("Place message here", "Place caption here",
        MessageBoxButtons.OK, MessageBoxIcon.Hand);
```

Example E.13:
```
MessageBox.Show("Place message here", "Place caption here",
        MessageBoxButtons.OK, MessageBoxIcon.Information);
```

Example E.14:
```
MessageBox.Show("Place message here", "Place caption here",
        MessageBoxButtons.OK, MessageBoxIcon.None);
```

Example E.15:
```
MessageBox.Show("Place message here", "Place caption here",
        MessageBoxButtons.OK, MessageBoxIcon.Question);
```

Example E.16:
```
MessageBox.Show("Place message here", "place caption here",
        MessageBoxButtons.OK, MessageBoxIcon.Stop);
```

Example E.17:
```
MessageBox.Show("Place message here", "Place caption here",
        MessageBoxButtons.OK, MessageBoxIcon.Warning);
```

We can also test and build new actions based on those responses received by those message boxes (see example E.18 – E.25).

Example E.18:

```
DialogResult result = MessageBox.Show("Place message here",
  "Place caption here", MessageBoxButtons.OK);

if(result == DialogResult.OK)
{PlaySound(@"C:\SourceCode\Fire.wav", 0, 0);}
```

Example E.19:
```
DialogResult result = MessageBox.Show("Place message here",
  "Place caption here", MessageBoxButtons.OKCancel);

if(result == DialogResult.Cancel)
{PlaySound(@"C:\SourceCode\Fire.wav", 0, 0);}
```

Example E.20:
```
DialogResult result = MessageBox.Show("Place message here",
  "Place caption here", MessageBoxButtons.YesNo);

if(result == DialogResult.Yes)
{PlaySound(@"C:\SourceCode\Fire.wav", 0, 0);}
```

Example E.21:
```
DialogResult result = MessageBox.Show("Place message Here",
    "Place caption here", MessageBoxButtons.YesNo);

if(result == DialogResult.No)
{PlaySound(@"C:\SourceCode\Fire.wav", 0, 0);}
```

Example E.22:
```
DialogResult result = MessageBox.Show("Place message here",
    "Place caption here", MessageBoxButtons.YesNoCancel);

if(result == DialogResult.Cancel)
{PlaySound(@"C:\SourceCode\Fire.wav", 0, 0);}
```

Example E.23:
```
DialogResult result = MessageBox.Show("Place message here",
    "Place caption here", MessageBoxButtons.AbortRetryIgnore);

if(result == DialogResult.Abort)
{PlaySound(@"C:\SourceCode\Fire.wav", 0, 0);}
```

Example E.24:
```
DialogResult result = MessageBox.Show("Place message here",
    "Place caption here", MessageBoxButtons.AbortRetryIgnore);

if(result == DialogResult.Retry)
{PlaySound(@"C:\SourceCode\Fire.wav", 0, 0);}
```

Example E.25:
```
DialogResult result = MessageBox.Show("Place message here",
    "Place caption here", MessageBoxButtons.AbortRetryIgnore);
```

```
if(result == DialogResult.Ignore)
{PlaySound(@"C:\SourceCode\Fire.wav", 0, 0);}
```

Example E.26:
```
DialogResult result = MessageBox.Show(this, "Place message here",
   "Place title here", MessageBoxButtons.YesNoCancel);

if(result != DialogResult.None)
{PlaySound(@"C:\SourceCode\Fire.wav", 0, 0);}
```
Note: We could have also inserted the MessageBoxIcon feature into any of these examples.

We'll also want to take advantage of two of the useful MessageBoxOptions namely RightAlign and RtlReading. These are essentially message alignment tools with RightAlign moving the message text to the far right (users perspective) and RtlReading moving the message to the left (placing the Icon on the right). We'll also want to set a default or pre-selected button, this default will not affect the users ability to choose, but it generally serves as the recommended option (see examples E.27 – E.29).

Example E.27:
```
DialogResult result = MessageBox.Show(this, "Place message here",
   "Place caption here", MessageBoxButtons.YesNoCancel,
   MessageBoxIcon.Question, MessageBoxDefaultButton.Button1,
   MessageBoxOptions.RightAlign);

if(result == DialogResult.Yes)
{PlaySound(@"C:\SourceCode\Fire.wav", 0, 0);}
```

Example E.28:
```
DialogResult result = MessageBox.Show(this, "Place message here",
   "Place caption here", MessageBoxButtons.YesNoCancel,
   MessageBoxIcon.Question, MessageBoxDefaultButton.Button2,
   MessageBoxOptions.RtlReading);

if(result == DialogResult.No)
{PlaySound(@"C:\SourceCode\Fire.wav", 0, 0);}
```

Example E.29:
```
DialogResult result = MessageBox.Show(this, "Place message here",
  "Place caption here", MessageBoxButtons.YesNoCancel,
  MessageBoxIcon.Question, MessageBoxDefaultButton.Button3,
  MessageBoxOptions.RtlReading);

if(result == DialogResultCancel)
{PlaySound(@"C:\SourceCode\Fire.wav", 0, 0);}
```

Note; it's also important to remember not to place message boxes such as these inside of OnPaint or other graphics handling methods. The result being a potential invalidating loop.

Appendix F: Graphics

Windows Forms has provided us with several methods used to produce everything from the basic shapes to some integrate designs. Here, we'll also want to introduce some of the alternative drawing tools and many of the techniques associated with the color references.

Points & Size

The first aspect to drawing is the point reference, this as its name implies describes the locations that delineate our shapes. A point is declared using the Cartesian coordinate system (also known as the x, y-coordinate system) where x is the horizontal position and y is the vertical position as in Point(*int* x, *int* y). Once our points our defined, we'll then need to include a size reference which also relies on a x, y scheme as in Size(*int* x, *int* y). Both Point and Size can be referenced as individual objects or as part of a specific shape (see example F.1).

Example F.1:

```
using System;
using System.Drawing;
using System.Windows.Forms;
namespace Appendix_F
{public class Form1 : System.Windows.Forms.Form
{public Form1() {}
protected override void OnPaint(PaintEventArgs e)
{Point point = new Point(10, 15);
 Size size = new Size(15, 200);
Brush GreenBrush = new SolidBrush (Color.Green);
Graphics MyText = e.Graphics;
Font Normal = new Font ("Times New Roman", 14, FontStyle.Bold);
MyText.DrawString ("TEST", Normal, GreenBrush,
   new Rectangle (point, size));
MyText.DrawString ("TEST", Normal, GreenBrush,
 new Rectangle (new Point (50, 15), new Size (15, 200)));}
static void Main()
{Application.Run(new Form1());}}}
```

Note: PointF and SizeF are used to indicate floating-point values which are necessary when drawing with pixels.

Brushes & Pens

We can also use what are known as brushes and pens to enhance our graphic and text supported displays. Brushes and pens are declared and accessed in basically the same manner with brushes being used for text and to fill rather than draw our shapes. Brushes are also abstract by definition and hence cannot be instantiated. There are, however, five derived classes used to create different types of brushes as in the HatchBrush, LinearGradientBrush, PathGradientBrush, SolidBrush, and TextureBrush. Pen is also derived for the abstract Brush class, it can be written to take advantage of all five of the derived classes, but it has a constant color rather than a gradient. For our purposes, we'll want to look at how to declare and reference both the basic SolidBrush and the Pen (see example F.2).

Example F.2:

```
using System;
using System.Drawing;
using System.Windows.Forms;
namespace Appendix_F
{public class Form1 : System.Windows.Forms.Form
{public Form1() {}
protected override void OnPaint(PaintEventArgs e)
{Graphics Figures = this.CreateGraphics ();
Brush RedBrush = new SolidBrush (Color.Red);
Pen BluePen = new Pen (Color.Blue, 3);
Figures.FillRectangle (RedBrush, 10, 10, 25, 25);
Figures.DrawRectangle (BluePen, 20, 20, 25, 25);}
static void Main()
{Application.Run(new Form1());}}}
```

Note: second value associated with the Pen statement as in Pen(Color, *int*) is used to reference its width.

Lines

Now that we have some basic points to reference and our pen in hand, the next logical step then would be to learn how to link those points to create lines and, of course, curves. Lines are straightforward enough with four basic reference as in DrawLine(Color, Point1, Point2), DrawLine(Color, *int* x, *int* y, *int* x_2, *int* y_2), DrawLine(Color, PointF1, PointF2), and DrawLine(Color, *float* x, *float* y, *float* x_2, *float* y_2) see example F.3.

Example F.3:

```
using System;
using System.Drawing;
using System.Windows.Forms;
namespace Appendix_F
{public class Form1 : System.Windows.Forms.Form
{public Form1() {}
protected override void OnPaint(PaintEventArgs e)
{Point point1 = new Point(10, 10);
Point point2 = new Point(250, 250);
PointF pointf1 = new PointF(125F, 10F);
PointF pointf2 = new PointF(125F, 250F);

Graphics Figures = this.CreateGraphics ();
Pen RedPen = new Pen(Color.Red);
Pen GreenPen = new Pen(Color.Green);
Pen BluePen = new Pen(Color.Blue);
Pen YellowPen = new Pen(Color.Yellow);

Figures.DrawLine(RedPen, point1, point2);
Figures.DrawLine(GreenPen, 250, 10, 10, 250);
Figures.DrawLine(BluePen, pointf1, pointf2);
Figures.DrawLine(YellowPen, 10F, 125F, 250F, 125F);}
static void Main()
{Application.Run(new Form1());}}}
```

Curves

Curves are a bit more complex with seven potential reference as in DrawCurve(Color, ArrayOfPoints, Offset, Segment, Tension), DrawCurve(Color, ArrayOfPoints, Tension), DrawCurve(Color, ArrayOfPoints), DrawCurve(Color, ArrayOfPoints, Offset, Segment, Tension), DrawCurve(Color, ArrayOfPoints, Offset, Segment), DrawCurve(Color, ArrayOfPoints, Tension), DrawCurve(Color, ArrayOfPoints) see example F.4.

Example F.4:

```
using System;
using System.Drawing;
using System.Windows.Forms;
namespace Appendix_F
{public class Form1 : System.Windows.Forms.Form
{public Form1() {}
protected override void OnPaint(PaintEventArgs e)
{PointF pointf1 = new PointF(125F, 10F);
PointF pointf2 = new PointF(125F, 125F);
PointF pointf3 = new PointF(250F, 250F);
PointF pointf4 = new PointF(250.0F, 150.0F);
PointF pointf5 = new PointF(150F, 100F);
PointF pointf6 = new PointF(250F, 200F);
PointF pointf7 = new PointF(125F, 125F);

PointF[] ArrayOfPoints =
{pointf1, pointf2, pointf3, pointf4,
pointf5, pointf6, pointf7};

Graphics Figures = this.CreateGraphics ();
Pen RedPen = new Pen(Color.Red);

Figures.DrawCurve(RedPen, ArrayOfPoints, 2, 4, 1.0F);
Figures.DrawCurve(RedPen, ArrayOfPoints, 0);
Figures.DrawCurve(RedPen, ArrayOfPoints);}
static void Main()
{Application.Run(new Form1());}}}
```

Drawing Shapes

Next, we'll definitely want to take advantage of all the potential shapes stored in the Windows Forms. Here we'll look at the basic Ellipse, Polygon, and Rectangle. We'll also want to have a look at the FillPolygon and FillPie (see example F.5).

Example F.5:

```
using System;
using System.Drawing;
using System.Windows.Forms;
namespace Appendix_F
```

```
{public class Form1 : System.Windows.Forms.Form
{public Form1() {}
protected override void OnPaint(PaintEventArgs e)
{Point point1 = new Point(10, 10);
Point point2 = new Point(250, 250);
PointF pointf1 = new PointF(125F, 10F);
PointF pointf2 = new PointF(125F, 125F);
PointF pointf3 = new PointF(250F, 250F);
PointF pointf4 = new PointF(250.0F, 150.0F);
PointF pointf5 = new PointF(150F, 100F);
PointF pointf6 = new PointF(250F, 200F);
PointF pointf7 = new PointF(125F, 125F);
PointF[] ArrayOfPoints =
{pointf1, pointf2, pointf3, pointf4,
pointf5, pointf6, pointf7};
Graphics Figures = this.CreateGraphics ();
Pen RedPen = new Pen(Color.Red);
Pen GreenPen = new Pen(Color.Green);
Pen BluePen = new Pen(Color.Blue);
Brush YellowBrush = Brushes.Yellow;
Brush OrangeBrush = Brushes.Orange;
Figures.DrawRectangle(RedPen, 10, 10, 100, 100);
Figures.DrawEllipse(GreenPen, 25, 25, 50, 50);
Figures.DrawPolygon(BluePen, ArrayOfPoints);
Figures.FillPolygon(YellowBrush, ArrayOfPoints);
Figures.FillPie(OrangeBrush, 40, 150, 70, 70, 40, 50);}
static void Main()
{Application.Run(new Form1());}}}
```

Appendix G: Colors

The Windows Forms colors are based on the Alpha-Blending Red Green Blue (ARGB) model. They are used with brushes, pens, backgrounds, and foregrounds... There are 140 predefined colors and one user-defined color. To use a color we must first define it as an instance and then assign it to as specific brush/pen (see example G.1).

Example G.1:

```
using System;
using System.Drawing;
using System.Windows.Forms;
namespace Appendix_G
{public class Form1 : System.Windows.Forms.Form
{public Form1()
{InitializeComponent();}
private void InitializeComponent() {}
protected override void OnPaint(PaintEventArgs e)
{Graphics test = e.Graphics;
Font AlgerianFont = new Font("Algerian", 10);
SolidBrush MyBrush = new SolidBrush(Color.Red);
test.DrawString("Salvatore A. Buono", AlgerianFont, MyBrush, 60, 25);}
static void Main()
{Application.Run(new Form1());}}}
```

Note: For a complete list of colors see table G.1.

We can also define our own colors using the static methods Color Color.FromArgb(*int* ARGB) , Color.FromArgb(*int* alpha, Color color), Color.FromArgb(*int* red, *int* green, *int* blue), and Color.FromArgb(*int* alpha, *int* red, *int* green, *int* blue) (see example G.2).

Example G.2:

```
using System;
using System.Drawing;
using System.Windows.Forms;
namespace Appendix_F
{public class Form1 : System.Windows.Forms.Form
{public Form1()
{InitializeComponent();}
private void InitializeComponent() {}
protected override void OnPaint(PaintEventArgs e)
{Graphics test = e.Graphics;
Font AlgerianFont = new Font("Algerian", 10);
SolidBrush MyBrush = new SolidBrush(Color.FromArgb(255, 0, 0));
test.DrawString("Salvatore A. Buono",
AlgerianFont, MyBrush, 60, 25);}
static void Main()
{Application.Run(new Form1());}}}
```

Table G.1:

AliceBlue	DarkOliveGreen	Indigo	MediumPurple	Purple
AntiqueWhite	DarkOrange	Ivory	MediumSeaGreen	Red
Aqua	DarkOrchid	Khaki	MediumSlateBlue	RosyBrown
Aquamarine	DarkRed	Lavender	MediumSpringGreen	RoyalBlue
Azure	DarkSalmon	LavenderBlush	MediumTurquoise	SaddleBrown
Beige	DarkSeaGreen	LawnGreen	MediumVioletRed	Salmon
Bisque	DarkSlateBlue	LemonChiffon	MediumBlue	SandyBrown
Black	DarkSlateGray	LightBlue	MintCream	SeaGreen
BlanchedAlmond	DarkTurquoise	LightCoral	MistyRose	SeaShell
Blue	DarkViolet	LightCyan	Moccasin	Sienna
BlueViolet	DeepPink	LightGoldenrodYellow	NavajoWhite	Silver
Brown	DeepSkyBlue	LightGray	Navy	SkyBlue
BurlyWood	DimGray	LightGreen	OldLace	SlateBlue
CadetBlue	DodgerBlue	LightPink	Olive	SlateGray
Chartreuse	Firebrick	LightSalmon	OliveDrab	Snow
Chocolate	FloralWhite	LightSeaGreen	Orange	SpringGreen
Coral	ForestGreen	LightSkyBlue	OrangeRed	SteelBlue
CornflowerBlue	Fuchsia	LightSlateGray	Orchid	Tan
Cornsilk	Gainsboro	LightSteelBlue	PaleGoldenrod	Teal
Crimson	GhostWhite	LightYellow	PaleGreen	Thistle
Cyan	Gold	Lime	PaleTurquoise	Tomato
DarkBlue	Goldenrod	LimeGreen	PaleVioletRed	Turquoise
DarkCyan	Gray	Linen	PapayaWhip	Violet
DarkGoldenrod	Green	Magenta	Peachpuff	Wheat
DarkGray	GreenYellow	Maroon	Peru	White
DarkGreen	Honeydew	MediumAquamarine	Pink	WhiteSmoke
DarkKhaki	HotPink	MediumBlue	Plum	Yellow
DarkMagenta	IndianRed	MediumOrchid	PowderBlue	YellowGreen

Appendix H: Algorithms

I'd also like to take a moment to demonstrate a more qualified version of an algorithm. Here, every detail must be documented and made as vivid as possible with no assumptions placed on the part of the programmer(s). Reasonable timelines should be developed with additional exit strategies placed on optional material and research. A text outline, drawings, and even some suggestive coding could be included with this model, but it should remain only a model.

Introduction

Pawns is a game I developed back in the late 80's as an alternative to the traditional Chess game. It resembles Chess down to its very last detail, but there's one key difference. In my version, the players are no longer considered to be the kings and instead are forced to choose alternative personas. They can select their own queen, a rook, bishop, knight, or any of their pawns, but if their player is captured, they're captured, that means that the game is over and the other player wins. Thus the true purpose of the game is not to capture the king, but instead to attempt to capture the other player's piece. Both sides should try their best to avoid revealing their identities, but at the same time they must defend the King and play the traditional game.

Basic Rules

The game is played on an eight by eight checked board with all sixty-four squares open for play (see figure H.1). Two players, one lighter and the other darker rotate between moves with the lighter player beginning the game.

Figure H.1:

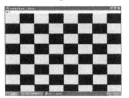

Each player begins with sixteen characters as in one King, one Queen, two Rooks, two Bishops, two Knights and eight Pawns. The players are lined up on opposite sides of the board with the lighter side placing its right-hand or King-side Rook on a lighter square. The arrangement of the key pieces is from left to right and is listed as follows; Queen-side Rook, Queen-side Knight, Queen-side Bishop, The Queen, The King, King-side Bishop, King-side Knight, and King-side Rook. The Pawns are then placed in the squares directly in front of them with their positions defining their identities as in Queen-Rook's Pawn, Queen-Knight's Pawn, Queen-Bishop's Pawn, Queen's Pawn, King's Pawn, King-Bishop's Pawn, King-Knight Pawn, King-Rook's Pawn, the darker side mirrors these positions (see Figure H.2). Note: The Queen's of each side should be lined up vertically with the lighter Queen placed on a lighter square and the darker Queen placed on a darker square.

Figure H.2:

Each player is only allowed one move per turn, no two piece may occupy the same square at any one time, and a player can only capture pieces form the opponents side. Once a piece is capture, the attacking piece takes that square and the turn is complete. At the beginning of the game each player is instructed to secretly choose a piece from their own set of characters which will represent them. The King is not considered a valid choice nor are any of the opponents pieces, if a player fails to select a valid character he automatically forfeits the game.

Once the game is in play it can only be terminated by one of four situations. One, a player's chosen piece is captured, which immediately ends the game giving the win to the player that captured the piece. Two, a King is placed in checkmate, which also immediately terminates the game, but this time it is considered to be a draw. Third, a player resigns forfeiting the game the win going to the remaining player. Fourth, both players agree to withdraw in this case the player who was ahead wins the game. And fifth, all players to either side have been captured except for the King and the player's choice, the game is then considered a victory for the player with the fewest pieces.

The King

Each piece has its own set of movements, beginning with the King, we find that he is subject to several limitations and one key exception. The King is only able to step a distance of one space, but he can move in any direction (see Figure H.3). He is not able to step onto a square controlled by his enemy nor can he remain on a square that his enemy has taken control over, this secondary situation is known as checking the King.

Figure H.3:

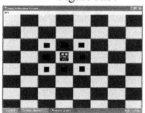

If the King is placed in check there are three potential solutions. One, he can move to an alternative space assuming there is one that is available that doesn't break the rules listed above. Two, he or another same side piece can capture the opposing piece assuming this secondary move can be done without leaving the King in any additional checks. And three, it may be possible to block the opposing players line of attack, this can be done by placing a lesser piece between the King and his opponent. Note: it is against the rules to cause a check by moving ones own pieces if they inadvertently reveal a check. However, if an opponent can open a path by remove one of his own obstacles, it would be considered legal or what is called a revealed check. If two or more piece are threatening the King (as in a double check) this second choice will be negated. Also, if the King is unable to relieve any and/or all checks he is considered to be checkmated and the game is terminated.

The one key exception to the King's one step rule is when he exercises his right to castle. Castling is a special maneuver wherein two pieces are actually displaced. First, the King is allowed to jump two spaces to either side and then the appropriate Rook is placed on the other side of him. Note: this means that the rook will literally jump over the King (see figures H.4 & H.5). There are several restrictions that may inhibit the maneuver; One, this must be the King's first move. Two, all spaces between the Rook and the King must be free of any pieces. And three, the King must not be in check and he must not pass or move onto a square that is controlled by the opponents side.

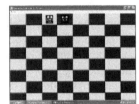

Figure H.4:

Figure H.5:

The Queen

The Queen is considered to be the strongest piece on the board, the assessment is based on her wide range of motion. She is capable of traveling across the entire board in one step, she can move vertically, horizontally, and diagonally (limited to only one direction per move). The Queens only obstacles are the other pieces, since she cannot leap or skip over occupied squares (see figure H.6).

Figure H.6:

The Rook

The Rook is the next strongest piece after the Queen. It is capable of traveling across the entire board in one step, it is capable of both vertical and horizontal movements (limited to only one direction per move). The Rook cannot leap or skip over occupied squares (see figure H.7).

Figure H.7:

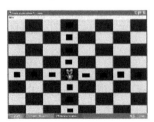

The Bishop

The Bishop is capable of traveling across the entire board in one step, it is only capable of diagonal movement (limited to only one direction per move). The Bishop cannot leap or skip over occupied squares (see figure H.8).

Figure H.8

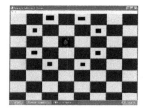

The Knight

The Knight is considered equivalent in strength to that of the Bishop. It is however, the only piece that can both changes directions while in play and jump over the other characters. It moves in what can be described as an "L" shaped pattern as in one to two squares in any directions followed by one to two squares on a left or right angle (again, for a total of three squares - see figure H.9).

Figure H.9:

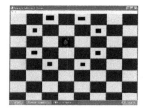

The Pawn

The Pawn can only move forward, straight for movement and diagonally to capture an opponents piece. The Pawn is only allowed one step per move, except on his first move, there he has the option of moving up to two steps (see Figures H.10 & H.11).

Figure H.10:   Figure H.11:

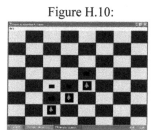 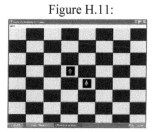

Pawns also hold a special right to capture other Pawns. This special case is known as the "en Passant," but two condition must be upheld. First, the capturing Pawn must be on the fifth rank (ranks counted from their players side). Second, the opponents Pawn must exercise his initial two step option. The adjacent Pawn can then step diagonally onto the unoccupied square and take the opponents Pawn. This special right can only be executed immediately after the two step advance. Also, if a Pawn reaches the other end of the board, he is then promoted, this can be to any one of the other ranking players namely a Queen, Rook, Bishop or Knight (see figures H.12 & H.13).

Figures H.12:   Figures H.13:

   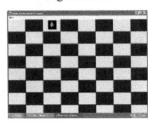

INDEX

P

Q

R

S

T

U

V

W

Z